Pedaling to Lunch

OHIO HISTORY AND CULTURE

All rights reserved • First Edition 2009 • Manufactured in the United States of America • All inquiries and permission requests should be addressed to the Publisher, The University of Akron Press, Akron, Ohio 44325-1703.

13   12   11   10   09   5   4   3   2

LIBRARY OF CONGRESS CATALOGING-IN-PUBLICATION DATA
Purdum, Stan, 1945-
   Pedaling to lunch : bike rides and bites in Northeast Ohio / by Stan Purdum.—1st ed.
      p. cm.
   Includes bibliographical references and index.
   ISBN 978-1-931968-59-1 (pbk. : alk. paper)
   1. Bicycle touring—Ohio—Guidebooks. 2. Ohio—Guidebooks. I. Title.
   GV1045.5.O3P87 2008
   796.6'404—DC22
                          2008026180

The paper used in this publication meets the minimum requirements of American National Standard for Information Sciences—Permanence of Paper for Printed Library Materials, ANSI Z39.48–1984. ∞

Cover design: Lan X. Le

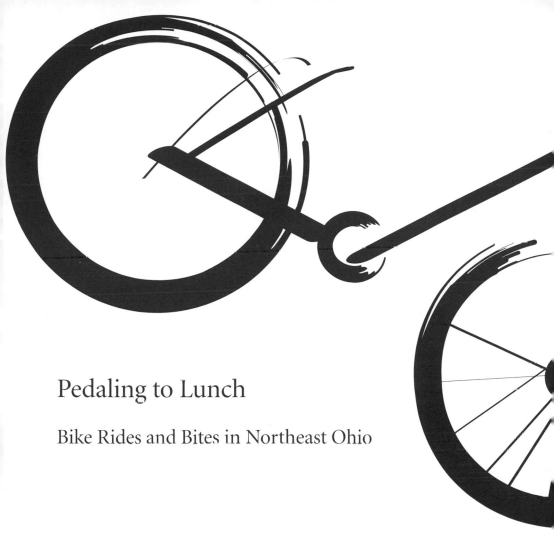

Pedaling to Lunch

Bike Rides and Bites in Northeast Ohio

Stan Purdum

Varsha Balachandran and Dan Von Holten
RESEARCH ASSISTANTS

 THE UNIVERSITY OF AKRON PRESS
AKRON, OHIO

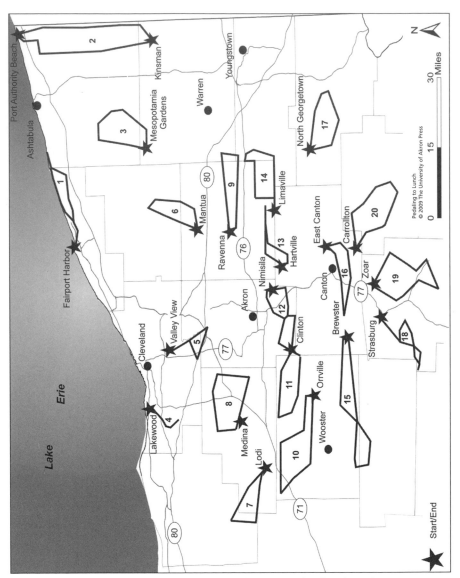

Twenty rides around Northeast Ohio. Numbers correspond to the ride number.

Contents

Acknowledgments

Companionship on the road made some of the rides in this book richer experiences. My thanks to my son, Scott Purdum, who rode the Metroparks Gorgeous Gorge ride with me, my brother, also named Scott Purdum, who joined me for the Arsenal's Edge ride, and Wayne Ostrander, who rode with me on the State Line and Granny's Delight rides.

Some of the enjoyment of these bicycle rides and information about the places I pedaled through came from people I talked to on the way. Thanks to Joseph M. Dyrcz, who told me about Rock Creek; to Doris Tolley, the officer in charge of the North Benton Post Office, who directed me to Chester Bedell's gravesite and filled me in on the tall tales about it; to Tim Miller who gave me a historical perspective on North Industry; to Larry Williams, who helped me find Battlesburg; to John Miday, who gave me a quick history of Petersburg and Algonquin Mill; to Bob, who for reasons of his own preferred not to provide his last name, but who told me a lot about the industrial pollution that now has put some ground near Fairport Harbor into Superfund toxic-waste cleanup programs; and to Jerry Walker, who gave me an excellent driving tour of Dungannon and the route of the old Sandy & Beaver Canal.

My gratitude and appreciation goes to my friend and fellow writer Wayne Vinson who read my manuscript, weeded out a bunch of typos, and made several helpful suggestions. Wayne also introduced me to Jerry Walker in Dungannon and accompanied us on the tour there.

I have been greatly helped by the clear guidance and professional direction of the staff at the University of Akron Press, including Interim Director Andrew Borowiec, who encouraged me to broaden the ride selection and guided the initial stages of the work; Director Thomas Bacher, who edited the book; Production Coordinator Amy Freels, who did the page design; Marketing Manager Julia Gammon; and Coordinator of Press Operations Carol Slatter.

My thanks also to graphic designer Lan Le, whose first-class cover design makes me proud to show my book. I am indebted as well to Kevin Butler, manager of the University of Akron's Geographic Information Sciences Research Department of Geography and Planning, and to graduate student Jeff McKee, whose work in the Laboratory for Cartographic and Spatial Analysis, Department of Geography and Planning, produced the maps. I am also indebted to graduate assistants Dan Von Holten, Varsha Arjun, and Tara Kaloz, and student assistant Kaitlin Trushel for their careful checking of the historical facts included in this book and the mileage guides in the map section. Thanks as well to student assistant Amanda Gilliland for providing the graphics for "Changing Gears" and for other help with the book.

And finally, but always, my love and appreciation for my wife Jeanine Purdum, who tolerates with good cheer my hours away from home while I'm wheeling down Ohio's back roads.

Introduction

I am a veteran of long bicycle rides. The year I turned fifty, I pedaled across America, from coast to coast. Five years later, I rode my bicycle the length of U.S. Route 62, from Niagara Falls, New York, to El Paso, Texas. I may yet take more extended bicycle journeys, but in the meantime, I have enjoyed exploring the byways closer to home. I live in Northeast Ohio, and my part of the state is loaded with scenery every bit as impressive as places I rode out west. Granted the scale is different, but the natural beauty of Ohio, especially when one gets off the main thoroughfares, is often grand.

This part of Ohio is filled with low-traffic back roads, small villages, and a wide variety of geography, from the relatively flat lands of Portage, Trumbull, and Geauga counties to the profusion of steep hills and sweeping vistas in Carroll, southern Stark, and Tuscarawas counties. The region also includes Ashtabula County, with its seventeen covered bridges, and Holmes County, with its many Amish farms, one-room schoolhouses, and horse-drawn buggies. Other counties in the quadrant have their unique and interesting sights as well.

What's more, some of these out-of-the-way places offer glimpses of the Buckeye State's history. On the routes described in this book you can see the site of an experiment in utopian communal living, a place where a colony of Native Americans was massacred, a "hollow" that was occupied by characters so notorious that lawmen refused to enter it, remnants of two canals and the historic Lincoln Highway, the childhood home of famed attorney Clarence Darrow, a couple of museum villages, and more.

In narrating the rides, I not only describe routes for cycling and sights, but also tell of my experiences actually pedaling these loops. I've done so intentionally so you get a feel for what bicycling beyond neighborhood boundaries and in less than ideal weather conditions can be. I rode on beautiful days, but also when I had to contend with very high and low temperatures, strong headwinds and variable road conditions, including melting snow. I've ridden in light and heavy traffic, travelled on city streets, country roads, and state highways, encountered unexpected pavement variations, found interesting objects on the roadside, and pedaled like mad to keep up with a faster rider. This range of experiences (and more) contributed to my memorable and enjoyable rides. Similar adventures can be part of your cycling stories as well, especially if you don't limit your trips to "perfect" days.

One thing the rides include, as the book title suggests, is lunch, roughly at the midpoint of each loop. That came about because I have always preferred to have a destination when I cycle. I've ridden plenty of excursions with no stop scheduled, jaunts simply for the fun and exercise of being out on the bike, but I enjoyed even more treks where a lunch stop was on the itinerary. There was also a practical reason: When I stopped to eat, I was able to ride longer distances. Of course, I could always have carried a lunch with me, and occasionally I did, but I like to dine in the little eateries off the beaten track as much to get the flavor of the place as the taste of entrees.

That said, this book should not be considered a directory to fine dining. The food is tasty in every one of the restaurants I suggest, and a few, such as the Spread Eagle Tavern in Hanoverton and Des Dutch Essenhaus in Shreve are outstanding, and but in most cases, the places chosen offer "everyday" fare, down-to-earth and filling, but not always epicurean, delights. In planning this book, I could have selected great restaurants and then figured out routes to include them, but my goal was always to find great rides and then locate acceptable lunch stops on those circuits. The fact that many of these cafes and diners are in small towns, where the need is simply for a place to get a bite to eat, often dictates the kind of menus available. In some cases, quite aside from the chow, being in the restaurants themselves are interesting experiences, such as in Sunrise Café in Geneva-on-the-Lake or in the Steel Trolley Diner in Lisbon.

I did have a couple of rules when picking lunch locations, however. First, I stayed away from fast-food and chain restaurants simply because such places give not the flavor of the community but the flavor of the franchise. And second, I did not pick any place where a person would feel unwelcome dressed in bicycle shorts or sporting "helmet hair."

Because these restaurants are located in small towns, they face the same problems of other businesses in low-traffic places, and can change their hours of operation without warning or even go out of business, so I have provided the phone number for each of them so that you can call ahead to verify that they will be open when you arrive.

In the event that you don't care for my selected eateries, several of the lunch-stop communities have other restaurants, and you may wish to sample them. Yet another option is to start the ride in the lunch-stop community and eat in the start-end location, which is possible on all but a couple of the rides.

In the end, of course, this book is not a guide for dining but a ticket to ride. Whether you stop for lunch or not, these are interesting routes that will give you miles of pleasure in Ohio's great outdoors.

Happy riding!

Before You Ride

Pedaling to Lunch

Cycling is fun. Unless you want to become a professional cyclist, weekend riding doesn't require a lot of expensive or fancy equipment, and almost anybody in reasonable health can pedal around. The following advice will make your cycling safer, more enjoyable, and more comfortable.

Safety

Always wear a helmet. While falls are not common, a good-quality helmet will spare you serious head injury. Several years ago, I was rolling downhill on a country road when my map suddenly blew out of my front pouch. Without thought, I hit the brakes hard to stop and retrieve it. I flew over the handlebars and tumbled several times on the gravel of the road's shoulder. My bike ended up with bent handlebars and a damaged rear wheel. I got a pulled thigh muscle, numerous cuts, scrapes, abrasions, and bent glasses. My head, however, was okay, but only because the helmet took the blow—a blow so hard that my helmet split. It "died" and I didn't. I was sore, but I was able to straighten the bent wheel and ride home.

I also suggest using a flashing taillight on overcast days and after dark. A headlight is a good accessory, too. Many of these and other items are reviewed in *Bicycling* (www.bicycling.com).

Mechanical Problems

Being prepared for minor mechanical problems will make your day of riding more enjoyable. If you keep your bike properly maintained to begin with, you are unlikely to have any problems major enough to derail your ride. And unlike a car, most of the things that can go wrong mechanically on a bike do not actually prevent you from continuing your journey. A broken spoke or two, a squeaky bearing, or even a broken shift-cable will rarely force you to stop. However, a flat tire will, literally, deflate your progress.

To prevent tire trouble, start out with good tires inflated to the pressure recommended on the tire itself. Since flats can occur nonetheless, I carry a spare inner tube, a set of three tire levers (the "spoon-shaped" tools for removing a tire from the rim to install the new tube), and a small air pump that mounts to my bike frame. (Alternatively, you can use a CO2 cartridge system for re-inflating the tire.) Since my wheels can be removed from the frame by opening quick-release levers (a common feature on most newer bikes), I need no other tools for dealing with a flat. If your wheels are attached to the frame with axle nuts, you'll have to carry the appropriate-sized wrench to remove the wheel.

Additionally, I carry a small combination Allen wrench (hex key) set that enables me to adjust any bolt on the bike, though I seldom have to use it. I also take along a chain-breaker tool for chain repairs, though I don't consider that essential for most riders. In the unlikely event of a broken chain, your best recourse may be to use your cell phone to call a friend for a ride. All of these tools come in small combination sets that can be found at bicycle shops.

Clothing

Prior to riding, I usually check the local forecast so I am aware of the temperature, wind speed and direction, and amount of sun I will encounter. This allows me to dress appropriately and avoid taking extra layers of clothing. If the weather conditions will be changing, I might have to take off one layer or bring an additional layer.

I recommend bicycle shorts for all rides (under other layers on cold days), but in warm and dry weather, you can get away with T-shirts and other everyday garments. Many riders don't cycle in colder weather, but if you do, it is wise to dress in layers and wear clothing made of the performance fabrics that wick moisture away from your body. The standard advice for cold weather riding is to think in terms of three layers: a base layer of wicking fabric, a middle layer of insulating fabric, and an outer layer of wind-breaking fabric. That advice is fine as far as it goes, but in practice, it is not precise enough to ensure comfort at different temperatures. Depending on the temperature, you may need to don two or three insulating layers between the base layer and the outer layer.

The best way to determine what you need to wear on cooler days is trial-and-error coupled with a little record keeping. Trial-and-error is not difficult if you have some arrangement on your bike to stash extra clothing, such as a rack, a pouch, or saddlebag. Then just take a bit more clothing than you think you are likely to need and see what actually keeps you comfortable. Unless your memory is exceptional, however, the key is to keep a written record of the temperature and the required number of layers. In my experience, for every five degrees the temperature drops below 65, I need to add a piece of clothing—long sleeves, gloves, a skull cap, an additional pair of socks, etc.

Comfort

The single most important item for comfort on long rides is a properly fitted saddle. Fit is far more important than padding. You can find saddles that feature lots of padding and that feel great for short neighborhood rides. But on longer hauls, the padding compresses and doesn't feel nearly as good. Saddles come in different widths, different material, and are structured differently for men and women. You might need to experiment with a few saddles, and some bike shops even have loaner saddles you can try. Personally, I've found that the classic leather saddle works best for me.

After you've chosen a saddle, have it properly adjusted. A professional at a local bike shop can do this for you, or you can also find instructions on the Internet or in your user's manual. Saddles need to be set for the proper height, tilt, and distance from your handlebars. You can find information on choosing and adjusting saddles at www.bicycling.com and other websites.

To stay comfortable during your ride, buy bicycle shorts. Shorts are important because they have a little padding, provide support, and are designed to reduce friction, rubbing, and to wick away moisture. Follow the manufacturer's instruction on proper wear.

Take at least two water bottles on rides. I usually fill one with a sports drink. I also carry an energy bar because cycling burns lots of calories. In hot weather, I take along pretzels to replenish my body's sodium level.

With attention to these few matters, you are all set for great adventure on northeast Ohio's byways.

Here are a few websites to check out:

Adventure Cycling Association
    www.adventurecycling.org
League of American Bicyclists
    www.bikcleague.org
Ohio Department of Transportation
    www2.dot.state.oh.us/bike
Pedestrian and Bicycling Information Center
    www.bicyclinginfo.org
Sheldon Brown's Bicycle Technical Info
    sheldonbrown.com

Ride 1
North Coast

Route: Fairport Harbor to Geneva-on-the-Lake loop
Counties: Lake, Ashtabula
Terrain: Relatively flat
Distance: 54 miles
Lunch: Sunrise Café, Geneva-on-the-Lake (440-466-8667)
Points of Interest: Lake Erie, seven parks, Fairport Harbor
  Marine Museum and Lighthouse, Geneva-on-the-Lake
How to Get There: Fairport Harbor Lakefront Park is located
  on High Street in Fairport Harbor, Ohio. Take State Route 2
  (SR2) to the Fairport Harbor/Richmond Street exit. Proceed
  north to the Richmond Street/State Route 283 (SR283)
  intersection. Proceed north to High Street. Turn right onto
  High Street to the park.

L AKE ERIE is the eleventh largest lake in the world by surface area, and it provides Ohio with an extensive north coast. This ride gives you an opportunity to explore some of that coast, as well as to visit seven parks situated on the shore, with a lunch stop at the resort town of Geneva-on-the-Lake.

Fairport Harbor Lakefront Park in the village of Fairport Harbor, a community of about 3,200 people, has water on two sides—Lake Erie to its north and the Grand River to its west. The town, part of Lake County, is a working harbor, shipping out salt, limestone, sand, and gravel. The first of these commodities comes from deep mines that extend as much as two miles out under the lake itself, making Ohio one of the top salt-producing states in the nation. The salt beds, the remains of a saltwater sea that covered the area in prehistoric times, are as deep as two thousand feet in some places. Fairport Harbor and Cleveland are the only two ports shipping out salt on the Great Lakes.

Changing Gears

Every summer, Fairport Harbor Lakefront Park hosts the Lighthouse Triathlon, which includes a twenty-kilometer bicycle circuit.

I park my truck in Lakefront Park, which is primarily a swimming beach, though it also has a picnic shelter and children's playground. I look out at the lake and see the breakwater barriers that form harbor channel guides. On the northern end of the western breakwater is a forty-two-foot lighthouse with a two-story attached keeper's house. These days, no one lives in the house, but the tower continues to aid navigation because it is fitted with an automated three hundred millimeter optic lens and operated by the Coast Guard.

I noticed another lighthouse as I drove into the park. The Old Fairport Harbor Marine Museum and Lighthouse sits at the top of the park's entrance road and has not operated since 1925, when it was replaced by the lighthouse out on the breakwater. The villagers rallied to keep the old lighthouse and the keeper's house from being torn down, and the complex now serves as a museum. This lighthouse and its predecessor on the same spot guided ships to the harbor for a full hundred years. The lighthouse

Fairport Harbor Marine Museum and Lighthouse. Courtesy of Lasse O. Hiltunen.

is sixty feet high and has a spiral staircase of sixty-nine steps. The museum displays artifacts related to life on the Great Lakes. The museum and lighthouse are open to the public, but only for afternoon hours on Wednesdays and weekends during the summer months. Since I am there on a Friday morning, I can't go in. Anyway, I am eager to get on the road.

Before heading out, I take a moment to gaze westward, looking across the Grand River. I can't really make out what I want to see, but the shaft of the Morton Salt mine is somewhere in the industrial cluster on the far side of the river, not very far from where I stand.

As I ride on Second Street, parallel to the shoreline, I pass a park belonging to the village. (I did not include this green space, which occupies a whole block, in the park count since it is not right on the lake.) I stop to look at the unusual monument on

Finnish Monument in Veteran's Park, Fairport. Courtesy of Lasse O. Hiltunen.

the lawn—a triangular red granite block, with two metal swans on the top. Rather than being a tribute to war veterans, as monuments in many parks are, this one pays tribute to the Finnish families who helped establish and grow Fairport Harbor. The stone of this monument was quarried and polished in Finland. Fairport Harbor also has a Finnish Heritage Museum on its main street.

As I pedal through the village, I am guided by a series of green-and-white signs marking the path of the Lake Erie Coastal Ohio Trail, a national scenic byway on public roads along the Lake Erie shore. For the most part, the first half of the North Coast ride, from Fairport Harbor to the lunch stop in Geneva-on-the-Lake, follows the Coastal Ohio Trail. The whole Coastal Ohio Trail is 293 miles long, extending from Conneaut to Toledo, along which are more than three hundred natural, historical, and cultural sites. Obviously I am cycling only a portion.

After I wend my way through Fairport Harbor along the Coastal Ohio Trail, I leave the village heading east on Fairport Nursery Road. This artery, State Route 535 (SR535), is not heavily traveled, perhaps because it passes through a region where no one would want to live. In terms of natural setting, the area is attractive enough and within sight of the lake, but the large, empty fields on both sides of the road are surrounded by high fences that clearly mean "stay out." Several of these fields were previously used as dumping grounds and "soup ponds" for toxic chemicals and industrial waste from companies once located along this road and have since become Superfund sites for toxic-waste cleanup programs. At least some of the cleanup has been successful. An area resident told me that a golf course and housing units will eventually be developed on some of this ground.

As I continue on Fairport Nursery Road, I pass Painesville Speedway, and then a stretch with houses on both sides. I don't see a nursery, leading me to wonder what has given the road its moniker.

As I draw near to State Route 2 (SR2), a four-lane superslab, I make my first departure from the Coastal Ohio Trail to avoid the traffic on North Ridge Road/US Route 20 (US20) which parallels SR2 on its south side and on which the trail runs. Just before the entrance ramp to SR2, I turn onto Blase-Nemeth Road. (I assume the first half of that name is pronounced "blaze" and not "blasé.") After a little more than a half mile, Blase-Nemeth crosses Bacon Road, and I see a "No Outlet" sign. That information, however, doesn't jibe with my map, so I continue on Blase-Nemeth. I find that "No Outlet" isn't quite true, though if you were driving a car down the road, you'd have to take the sign seriously. At the east end of the road, Blase-Nemeth becomes one-way, westbound. Coming from the west, however, Blase-Nemeth is a through street all the way.

The one-way eastbound portion of Blase-Nemeth is only two-tenths of a mile long, and it has a wide-paved shoulder, so

I simply continue on the shoulder, riding this short distance the "wrong" way but not competing with the traffic at all.

At the end of Blase-Nemeth, I move onto Ridge Road for a short time, but I am well beyond the SR2 exit ramps and have significantly reduced my stint on the busier thoroughfare.

I turn off North Ridge Road and cut north on Lane Road. I make my way toward the lake in a series of stairstep turns that eventually brings me to Parmly Road and Perry Township Park, the second of the seven lakefront parks. Much of the space in this one is devoted to playing fields, but being right on the lakefront, the green space also gives me access to the lake. I ride into the park on its paved lane and follow it right to where I have a splendid view of the water. After stopping for a good look, I continue on the lane and follow it back to Parmly Road, where I resume my journey.

I follow Parmly Road back down to North Ridge Road. When I reach North Ridge Road, I hop back on that artery for nine-tenths of a mile, until I reach the next north-running road, Antioch, which allows me to return to the shore. Antioch Road ends at Lockwood Road, which is the closest through street to the lake at this point.

Immediately across Lockwood from where Antioch ends, I find the third of the seven parks, this one called Lakeshore Reservation, which belongs to the Lake Metroparks system. An eighty-

Lakeshore Reservation

Lakeshore Reservation was once owned by ten individuals who had summer or permanent residences along Lake Erie. Several property boundaries are still visible because of treelines that remain. The property was developed as a park because the site had the most naturally stable beach conditions with a mature stand of trees along Lake Erie in Lake County. A memorial was dedicated on October 29, 1978, to Luanna Strock, wife of the park system's first naturalist, Don Strock. The memorial includes a sculpted sundial, a cable bridge, and a bronze cast of the area.

From the Lake Metroparks website (www.lakemetroparks.com)

four-acre site, for day use only, the park features a sculpture garden, picnic facilities, a hiking trail, and access for fishing. I pedal into the park, take the right fork of the access road, and follow it a short distance to where it ends in a parking lot. Between the lot and lake is a grassy mall, and I head down its path toward the lake, walking my bike. The mall ends on a bluff overlooking the lake. If I had wanted to get down to the shore level, I could have trod one of the side trails to a set of steps. I am content, however, to view the water from the bluff.

Lakeshore Reservation, and the others similar to it, provide access to and unobstructed views of the lake. Without these parks I would only be able to glimpse Lake Erie, because many homes have been built between the road and the water. And naturally, those homeowners wouldn't welcome strangers traipsing across their properties to get to the lake.

Heading out of the Lakeshore Reservation, I continue east on Lockwood Road. The further due east I go, however, the further the lakeshore, which also moves north as it extends east, moves from me, so shortly after leaving Lakeshore Reservation, I turn left onto McMackin Road, and then right onto Chapel Road.

I barely take more than a few strokes of the pedals on Chapel when park number four comes into view. Bill Stanton Community Park is a thirty-three-acre site that includes an in-ground

---

Bill Stanton Community Park

With twelve hundred feet of scenic Lake Erie shoreline, this thirty-three-acre former church camp was under imminent threat of development when it was protected with the help of the Trust for Public Land. At the time it was protected, the property was the largest privately-held undeveloped lakeshore in northeast Ohio. Generations of Greater Clevelanders have fond memories of the property as Camp Isaac Jogues. Today, it is a community park for Madison Township. The park is named in honor of Bill Stanton, who was the longtime congressman from the area.

From the Trust for Public Land (www.tpl.org)

swimming pool, basketball and tennis courts, a playground, beach access, a picnic pavilion, a banquet hall, and cabins that can be rented for public and family events. I loop through the park, pause at the lakeside vista point, and then return to Chapel Road.

I continue riding, moving east and north to stay near the lake. One of my next uninterrupted views of Lake Erie comes at the fifth park, which belongs to Madison Township. This park sits at the water's edge right where Hubbard Road ends and has the look and feel of a village park, with ball diamonds and a picnic shelter. There are several dining establishments facing two sides of the park (Madison Township Park). This point on the route makes a good lunch destination if you want to head back to your car. Simply eat here and then ride south on Hubbard Road to Middle Ridge Road. Doing so will cut the trip from fifty-four to thirty-six miles.

Changing Gears

Dining near Madison Township Park:
The Landing; Romans IV; Flying Burrito Cantina; Wagon Wheel; Spinnaker Dining Room; Max's Carry Out; Holiday; Karen's Pizza, Subs, & More

I press on, however, and turn north onto Dock Road. Up the road about four-tenths of a mile, in the very northeast corner of Lake County, is Arcola Creek Metropark. Unlike the other parks, this one exists more for the benefit of wild creatures than tame recreationalists. It does accommodate fishermen, but it func-

Arcola Creek

The town of Ellensburg was built at the junction of Arcola Creek and Lake Erie. It was a thriving community of shipbuilders, fishermen, and commerce. The Arcole Iron Works was located south of the mouth of the creek (then called Cunningham Creek after Captain John Cunningham, who purchased property there in the early 1800s). Arcole Iron Works was, at one time, the largest industry in Ohio. Bog iron, discovered in Madison Township near North Ridge Road in 1812, and the abundance of timber provided the raw materials for iron furnaces. Iron stoves, kettles, hollowware, and other heavy castings were made at the foundry.

From the Lake Metroparks website (www.lakemetroparks.com)

tions mainly as a wildlife habitat. The park encompasses the estuary for Arcola Creek, which empties into Lake Erie at this point, but in the days when Ohio was being settled, the land around the creek was turned into a center of commerce. Before the arrival of Europeans, this estuary, along with several others, hosted swamps, marshland, and abundant wildlife, but the early settlers dredged many of them to provide better transportation routes. While pushing a roadway through the Arcola Creek marshland, the workers discovered iron ore, and soon iron furnaces were set up nearby to exploit the material. Hotels, stores, shipbuilding yards, and housing followed. Once the ore played out, people moved away and the land gradually reverted to its natural state.

Changing Gears

Arcola Creek Park is a place where the fresh waters of the creek mix with the waves of Lake Erie. It is one of the last remaining natural estuaries in Ohio.

From the Lake Metroparks Website

I pull into the park, dismount and walk to the nearby viewing deck and gaze at the marsh-and-sand-dune habitat in front of me. The area is known for its flora and fauna. I look at Mother Nature's beauty a moment or two and follow the footpath to the lakefront for a different vantage point. Satisfied, I return to my bike and retrace my route on Dock Road to the next road heading east, Cashen Road. A bridge on this road takes me across Arcola Creek and I enter Ashtabula County.

Changing Gears

Geographically, Ashtabula County is the largest county in Ohio, while Lake County is the smallest.

I pedal north eight-tenths of a mile on County Line Road to Lake Road and make my way to the last of the seven parks. Geneva State Park is a seven hundred-acre reserve right on the shore of Lake Erie. Lake Road runs directly through the extensive park, which features two miles of lakefront and a natural sand beach. The park also offers camping, cabins, hiking trails, picnic facilities, a boat ramp, and a lodge with a restaurant and conference center. Most of the facilities are not visible from Lake Road. I ride through the woods, a pleasingly natural jaunt.

After a two-mile cruise through the park, I head north again and pedal into Geneva-on-the-Lake. The main street of this vil-

The Lodge at Geneva-on-the-Lake. Courtesy of the Lodge at Geneva-on-the-Lake.

lage is a cross between a circus midway and an old-fashioned seaside resort. Set up to entertain tourists, Geneva-on-the-Lake is a community that lives for summer and rolls up its sidewalks in winter.

The beaches and excellent sturgeon fishing in the area of what is now Geneva-on-the-Lake led to the rise of Ohio's first summer resort. In 1869, two young men opened a public picnic area,

Geneva-on-the-Lake

And after Ashtabula, which was as charming as any of these little cities to look at, with wide shady streets of homes and children playing gaily on lawns and in open lots everywhere, came Geneva-on-the-Lake, or Geneva Beach, as it seemed to be called—one of those new-sprung summer resorts of the middle west, which always amuse me by their endless gaucheries and the things they have not and never seem to miss. One thing they do have is the charm of newness and hope and possibility, which excels almost anything of the kind you can find elsewhere.

From A Hoosier Holiday, *Theodore Dreiser, John Lane Company, 1916*

*Thomas Edison, John Burroughs, and Henry Ford, full-length portrait, standing,
facing front, at Edison's home in Ft. Myers, Florida, 1914.
Courtesy of the Library of Congress, Prints and Photographs Division.*

which was followed in short order by a horse-powered carousel,
campgrounds, cottages, a dancehall, hotels, a golf course, and a
"strip" of eateries, nightclubs, and various amusements. Initially,
Geneva-on-the-Lake was a vacation spot for the wealthy seeking
to get away from the heat and bustle of the cities in the summer-

Henry Ford

John Burroughs, Edison, and I with Harvey S. Firestone made several vagabond trips together. We went in motor caravans and slept
under canvas. Once, we gypsied through the Adirondacks and again
through the Alleghenies heading southward. The trips were good
fun—except that they began to attract too much attention.

From My Life and Work, Henry Ford, *Doubleday, 1922*

The Sunrise Café, Geneva-on-the-Lake. Courtesy of S. Hupertz.

time. In the early 1900s, John D. Rockefeller, Harvey Firestone, and Henry Ford came to the area to camp out (with the assistance of a bevy of servants). The coming of the automobile eventually made the community a feasible destination for working families as well. Today, the community is a destination to folks from all walks of life.

My immediate interest in the community is not as a source of entertainment, but as a source of food. Having pedaled twenty-nine miles in brisk lake air, I am famished.

I choose the Sunrise Café because on a previous midwinter drive through Geneva-on-the-Lake, I found that the Sunrise Café was the *only* eatery open at that time of year. On that trip, I ordered a dish called "Chili-Mac with Cheese" and found it absolutely delicious, not to mention reasonably priced. So now, faced with lots of choices for dining, I return to the location of my previous culinary delight.

SUNRISE CAFÉ, GENEVA-ON-THE-LAKE
5367 Lake Road East, Geneva, OH 44041
440-466-8667
Open year-round

HOURS
Summer: 7:00 A.M. to 3:00 P.M.
Winter: 8:00 A.M. to 2:00 P.M.
Closed Monday and Tuesday

SPECIALTIES
Buffalo Burgers, Messy Meal, Biscuits and Gravy

The Sunrise Café is in small quarters. I sit at the counter where there are a few stools to watch my food being prepared, and chat with the cook.

The café serves breakfast all day and lunch, too. Lunch offerings include sandwiches and fries, plus several dishes based on chili. After eating my chili-mac meal on my first visit, I mentioned to the cook, who I gathered was part of the family that owned the place, that the seasoning was just right in the dish. "Well," he said, "when I was making it, I let the guys at the counter have a taste from time to time. When they say it tastes right, I stop adding seasoning."

Several of the people in the restaurant are apparently regulars, and there is a lot of jesting and bantering going on. I am soon included. I shouldn't have been surprised, as one comment on the menu notes, "Most meals at Sunrise come with a side of sarcasm. Feel free to join the fun and know that if we pick on you, it's because we love you (or it's REALLY early)." Another read "If you're truly in a hurry and can't stick around, you can call ahead and have any menu item made 'to go.' (Sorry, only *small* helpings of abuse come with 'to go' orders.)"

If your ride on the North Coast route is during late spring or summer, you will find the Sunrise open no matter what day you visit, from 7 A.M. to 3 P.M. In the off season, it's closed Mondays and Tuesdays, but open the rest of the days of the week from 8 A.M. to 2 P.M.

Full and happy, I climb back on my bike for the rest of the ride. The first part of the return requires retracing my route through Geneva State Park and back across the line into Lake County. But when I reach Dock Road, I turn south and wheel down Dock Road, cross North Ridge Road, and take Arcola Road to Middle Ridge Road, where I head west. Although Middle Ridge roughly parallels North Ridge Road, it is not as heavily traveled and it offers me a friendly passage.

Middle Ridge runs past several large nurseries, with acres of plants and row after row of greenhouses. I didn't know it at the time, but Lake County is home to more than one hundred wholesale nurseries, which supply plants to garden centers in several states. The rich soils deposited here by ice-age glaciers and Lake Erie's moderation of the climate make it feasible to grow a wide range of plants.

After seven miles on Middle Ridge, I ride through the edge of Perry. I see a sign announcing that the village had been the home of Hugh Mosher (1819–1896), the man who was the fifer in the famous "The Spirit of '76" painting by another Ohioan, Archibald M. Willard, who lived in Wellington (the lunch destination for ride 7; see page 80).

I pedal out of Perry on Narrows Road to North Ridge Road and I ride two-tenths of a mile to Blase-Nemeth Road. Blase-Nemeth funnels me to Fairport Nursery Road and on to Fairport Harbor. I complete my journey of Ohio's North Coast.

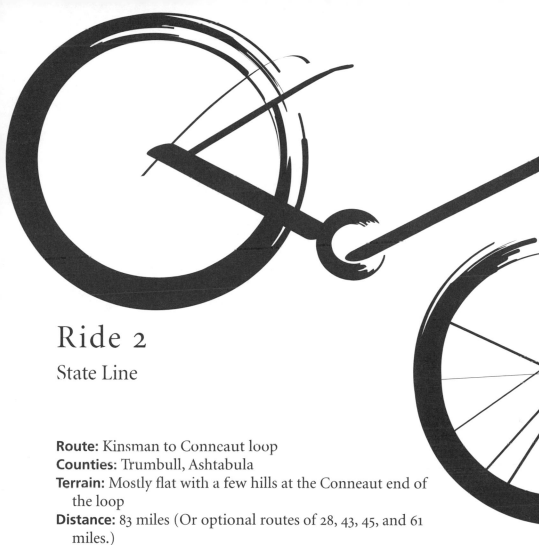

Ride 2
State Line

Route: Kinsman to Conneaut loop
Counties: Trumbull, Ashtabula
Terrain: Mostly flat with a few hills at the Conneaut end of the loop
Distance: 83 miles (Or optional routes of 28, 43, 45, and 61 miles.)
Lunch: State Street Diner, Conneaut (440-593-5061) or Times Square Restaurant, Kinsman (330-876-3241)
Points of Interest: Pymatuning Lake State Park, covered bridges, Clarence Darrow octagon house
How to get there: *Kinsman*: The Kinsman Public Library is located on Church Street in Kinsman, Ohio. Take State Route 7/5 (SR7/SR5) into Kinsman. This becomes Main Street. Turn West onto Church Street.
Conneaut: The Conneaut Port Authority is located on Broad Street in Conneaut, Ohio. Take SR7 north into Conneaut. Turn east (right) at the State Street intersection. State Street will intersect with Broad Street (SR7). Turn north (left) onto Broad Street.

A T eighty-three miles, this state line ride is the longest one in this book, but since it is relatively flat, it is by no means the toughest. Unless you happen to ride on a windy day, the main challenge is distance. Cyclists who ride regularly will like the extended duration.

If you don't have the time or the inclination for a ride of this length, but still want to ride in the state line area, you can shorten the ride easily. One approach is simply to cut the ride in half, using Footville–Richmond Road as a crossover link (marked on the map as an optional crossover). In this way, you will have effectively made State Line into two rides of approximately forty-three to forty-five miles each, one starting and ending in Conneaut and one starting and ending in Kinsman. I have offered a restaurant suggestion in both Conneaut and Kinsman for this reason, and for those who ride the entire route, you might be inclined to have breakfast in one eatery and lunch in the other.

A second option for shortening the route is to cut through Andover on US Route 6 (us6) and State Route 85 (sr85) (marked on the map as an optional crossover). If you start in Kinsman, the ride would be about twenty-eight miles; if you started in Conneaut, the ride runs about sixty-one miles. In either case, Andover would be the place to grab lunch since I don't know of any other location between Conneaut and Kinsman offering a place to dine.

If you bike the entire route, you will visit a working harbor town (Conneaut), view several covered bridges, see a quintessential Western Reserve village (Kinsman), pedal through miles of countryside, and ride beside a beautiful lake (Pymatuning), where you can even stop for a swim. (Depending on where you live, it might be more convenient to start at Conneaut or Kinsman. I have provided two sets of "Miles and Directions," for both start points.)

I started from Kinsman. I am riding this route with my friend and cycling buddy, Wayne Ostrander. We leave my truck in the parking lot of the public library on Church Street and take a moment to look at the Presbyterian church across the street. Like other Western Reserve communities, Kinsman has a New England feel. The church was modeled on the Old North Church in Boston, the one with the famous steeple where the signal lanterns were hung to set Paul Revere off on his midnight ride to warn the American colonists that the British troops were coming.

From the library, we pedal two blocks south to the public square for the official starting point of the jaunt. We had eaten before leaving home, but we could have ridden another block south to Times Square Restaurant, which is open all day long and serves, besides breakfast, a selection of sandwiches and dinners. Times Square is the recommended lunch stop for riders who start in Conneaut. From the square, Wayne and I head north on State Route 7 (SR7).

Kinsman is named for the original owner of the town site, John Kinsman, who arrived there in 1799. Since the community is unincorporated, there are no population figures available, but there are about two thousand people in the whole township, somewhat fewer in the village proper.

After a few turns of our wheels, we pass a two-story octagon-shaped house on the left-hand side of the street. While the structure is notable for its unique architecture, it was also the boy-

TIMES SQUARE RESTAURANT
8078 Main Street, Kinsman, OH 44428
330-876-3241
Open year-round

HOURS
6:00 A.M. to 9:00 P.M.

SPECIALTIES
Homemade pies

Clarence Darrow House. Courtesy of Leon Reed.

hood home of Clarence Darrow (1857–1938), the most famous trial attorney in the United States in the 1920s. Darrow's reputation came in part because of his defense of John Scopes, a schoolteacher who had been charged with violating Tennessee law by teaching evolution. Because evolution, in effect, was on trial, the 1925 case became known as the "Monkey Trial."

Clarence Darrow

Down the hill on the edge of the stream stood a log cheese-house,—at least, it seems so now,—and back of this cheese-house beside the brook must have been a favorite spot for me to wade and fish, although I have no remembrance that I ever caught anything. . . . Beyond the stream was an orchard. I am uncertain whether or not it belonged to my father, although I rather think it must have been owned by somebody else, the apples always looked so tempting and so red. . . . Anyhow, this orchard stands out very plainly in my mind. It was a large orchard,—in fact, a great forest of trees; and I remember that I always stole over the fence intending to get the apples on the nearest tree.

From Farmington *by Clarence Darrow, B. W. Huebsch, 1919 (third edition)*

*Portrait of Clarence Darrow, circa 1922. Courtesy Library of Congress,
Prints and Photographs Division.*

Continuing north, but still within the village limits, we pass
the home of a formerly well-known person, James McGranahan
(1840–1907). Although little remembered today, McGranahan
was popular within Christian revival circles during his lifetime.
He was a singer-songwriter who accompanied the evangelist
Dwight L. Moody on several campaigns. In fact, McGranahan
was to Moody in the nineteenth century what George Beverly
Shea was to Billy Graham in the twentieth century. McGrana-

Review of *The Gospel Male Chorus Book* by James McGranahan

The first ground of recommendation is simplicity. The second is charm
of harmony, for with all the simplicity the harmonies are very chaste
and sweet. The third is utility. We can imagine no more delightful
occupation for the members of a Young Men's Christian Association
than spending one or more evenings a week in extemporized con-
certs from these choruses. Fourthly, elevating tendency. The words
are all of evangelical impart. . . . We would suggest as some of the
choicest pieces—"In the Silent Midnight Watches," "Ye must be Born
again," "Memories of Galilee," and "There's a Home."

From The Preacher's Analyst, *E. Stock, 1884*

han's best-known song, "There Shall Be Showers of Blessings," is still sung in churches today. McGranahan spent the final twenty years of his life in Kinsman, constructing the home in 1887. The building, which is a sizeable mansion by most measures, today houses Baumgardner Funeral Home.

Out of Kinsman, we continue on SR7 and turn onto Kinsman–Pymatuning Road toward the easternmost road in this part of Ohio. That road, which parallels the Ohio–Pennsylvania border, occasionally ends at a crossroad only to resume again a short distance to the right or left with a new name. We pick up the road where it is called Ward North Road, but after a small jog on a crossroad, it continues north as Simons South Road. (Yes, Simons South is *north* of Ward North, but don't blame me. *I* didn't name them!) Farther on, after a jog on Slater Road, the byway becomes Pymatuning Lake Road (CR274), a name it retains as it edges along Pymatuning Reservoir and beyond until it ends at US6. Another jog right and the route continues on as Creek Road (CR340), jogs again to become Middle Road, and, after one more jog, finishes in Conneaut as Furnace Road.

Pymatuning

Pymatuning: An Algonquin word of the Delaware dialect applied to a person whose mouth was crooked.

From Handbook of Tribal Names of Pennsylvania, *S. N., 1908*

On this northbound thread, the only piece that we find to be a bit of an anomaly—not running due north—is Creek Road, which connects US6 and Marcy Road. Creek Road tracks north–northwest, so that when it arrives at Marcy Road, the jog to the east to pick up northbound Middle Road is nearly a mile and a half. When you first bike onto Creek Road, continuing straight north might tempt you, but I recommend against that route,

the road is not maintained during the winter and another indicates "travel at your own risk." Take Creek Road and the Marcy jog for safety.

Before getting that far north, we find ourselves pedaling alongside Pymatuning Reservoir, close enough for occasional good views of the expanse. Pymatuning is a seventeen thousand-acre lake that traverses the border between Ohio and Pennsylvania. It was formed in the 1930s by the damming of the Beaver and Shenango Rivers. *Pymatuning* is an Indian word meaning either "the man with a crooked mouth" or "whispering waters." The first interpretation lends itself to a more interesting story line.

On the Ohio side of the lake, much of the shoreline is given over to a state park, also named Pymatuning, which offers opportunities for camping, swimming, fishing, boating, hiking, and cabin stays. Andover is the closest community, and though it has a year-round population of only about 1,200, some thirty thousand vacationers descend on the area in the summertime, supporting several businesses and eateries in the village.

We bike closest to Andover at the point where Pymatuning Lake Road crosses SR85, which is only a little more than a mile from the center of Andover. Just before coming to that intersection, we see the entrance to the state park swimming beach. The day is hot already and the temperature is forecast to go into the nineties by midday with high humidity. A swim might feel good, but we have miles to go.

Origins of Andover, Ohio

Andover was established in 1883 when the Lake Shore & Michigan Southern Railways built a line branching from Ashtabula to Youngstown. This brought work and prosperity to Andover. Railroad families, retired farmers, merchants, and other business people mostly populated this area.

From Andover Area Chamber of Commerce

State Street Diner. Courtesy of Rich McBride.

State Route 85 continues straight east across the lake on a causeway into Pennsylvania, where the road becomes Route 285. Pennsylvania also has a state park named Pymatuning on its side of the water.

Wayne and I weren't planning to visit Andover, but I had been there previously. I had also read that the hamlet was officially founded in 1883 after some five hundred area residents signed a petition to incorporate the mile-square area. Clarence Darrow made sure all the *i*'s were dotted and all the *t*'s were crossed before he submitted the petition to the county commissioners.

Our ride north of Pymatuning Lake is on quiet country roads and the south wind helps us eat up the distance. Finally nearing Conneaut, we cruise down a long hill and descend into the community. We arrive in Conneaut on Furnace Road and make our way to US Route 20 (us20), a major highway. However, since Interstate 90 (i-90) parallels us20 (we had pedaled beneath the interstate on Furnace Road on our way into Conneaut), us20 carries mostly local traffic. Our mile ride into Conneaut's small downtown goes smoothly.

The Seneca Indians called the creek that empties into Lake Erie at this point *Konyiat,* which was anglicized as "Conneaut." *Konyiat* means either "place of many fish" or "place of the late snows." An early missionary in the area suggested that the name could have been a corruption of *gunniate*—"it is a long time since they have gone." I'm not sure what connection the third of those options might have to the place, but since Conneaut is a harbor community, the fish name seems logical, as is the snow reference, since Conneaut sits squarely in Ohio's snow belt. When white settlers arrived in Conneaut in 1799, they found some twenty to thirty Indian cabins. Reportedly, problems arose between the two groups and the Indians left. The community was incorporated as a village in 1832 and as a city in 1902. Today, about 12,500 people live in Conneaut.

We pull into the State Street Diner for lunch. The establishment is painted a can't-miss aqua color. Wayne and I are hungry. Wayne eats spaghetti and meatballs, and I have a chicken-fried steak dinner with a very tasty coleslaw on the side. (One benefit of rides of more than fifty miles is that you can eat as much as

STATE STREET DINER
251 State Street
Conneaut, OH 44030
440-593-5061
Open year-round

HOURS
6:00 A.M. to 8:00 P.M.

SPECIALTIES
Breakfast, Sandwiches, Macaroni Salad

NOTES
The owner takes pride in serving large portions.

Conneaut Waterfront. Courtesy of Irene Coxton.

you want because you usually burn more calories than you can consume.)

At the start of our ride, Wayne and I had each taken a bottle of sports drink and two bottles of water, but by the time we hit Conneaut, we had both gulped almost all the liquid, as well as several pretzels to replace the salt we were sweating out. At lunch, we rehydrate with big glasses of ice water and refill our bottles with more ice water that the waitress is kind enough to supply. That neither of us require a bathroom break tells us we need to be careful to guard against dehydration as we continue our ride.

 **Changing Gears**

Every summer, a reenactment of the D-Day landing in Normandy is held in Conneaut Township Park.

www.ddayohio.us

After lunch, we turn north from the diner, stop at a convenience store to purchase another bottle of a sports drink each, and pedal a little more than a mile and a half to Lake Erie and the harbor. We see many small boats in the marina, but no large ships at dock. Free public parking is available here, making it a perfect spot to leave your vehicle if you are beginning this ride from Conneaut.

Turning around, we make our way back to the business district where a sign on a local bank indicates the temperature is now ninety-five degrees. We ride a few blocks west, where we exit town on Center Street, which becomes Center Road. This road apparently continued out of town previously, but now it is severed into two pieces by I-90. We use a cutover street to get to SR7 and ride carefully when we come to the interstate's exit ramps. Once I-90 is behind us, we cut back over to the southern section of Center Road.

Changing Gears

Ashtabula County holds a covered bridge festival every fall.

www.coveredbridge festival.org

When I first examined a map of Conneaut while planning this ride, I had spotted two other routes out of town that would bypass the interstate interchange. Unfortunately, upon checking, I discovered both included long stretches of gravel roads that are not friendly to skinny-tired road bicycles.

Eventually we are able to turn west on Hatches Corners Road to State Road and a covered bridge. Covered bridges were once common in Ohio. Many have disappeared, but Ashtabula County still has seventeen of them; the last opened in September of 2008. The route selected for the return trip to Kinsman will take us past four of them.

Conneaut and Mormonism

Conneaut is also interesting in its connection with the first great conference of Mormons in the year 1834. . . . The village of Conneaut is a mile from Conneaut Station on the Lake Shore Railroad. It is the county seat and in its thrift and general appearance greatly resembles a New England town of the best type. At the eastern side of the village is the broad ravine through which the Conneaut River or Creek flows down to Lake Erie which is picturesque and beautiful. . . . An evening at Mr. Lake's residence was spent in hearing his reminiscences of certain circumstances in connection with the Spaulding's many facts. . . . There is no trace of this primitive homestead now or of the earth mound close to it but there are many people living in Conneaut who remember both.

From New Light on Mormonism, *Funk & Wagnalls, 1885*

The first covered bridge is a few hundred yards north of where Hatches Corners Road tees into State Road. At this intersection, we turn north on State to the bridge and ride through. We dismount for a better look at the structure, one obviously maintained and capable of carrying motor vehicles.

We remount, pedal back through the bridge, and head south on State Road up a long hill. Unlike the series of roads we used to make a continuous path north, the road we are now on will bring us all the way back to Kinsman without any shifts in direction. At some point after we cross SR84, State Road changes to Stanhope–Kelloggsville Road, though there is no sign to tell us exactly where that occurs. After crossing SR84, we roll into a small cluster of homes that is Kelloggsville, so it is likely the new moniker takes effect there. The other half of the name comes, not surprisingly, from a place called Stanhope, little more than a blip on the map about three miles north of Kinsman. The road retains the name all the way into Kinsman and ends at the village square.

Early Travel in the Mahoning Valley

In 1817 the first stage coach made its appearance in the Mahoning Valley, coming one year before the completion of the Ashtabula Turnpike, which was the first real road in the Western Reserve and connected the Lake with the Ohio, its southern terminus being at Wellsville. . . . The trip from Conneaut, where boats from Buffalo and Erie landed passengers for the west, to Wellsville, covering 100 miles, required twenty hours and cost the passengers, exclusive of their meals, $4.00. . . . Gradually the roads were improved and extended to all parts of the valley, as well as in all directions from it to points of importance. The paths through the woods were exchanged for earthen highways laid out, usually on land lines where this did not involve impossible grades, and banked in the middle to furnish drainage. The streams were crossed by wooden bridges, some of the more pretentious being covered. Wagons soon became common, and the more wealthy citizens began to appear in buggies and carriages.

From History of Youngstown and the Mahoning Valley, Ohio,
American Historical Society, 1921

The next three covered bridges are all on side roads joining Stanhope–Kelloggsville Road from the east, spanning a creek that runs beside our southbound course and making it easy to view them without wandering far from our route. The roads with bridges are Root, Graham, and Caine Roads. Each bridge is unique, but the one on Graham Road is no longer in service; the road crosses the stream on a newer, traditional bridge. The covered bridge is not visible from Stanhope–Kelloggsville Road, but if you turn onto Graham and pedal just a few strokes, the bridge will come into view.

Because Stanhope–Kelloggsville rolls uninterrupted to our final destination, we are able to ride the rest of the journey without any further fussing with the map. As we continue on, we pass through other places like Kelloggsville that once aspired to be communities in their own right. These include Gould, Steamburg, Leon, West Andover, West Williamsfield, and the previously mentioned Stanhope. In West Andover, there are a number of homes and a white frame church, which give the place the feel of a hamlet. West Williamsfield has an increased concentration of homes, but the other places exist as little more than names. When Ohio imposed its highway numbering system, Stanhope–Kelloggsville Road was not selected to be one of the routes, and without sufficient traffic, businesses did not flourish. On the other hand, the lack of traffic makes these roads great cycling routes.

Cider Production

To illustrate the fruitfulness of the land, Mr. Howells showed me thirty-six pears clustered on a single stem only about twenty inches long; the entire weight was eleven pounds. He told me that this county last year raised 587,000 bushels of apples. One cider factory, that of Woodworth, at West Williamsfield, sent off in 1885 twenty carloads of sixty barrels each, fifty-two gallons in a barrel—in all 62,400 gallons.

From Historical Collections of Ohio, *H. Howe & Son, 1898*

By the time we are halfway back to Kinsman, we are both feeling the effects of the heat, especially since heading south means we are cycling into the wind with its strong gusts. Four times we stop in shady spots on the return journey for rest and cooling down, something we did not do on our trip to Conneaut. One stop is on the front lawn of a house whose owner kindly refills our water containers. We are grateful, because by that point, we are down to the dregs in all of our bottles.

We pedal the final miles a bit more slowly and arrive in Kinsman with plenty of daylight left. Although a bit exhausted, we are content with the miles we put on our bikes.

John Brown in Ohio

On June 18 [1859], he [John Brown] was again with his son, John, at West Andover, Ohio. This entry in his journal of that date is of interest:

"Borrowed John's old compass and left my own* together with Gurley's book, with him at West Andover; also borrowed his small Jacob staff; also gave him for expenses $15.00. Write him under cover to Horace Lindsley, West Andover."

*This compass is now in the Museum of the Ohio State Archaeological and Historical Society.

From Ohio History, *Ohio Historical Society, 1921*

Note: On October 16, 1859, John Brown led 21 men on a raid of the federal arsenal at Harpers Ferry, Virginia.

Ride 3
Grand River Valley

Route: Mesopotamia to Rock Creek loop
Counties: Trumbull, Ashtabula
Terrain: Relatively flat
Distance: 42 miles
Lunch: Pasta Oven, Rock Creek (440-563-9529)
Points of Interest: Mesopotamia Commons, octagon house
How to get there: The south end of Mesopotamia Commons
is located at the juncture of State Route 534 (SR534) and
State Route 87 (SR87). Take either road into Mesopotamia
and you will reach Mesopotamia Commons.

THIS trek is a flatland ride that will take you to one of Ohio's oldest villages, Mesopotamia, and one of its newest, Roaming Shores. The route is mostly through rural land on low-traffic roads allowing you to move right along and get a good look at the scenery, a good lunch, and a good workout.

The ride starts in Mesopotamia, the heart of which is a long oval park called the Commons. The northbound lane of State Route 534 (SR534) passes around the east side of the Commons and the southbound lane passes around the west side. There are twenty-eight buildings, including a church and general store surrounding this green space and twenty-one of them were built before the Civil War. Most are still in use. The entire district including the park and the structures are included on the National Register of Historic Places. The store has been in continuous operation since the 1840s.

Changing Gears

The local nickname for Mesopotamia is "Mespo."

If you are in the Commons area, you will likely see Amish people. In fact, the Commons includes a small parking area for cars and a larger area with hitching rails for horse-drawn buggies. Mesopotamia, along with Middlefield and Burton in adjacent Geauga County, contains the second largest settlement of Amish people in Ohio, and the fourth largest in the nation. The village is unincorporated, so no population figures are available, but approximately three thousand people live in Mesopotamia Township, and about 60 percent are Amish.

A sign posted at the south end of the Commons explains that the first clearing of the area took place in 1799, and the first cabin was built in 1800. A story on the website of the "End of the Commons" store reports that mail service to the village began in 1809. Letters, at that time, were left in the hat of Seth Tracy, one of the first settlers. (What it doesn't explain is why Mr. Tracy's hat wasn't on his head.)

Changing Gears

The Mesopotamia Commons is home to a fourteen-foot tall wooden sculpture of a horse and buggy.

The mail deliveries reportedly played a role in how the village got its name. Originally, the place was called Troy,

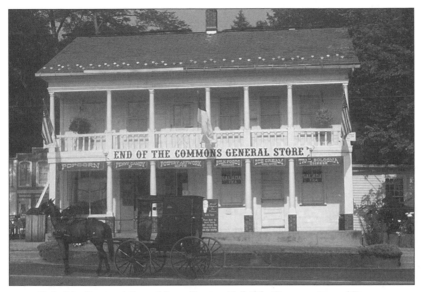

End of the Commons General Store. Courtesy End of the Commons General Store.

but since there were two other towns in Ohio named Troy, mail mix-ups occurred. After ten years of confusion, the residents renamed the village Mesopotamia—"land between two rivers." The Mesopotamia of antiquity was situated between the Tigris and Euphrates Rivers, and its Ohio namesake is situated between the Grand and Cuyahoga Rivers. At least that's the story. In real-

Seth Tracy's Land

Seth Tracy took up seven hundred acres of land in lots lying near the center [of Mesopotamia, Ohio]. On the four acres first cleared, the first orchard in the township was set out about the year 1806, in rows exactly two rods apart each way. Most of the trees are still living. They were procured from Detroit by David Barrett, who made a nursery on Mr. Tracy's land, and cultivated it until the trees were large enough to be planted in an orchard. Seth Tracy was the first justice of the peace in this section and a very active man in his day. He died in 1827 at the age of seventy, and his wife when eighty-five.

From National Cyclopaedia of American Biography, *J. T. White, 1893*

ity, Ohio's Mesopotamia is much closer to the Grand than the Cuyahoga and is part of the watershed area of the former.

I arrive in the village to ride the loop from there to Rock Creek on March 3, 2008. I mention the date intentionally because the day was sunny and the temperature was in the upper fifties for the first time since the previous fall. The Ohio winter had been long, and February had been especially cold. I was suffering cabin fever. Not knowing if the spring-like weather would continue, I canceled other plans and decided to ride. I cycle year-round, but in the winter months, it is generally too cold and gets dark too early to stay on the road for extended periods.

I park my truck in the vehicle area near the picnic shelter in the Commons and pedal to the south end of the park. I set my odometer and start cruising north on sr534.

State Route 534 is the major north–south artery for five miles in either direction, but north of Mesopotamia, it is not heavily traveled. In fact, between Mesopotamia and Windsor, a five-and-a-half mile stretch, only one semi-truck and five cars pass me, and since there is even less traffic southbound, those drivers have plenty of room to move over as they speed by. Trekking the route in other seasons might include additional traffic.

There is still plenty of snow on the ground, but the roads are clear. I wear sunglasses to cut down on the glare. As I ride, the melting snow is filling up the roadside ditches. I am mildly concerned because the return leg of the loop passes across an area that routinely floods. I have an alternative route mapped out for this circumstance, but this will put me on a busy highway. I hope my luck holds up.

Much of the scenery on this route is of farms, rural residences, and woods—actually a surprising amount of woods. Over the course of the whole ride, I will wheel past at least three sawmills.

At mile four, I come to a large octagon-shaped house on the left. The Highley-Pelen house, built in 1860, is a two-story building with a porch wrapped around the front half and a cupola on top. In an area where there are many buildings of a similar era, this place is remarkable for its unusual shape. It is obviously occupied, with a couple of cars in the driveway and dog in the yard that barks at me as I go by. Whether Highley-Pelen is the hyphenated name of one family or the names of two early owners is a mystery.

I arrive shortly at Windsor, a small crossroad community at the intersection of SR534 and US Route 322 (US322). The town was settled in 1810 and was once a thriving place with a grocery, a hotel, a gas station, a church, and a restaurant. Today, while those structures remain, only the church is still operating. Windsor Corners is listed on the *National Register of Historic Places*.

After crossing US322, SR534 veers northwest, and the path that continues straight is Noble Road. I pedal onto Noble Road and up a little hill. I had encountered one small hill after leaving Mesopotamia Commons, and now I ride up this one, knowing as I continue to Rock Creek that the roads will be reasonably flat. (Even on the way back to Mesopotamia, I will meet only a couple small, quick upgrades.) Flat terrain is a benefit, in most cases, but does not provide protection on windy days.

As I head north, I notice that I am getting a push from the air current, which means I will likely be working against a headwind on the return journey. When I ride with no particular destination in mind, I often determine which way the wind is blow-

Octagon House

[The Octagon House] combines comfort and convenience in the interior, with neatness and beauty in the exterior. It shows conclusively that in order to secure these excellences in a country residence, it is not necessary to erect a vast and expensive mansion. It is rich in appearance, yet it is a style not beyond the reach of moderate means. Simplicity is becoming the order of the day in building, as well as other things.

From The Christian Parlor Magazine, *Darius Mead, 1855*

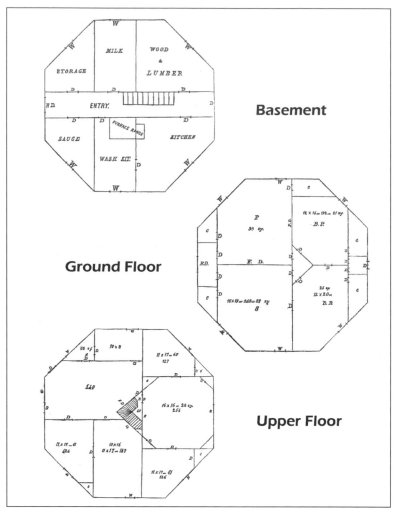

Floor plan of an octagon house. From The Poor Man's Home
and Rich Man's Palace, *Applegate & Company, 1854.*

ing and then plot my journey so that I am riding into it on the outbound leg and have it pushing me on the return when I have less energy.

I soon turn east on New Hudson Road, and after a mile, turn north on Windsor–Mechanicsville Road, a straight and level path that will take me the rest of the way eight miles north. Windsor–Mechanicsville Road is an ideal road for cycling because it is well-paved, level, and has little traffic. During the eight miles, only one car passes me. Probably because there was no competing traffic, that driver was traveling at a fairly high rate of speed, but because the sight lines were so unobstructed, he moved over into the other lane well before getting to me.

Early Description of Windsor, Ohio

Windsor [is] a flourishing post township, (post office same name), and the southwestern most in Ashtabula county, lying immediately north of Mesopotamia, in Trumbull county, twenty-four miles southwest from Jefferson, and nearly 180 northeast of Columbus. It was organized about the year 1810; and was so called from Windsor, in Connecticut. It contains one store, two flouring mills, and three saw mills; and had 666 inhabitants at the last census. Here is also said to be a quarry for grindstones.

From The Ohio Gazetteer and Traveler's Guide, *I. N. Whiting, 1839*

At another tiny crossroads community, East Trumbull, I turn east off of Windsor–Mechanicsville Road onto Footville–Richmond Road. About halfway between the East Trumbull intersection and the village of Rock Creek, I pass over the Grand River. With no leaves on the trees, I have an especially good view of the stream as it snakes around a couple of bends on the north side of the road. The Grand River rises in Geauga County near Parkman, but initially runs east into Trumbull County where, about five miles below Mesopotamia, it curves north and then slithers in that direction to a spot about five miles above Rock Creek. At that point, the river makes a ninety-degree turn and runs west for several miles before turning north again near Painesville and finally emptying into Lake Erie at Fairport Harbor. (See ride 1.) From below Mesopotamia to above Rock Creek, the Grand flows north, and I have been roughly paralleling its course since the start of the ride, though this is the first time I had been near enough to see it.

As I proceed to Rock Creek (the village), I see a smaller waterway on the south side of the road, which is Rock Creek (the stream), rushing west to unite with the river not far below where I had crossed the Grand. A few minutes more of pedaling, and I am in the center of Rock Creek and head a half block north to Rock Creek Grille.

I park my bicycle out front, walk in, and take a seat at the counter. The menu offers an assortment of sandwiches and several full dinners. Breakfast is available all day. I order a Philly omelet with fried red potatoes and toast.

While I wait for the meal to come, an older man seated at a table behind me strikes up a conversation and tells me about the town. When I ask him if he lives there, he tells me he is a resident and a trustee of the township in which the village sits. (Although the village has only about six hundred residents, it has been incorporated since February of 1849. He reaches into his shirt pocket, pulls out a wooden nickel, and hands it to me. It identifies him as Joseph M. Dyrcz, trustee of Morgan Township.

I am glad to meet someone who is interested in the area since I wanted to find out more about a rail-to-trail path called the Greenway Trail (see www.ashtabulacountymetroparks.org/trail map2003.htm) that runs through the village. Intended eventually to extend from Ashtabula to East Liverpool as a lake to river multi-use route, the trail is paved and in service in some places but awaiting monetary grants for completion in others. (See ride

The Grand River

The majestic Grand was designated Ohio's second Wild and Scenic River in 1974. This 712-square-mile watershed covers 455,680 acres and supports an incredible array of fish, birds, mammals, reptiles, amphibians, and numerous rare plant species. Its intact biological ecosystem and streamside forests of statewide significance make it one of Ohio's finest examples of a natural waterway.

From The Nature Conservancy website (www.nature.org)

17.) I know that the section immediately south of Rock Creek is paved, but only for a couple of miles, so I ask Joe if he has heard of any plans to complete the unpaved stretch from that point south to Orwell, where the paving resumes. He doesn't know a scheduled date, but he has heard that the estimated cost for paving is $425,000, which strikes him as a questionable expenditure. (When the trail is complete, it will make a good alternative return route for this ride.) I wonder aloud about using the section that is paved for part of my return leg, but a woman who is seated with Joe speaks up and says she doesn't think the Greenway is plowed.

A few seconds later, my omelet arrives and the woman tells Joe to stop talking and let me eat. The meal is delicious, and I relish every bite.

(On my most recent visit to Rock Creek, I found that Rock Creek Grille has closed. I ate instead at Pasta Oven, which is diagonally across Main Street from the Rock Creek Grille location, right on the corner. Pasta Oven is a full-menu sit-down eatery, offering sandwiches, dinners, subs, and pizza. It is open seven

Incorporation of Rock Creek

Be it enacted by the General Assembly of the State of Ohio, That so much of the township of Morgan, in the county of Ashtabula, as is comprised within the following boundaries, to wit: the whole of original lots, number one hundred and fifteen, one hundred and sixteen, one hundred and twenty-five, one hundred and twenty-six, and the south half of lots number one hundred and five, and one hundred and six, be, and the same is hereby created into, and constituted a town corporate, to be known and designated by the name of "the town of Rock Creek," and the same shall in all respects be governed by the provisions of an act entitled an act for the regulation of incorporated towns, passed February sixteenth, one thousand eight hundred and thirty-nine, and the several acts amendatory thereto, except as is hereinafter provided.

From General Acts Passed and Joint Resolutions Adopted by the Forty-seventh General Assembly of the State of Ohio, *N. Willis, 1849*

PASTA OVEN
3311 Main Street, Rock Creek, OH 44084
440-563-9529
Open year-round

HOURS
Summer
Monday–Thursday: 6:00 A.M. to 10:00 P.M.
Friday–Saturday: 6:00 A.M. to 11:00 P.M.
Sunday: 7:00 A.M. to 9:00 P.M.

Winter
Monday–Saturday: 6:00 A.M. to 10:00 P.M.
Sunday: 7:00 A.M. to 9:00 P.M.

SPECIALTIES
Pizza, Pasta Burger, Wings

days a week from early morning to late evening. There for lunch, I had a delicious Italian sausage sub and a side salad.)

Before leaving the village, I decide to ride east on Water Street to see where the Greenway begins. It is well marked, and I find it easily enough, but the woman in the restaurant is right and the trail is not plowed. A thick layer of heavy, wet snow covers the area and it looks like it has been used by snowmobiles.

I'm not disappointed since I wasn't planning on using the trail. Bike paths are an excellent and safe idea, especially for people who will not otherwise get out on their bikes. As someone who tours by bicycle, I often find the scenery along roads more interesting and the topography more challenging. Moreover, I frequently intend to go places and see things that are not accessible on bike trails. I make use of trails when it is reasonable (and several of the rides in this book spend some time on trails), but I don't rely on them as my major cycling thoroughfares.

This ride has so little vehicular traffic that the existence of the trail beside it is almost superfluous. However, when the trail is completed, the Grand River Valley loop will be reduced by over three miles, so you might want to give it a try.

Returning to the center of Rock Creek, I head south just a short distance on Main Street to Rome–Rock Creek Road and turn east toward Lake Roaming Rock, a five hundred-acre body of water created in 1968 by the damming of Rock Creek. A private, planned community called Roaming Shores Village was established around the lake. When it was incorporated in 1979, it was the first new community in the county in over fifty years. The Roaming Shores name refers to the government of the village, but residents also must join the Roam Rock Association, and the two entities together make up Roaming Shores Village. People not intimately familiar with the naming scheme have a hard time keeping it straight, and so the village sometimes gets called Roaming Rock or Rome Rock, but its name is Roaming Shores.

Changing Gears

Fenders can help you stay dry in wet conditions. They also protect you and your bike from road grime.

The road I am on does not take me near the "downtown," if indeed there is one. Instead, it soon swings south and rolls alongside the lake and the Roaming Shore houses that front it. I see the lake occasionally and realize that the Greenway Trail would have bypassed this area.

After cutting through a couple of village streets, I cross US Route 6 onto Dodge Road. Unfortunately, the pavement on the

Western Reserve Greenway

The Western Reserve Greenway is the former PennCentral right-of-way, which was closed in April 1976. The line at one time was also known as the USRA 714 rail line. The right-of-way, which served industry then, is now set to help serve the recreational needs of Ashtabula County.

From the Ashtabula County Metroparks
(www.ashtabulacountymetroparks.org)

first couple of miles of Dodge is rough, and the water from the melting snow doesn't improve matters. Still the ride isn't very bad and I am able to dodge (no pun intended) the potholes rapidly filling with water.

After about two miles, Dodge Road becomes a smoothly paved road. I don't see any signs, but guess that I have crossed a township jurisdictional line (and Dodge is a township roadway). The smooth surface doesn't eliminate the headwind I've been pedaling against since leaving Rock Creek, however. In the larger puddles, I see ripples on the surface of the water from the wind. Thanks to the wind, my progress is slower than normal and I am tiring.

Experienced riders prefer hills to headwinds, be-cause you eventually get to the top of the hills. Wind, however, doesn't abate over the long haul. I could have waited for a day with lighter or no wind, but the sunshine and warmth of the day are a gift. I'd rather be battling a headwind than sitting at home.

From the end of Dodge Road, the rest of the return route consists of a series of turns—first west, then south, then west, then south, and so on—Each time I turn west, I face a cross breeze, pedaling is easier, and I have a chance to rest.

One of these turns takes me into the village of Orwell, home to about 1,500 people, and if the snow was cleared, I could have jumped on a paved section of the Greenway Trail. Instead, I choose Penniman Road, which is paved, clear of snow, and free

Changing Gears

The World of Wildlife Bicycle Tour takes place on the Greenway Trail in August. Check the Trumbull County MetroParks website for registration deadlines and other information.

of traffic. For two miles, Penniman and the trail run close enough that a rider on one could converse with a rider on the other. Penniman ends where the blacktop turns west and becomes Winters Road. The trail continues south, but had I been on it, I'd have had to get off it at Winters Road anyway to continue my planned route.

Winters Road ends at State Route 45 (SR45). Directly across the road is a multi-acre complex with a statue of a Roman warrior guarding each side of the entrance. A sign identifies the place as King Training Camp and indicates that it is closed to the public. The boxing promoter, Don King, owns the facility and uses it as a camp for his famous pugilists and his novice fighters, too.

After a few more south-to-west jogs, I am westbound on Flagg Road, a stretch that has a long downhill glide to floor of the Grand River valley. I pedal on Bloomfield–Geneva Road to Donley Road for my final sprint west. Donley is the road I have been concerned about from the beginning of the ride because it might be closed due to high water. I am relieved to see that the amber light at the top of the signpost is not flashing, meaning the road is open.

On Donley Road, I roll through water about a half-inch deep. The area adjacent to the road is woodland and looks like it floods too often to be farmable, and I am surprised to see that a few houses are built along this road. I would have thought the flood risk would keep people from homesteading. Riding by, I notice several yards are now ponds.

Eventually I come to a bridge crossing a rushing watercourse. This is the Grand River again.

I press on, and as I near SR534, Donley Road begins a gradual climb out of the river bottom. By the time I reach the highway, I am back to higher ground. I turn south on SR534, and within minutes, roll into Mesopotamia.

Note: A day later, a snow storm with freezing rain hit the whole region shutting down schools and postponing most public events. I'm glad I got my sunny ride in before winter returned.

Ride 4
Gorgeous Gorge

Route: Rocky River to Berea and back
Counties: Cuyahoga
Terrain: Relatively flat
Distance: 29 miles
Lunch: Sandwich Delights, Berea (440-234-3322)
Points of Interest: The Emerald Necklace
How to get there: The entrance to the Rocky River Reservation is located on Valley Parkway in Rocky River, Ohio. From Interstate 90, take exit 162 (Hillard Boulevard). Turn west onto Westway Drive. At the intersection of Westway Drive and Wagar Road, turn north (right). Wagar will intersect with Detroit Road (SR2). Head northeast (right) on Detroit Road. Valley Parkway is the intersection immediately after the bridge. Turn south (right) onto Valley Parkway.

THIS ride is unique since it is an "out-and-back" ride rather than a loop. The path to Berea is the same path that returns to Rocky River. The ride through the Cleveland Metroparks takes you along a scenic valley via a multi-use trail without motor vehicles. Vehicles use the parks—on the road that parallels the trail—but due to the low speed limit (30 mph), the parks are avoided by most commercial traffic.

The parks are a linear system. They essentially form a semicircle around Cleveland, which is why the Metroparks are often referred to as the "Emerald Necklace." In order to create a loop ride, city streets would have to be used, and frankly, the traffic density would have diminished the trek's enjoyment.

(I actually spent a good bit of time researching the return leg to make this a loop ride. I was able to identify some residential streets on which traffic would not hinder cycling. However, wheeling down suburban street after suburban street with similar houses seemed quite boring. On the other hand, the cruise through the parks is a treat for the eyes and a balm for the soul, enjoyable in both directions. So out and back we go, with a pleasant lunch stop at the turn-around point.)

The Cleveland Metroparks is comprised of fourteen separate tracts, called "reservations," not all of which are contiguous, though several are. This ride will take you through two that are: Rocky River Reservation and Mill Stream Run Reservation. They, in turn, link up with three other reservations, forming part of the necklace.

The parks are reservations in the best sense of the word. The Metropark system was created in 1917 to make the natural valleys of the area "reserves" against commercial and residential development, as well as to provide green space for the people of greater Cleveland. Today, the parks are used year-round by hikers, horse enthusiasts, bird watchers, exercisers, picnickers, archers, and cyclists, and used seasonally by cross-country skiers, ice skaters, fishermen, sledders, boaters, and others. There are seven golf

Building on a portion of the old bridge over the Rocky River. Courtesy of the City of Rocky River.

courses within the system as well as the Cleveland Metroparks Zoo.

Our ride begins at the northernmost end of the western side of the necklace in the community of Rocky River and uses the paved multipurpose trail. I actually rode this route in the summertime with my son Scott and in late winter by myself. I mention the latter especially because unlike some parks, the Metroparks are truly parks for all seasons. After snowfalls, the roads and the multipurpose trail are plowed. The restrooms are open year-round, as well.

Winter has come to Cleveland as I enter Rocky River Reservation from Detroit Road, the main street of the city of Rocky River. The entrance road descends quickly into the valley, and I park my truck in the lot provided at the foot of the descent. This area is also adjacent to a boat launch ramp and the Emerald Necklace Marina.

45

Ice on the Rocky River. Courtesy of Jennifer Goellnitz.

Mounting up, I wheel out of the lot onto the paved trail and head south between the road and the river. I mentioned earlier that the road parallels the trail, but "parallels" needs to be applied loosely. The trail meanders more than the parkway, tending to stay near the river, especially at the north end of this route. If you were to drive the parkway rather than pedal the trail, your mileage would be a bit less. On my summer ride, using the trail, my outbound distance to Berea was 14.6 miles; on my winter ride, using the road on the inbound leg, I pedaled 13.9 miles.

The river running through the valley snakes even more than the trail and the road, so a canoe route would no doubt be even longer. The stream is the Rocky River, which also gives its name to the nearby city and to the reservation. Although I am pedaling south, the river is flowing north, heading for Lake Erie. The river is never out of sight for long.

Over eons, the river had cut the gorge through which I now pedal. On my winter ride, with the foliage gone, I am able to see clearly the massive shale cliffs. During my summer ride, the sense of being in a gorge wasn't as evident because the view of the cliffs was somewhat obstructed by the trees growing from the valley floor, but they were still noticeable, and where the river made sweeping bends, the shale precipices were plainly in view.

The other scenery is mostly natural panoramas of forest, meadow, river, and rock, but here and there are fields marked as picnic areas, some containing multi-use spaces.

One way I mark progress on this ride is by noting the streets and highways I pass under (signs in the park identify the thoroughfares on the high bridges above) and by the occasional entrance and exit roads that tee into the parkway or cross it at an intersection. One of the latter is Cedar Point Road (no connection to the amusement park of that name), intersecting the parkway about ten miles from the northern end. If I had turned west on this road, I would have come to a museum village called Frostville, consisting of seven pioneer-era buildings (six of which were moved onto the site). Frostville is maintained by the Olmstead Historical Society. I do not make the detour because the village is not open in the winter. Below Cedar Point Road, two tributaries come together to form the Rocky River, though I cannot see the confluence from the trail. The western branch, which is not in the Metroparks, rises in southeast Lorain County. The eastern branch, along which the trail and road follows upstream from this point, has its source in the Cleveland suburb of North Royalton to the southeast. Near the southern boundary of Rocky River Reservation, the elevation rises, and there is a small parking area on the left hand side with a viewing deck. This vantage point provides a view of the waterfalls in the river at Berea (Berea Falls Scenic Overlook). In the summer, I found the

> **Changing Gears**
>
> Frostville
>
> Open Saturdays May–November
>
> Check the Olmsted Historical Society for events.
>
> *www.olmsted historicalsociety.org*

47

Clock tower in Berea Commons. Courtesy of Berea City Hall.

view enchanting. Returning now, when the river is swollen with
melting snow, the sight is powerful.

At his point, Rocky River Reservation ends and after a small
gap, Mill Stream Run Reservation begins. This transition is barely noticeable except for the crossing at busy Bagley Road, which
is aided by a traffic light. Valley Parkway briefly runs concurrent
with a city artery called Barrett Road, but after crossing Bagley,
Barrett Road becomes Valley Parkway and runs through a green
corridor.

The park narrows down soon after to only the parkway and
the trail. The trail is no more than a sidewalk. The cliffs, close
on each side, are not high, and from the trail, I can see buildings

SANDWICH DELIGHTS, BEREA
1 Berea Commons, Berea, OH
440-234-3322
Open year-round

HOURS
Monday–Saturday: 10:00 A.M. to 7:00 P.M.

SPECIALTIES
Turkey Sandwich, Vegetarian Options

in the adjacent community. Though constricted, I am protected from the city traffic. Within a couple of minutes, I am back on the broad valley floor, rejoined by the river and in the full expanse of park.

Hungry, I turn left onto North Quarry Lane. I pedal up into Berea Commons, which is the hub of the original town. On the community triangle, I find a small shop called Sandwich Delights. (During my summer ride with Scott, we only looked around the triangle and did not stop for lunch since we had eaten before the ride.) I enter the shop and delight in an excellent hot roast beef sub with a side of potato salad.

Baldwin-Wallace College

Baldwin University was founded in 1846. In 1858, a German department was established, which was reorganized in 1864 as the German Wallace College, in honor of its most liberal patron, James Wallace. The consolidated institution, known as Baldwin University and German Wallace College, is under the auspices of the Methodist Episcopal church.

From History of the Western Reserve, *Lewis Publishing Company, 1910*

Berea was named by a circuit-riding Methodist preacher named Henry O. Sheldon. He arrived in the Berea area in 1836, and soon became the first postmaster of the settlement taking root there. With a post office, the place needed an official name, so Sheldon thought of two possibilities from the Bible. One was Berea and the other was Tabor. Having no strong preference for one over the other, he chose Berea by flipping a coin.

For about a hundred years, beginning in 1840, Berea was the center of a thriving sandstone business. Building blocks and grindstones were cut from the banks of the appropriately named Rocky River. Today, Berea is better known as the home of Baldwin-Wallace College.

It was now time to retrace my route back to the starting point. Should you want to extend the ride, it is a simple matter to continue deeper into Mill Stream Run Reservation and beyond

Berea Grit

On the arrival of my father at Berea, from New York City, the first work in hand was to lay out the proposed Lyceum village, in streets and squares, on the property Mr. Baldwin had used for the community. After a forenoon had been spent in running lines with the compass, and the party had partaken of dinner, father suggested to Mr. Baldwin, since they had been delayed in their work by a dull axe in sharpening the corner stakes, that they should go out and grind the axe. Mr. Baldwin proposed to turn the grindstone while father held the axe. Grinding and talking for some little time father failed to look at the axe. In turning it over to examine it, he was astonished to find what an amount of steel had been ground away.

Said he: "Brother Baldwin, where did you get this grindstone?"

"Down in the creek below here."

"In the creek below here?"

"Yes, the whole country is based on this kind of grit."

"Is that so? You have a fortune more substantial than the Bank of England underlying your possessions."

This was the discovery of the famous Berea grindstone grit.

From Reminiscences of the Happy Life of a Teacher,
Elm Street Printing Company, 1885

Baldwin-Wallace May Day circa 1907.
Courtesy Library of Congress, Prints and Photographs Division.

if you wish and turn around later. But don't count on finding lunch below Berea, as there are no conveniently placed eateries for the next several miles.

When I head back north, I notice vistas I had not observed on the way down. Even though my ride is along the same route, the depth of images is stunning. The gorgeous gorge of the Emerald Necklace changes by season, by light of day, and by condition. This trek is straightforward and fun.

Ride 5
Cuyahoga Valley Sampler

Route: Canal Visitor Center to Peninsula loop
Counties: Summit, Cuyahoga
Terrain: Relatively flat to hilly
Distance: 31 miles
Lunch: Fisher's Café and Pub, Peninsula (330-657-2651)
Points of Interest: Ohio & Erie Canal, Canal Visitor Center,
   Alexander's Mill, Brandywine Falls (on optional route)
How to get there: The Canal Visitor Center is located at
   Hillside Road and Canal Road in Independence, Ohio.
   From Interstate 77 (I-77), take exit 153 for Independence.
   Head east on East Pleasant Valley Road. Turn north (left)
   at Brecksville Road (SR21). At the intersection of Brecksville
   Road and Hillside Road, turn east (right). The entrance to
   the Canal Visitor Center will be just before the intersection
   with Canal Road.

T HE Cuyahoga Valley National Park is a rich treasure of natural beauty. It provides a green refuge from the busy urban and suburban regions on its sides. The late Congressman John F. Seiberling, whose grandfather founded the Goodyear Tire & Rubber Company, Congressman Ralph Regula from Navarre, and former Republican National Committee Chairman Ray Bliss from Akron, were instrumental in creating the national park. Visitors use the area year-round, enjoying activities from bird watching and picnicking to tobogganing and snowshoeing.

Cuyahoga means "crooked," and so the river is. The river rises thirty miles south of Lake Erie, but the river is ninety miles long. Approximately twenty-two miles are within the national park. The river valley provides the varied setting for this ride.

The Cuyahoga Valley's history was written by advances in transportation. The river was used by natives of the region, the Iroquois and other tribes, and early settlers. The Ohio & Erie Canal extended the reach of commerce to new areas. The railroad speeded up progress, and roads extended the reach of development.

Before the arrival of settlers, the river was an important transportation artery for natives. The Cuyahoga flows north and the Tuscarawas River flows south from a divide in an area near what is now Akron. A short portage between the two rivers permitted canoe travel from the Lake Erie to the Ohio River. Frontiersmen and early settlers also took advantage of this route.

The Ohio & Erie Canal, connecting Lake Erie at Cleveland to the Ohio River at Portsmouth, was routed through the Cuyahoga Valley in the early 1800s and was completed in 1832. The canal permitted a much greater movement of materials and goods through the region and spurred urban development and industry.

Changing Gears

Use of the portage was discontinued in 1827 when the Ohio and Erie Canal was built along the old trail. Today, modern Akron streets—Portage Path and Manchester Road—follow the approximate route of the original portage.

From Summit County Historical Society (www.summithistory.org)

In 1873, railroad lines were laid through the valley, eventually spelling the end of the canal, but furthering development. The great flood in 1913, which seriously damaged the canal, was the final blow to that artery.

Not long after the turn of the last century and the emergence of the automobile, roads were paved through and across the valley. In time, trucks diminished the need for trains to transport freight and cars reduced the need for passenger rail services.

In the early 1960s, as development threatened to overrun the natural settings in the valley, citizens joined forces with state and local governments to preserve the area. In 1974, Congress created the Cuyahoga Valley National Recreation Area. In 2000 the name was changed to Cuyahoga Valley National Park, making it more recognizable as a unit of the National Park System.

This ride, the Cuyahoga Valley Sampler, rolls over both the canal towpath and Valley Road and runs alongside the river and the rails.

I began my ride east of the community of Independence at the Canal Visitor Center, which is located in the park at the

> **Changing Gears**
>
> There are two historic site markers for the old portage path:
>
> *North:*
> Merriman Road and Portage Path
> *South:*
> Near Carnegie Avenue and Manchester Road

The Cuyahoga Valley

The Cuyahoga valley, which begins at Akron, expands as it approaches the northern limits of the county, and thereafter, in Cuyahoga county, loses much of its impressiveness and beauty. The gorge of the Cuyahoga which extends from Cuyahoga Falls, three or four miles westward nearly to the joining of the Big and Little Cuyahoga rivers, is famous throughout the West both for the ruggedness of its beauty and the power which it furnishes to the great manufactories along its precipitous banks. In summer its banks are graced with oaks, maples, and elms, ash and evergreens, and in the winter months present to the visitor, especially in the vicinity where manufactories are found, fantastic and changing formations of ice, snow and frost.

From History of the Western Reserve, *Lewis Publishing Company, 1910*

intersection of Hillside and Canal roads. The visitor center is a good place to begin because its displays give me an introduction to the canal: the construction, its operation, its decline, and its restoration as a towpath for recreational activities. After spending time viewing the information, I go outside, get my bike, and head south on the Towpath Trail.

The trail runs like a backbone on a north–south course through the entire length of the national park along the path of the old Ohio & Erie Canal towpath. The trail covers 101 miles from Cleveland to New Philadelphia, Ohio, and is a key component in a historic corridor known as the Ohio & Erie Canal Heritage Canalway. Begun in the late twentieth century, the trail is, as of this writing, open and operating over 80 percent of its length, but 100 percent of the trail within the national park is open.

Most of the trail is covered with finely crushed limestone. Some areas are paved with asphalt. In dry weather, the limestone is a decent rolling surface. My ride is on the first sunny day after three days of rain, and I notice that the soaked limestone sec-

The 1913 Flood

The huge volume of water which had been gathering in the three hundred-acre reservoir caused a report that there was danger of the concrete walls bursting. Most of those living near the canal sought refuge in Akron. When the heavy rain continued over night the dam began to show signs of wear. Cracks in the concrete appeared. All during the night horses were kept saddled to carry the news ahead if the danger became imminent. When the masonry showed flaws Thursday morning, the riders were sent out. They started several hours before the dam collapsed, and warned everybody near the canal in time for them to escape. The rush of water from the broken dam struck the city within a few minutes after the break. Most of the bridges in the county were swept away. The city was in total darkness at night, and telephone and telegraph connections were destroyed.

From The True Story of Our National Calamity of Flood, Fire and Tornado, *Hampden Publishing Company, 1913.*

Riders on the Towpath Trail. Courtesy of Christina Getrost.

tions create a bit of resistance. I definitely feel the improvement each time I ride across one of the blacktopped stretches.

The canal is not fully intact, but sizable sections are filled with water. In those places, the view from the towpath is much like it was in the nineteenth century when the canal was in operation. In other places, the canal is nothing more than a ditch with wild vegetation growing in it, and at times the remnants of the canal are not visible. Vestiges of several canal locks exist along the trail, and I stop to study them and read the signs detailing information about each one. Although there are no working locks within the park, the Canal Visitor Center offered an exhibit detailing how the locks had enabled boats to follow the rise and fall of the land.

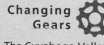

Changing Gears

The Cuyahoga Valley Scenic Railroad offers a special $2.00 rate for cyclists. The Bike Aboard program allows cyclists to ride the train one direction along the Towpath Trail.

See www.cvsr.com for schedules.

About a mile and a half south of the visitor center, the trail passes under Pleasant Valley Road, and from that point south,

The Cuyahoga Valley Scenic Railrost. Courtesy of Christina Getrost.

the trail is one of four threads sharing the passage down the valley. The Towpath Trail is the easternmost of these threads, and west of the towpath are the Cuyahoga River, the railroad tracks, and Riverview Road. The four remain in that configuration until about a mile outside of Peninsula where the river and the trail cross under the tracks, making the rails the eastern thread.

About four and a half miles below the visitor center, I pass under a high bridge on which State Route 82 (SR82) crosses the valley. A short distance later, I come to the Station Road Bridge, a wrought-iron truss bridge built in 1881. It is closed to vehicle traffic but open to hikers, cyclists, and horseback riders.

Across Station Road Bridge is a stop for the Cuyahoga Valley Scenic Railroad. The bridge is also the point at which one can leave the Towpath Trail to access Riverview Road or enter the Brecksville Reservation, a part of the Cleveland Metroparks Sys-

Brandywine Falls. Courtesy of Paul L. Csizmadia.

tem. (If you want to shorten the ride, you can easily cut across to
Riverview Road and follow the directions back to the Canal Visitor Center, or you can start the ride at the parking lot beside the
station and pedal just the lower section of this route.)

I continue south on the towpath. A couple of miles further
on, I come to a side trail to the left that offers an extension of
about four miles to the ride (which I have marked on the map as
an optional side trip). I could have pedaled up and out of the valley to Holzhauer Road and picked up the Bike and Hike Trail, a
path on a former railroad bed that is administered by the Summit County Metro Parks. This trail takes you to Brandywine
Road and Brandywine Falls, a sixty-foot "bridal veil" cascade
that is one of the most scenic places in the entire park. After seeing the falls, turn off of Brandywine Road, continue on the Bike
and Hike Trail to Hines Hill Road, and turn west to rejoin the

Towpath Trail at the Boston Mills Road Trailhead. Since I had visited Brandywine Falls previously, I remain on the towpath all the way to the trailhead in the village of Peninsula (population six hundred). There, after leaving the trail, I cross the tracks, ride along a couple of village streets, and land at Fisher's Café and Pub.

Changing Gears

Brandywine Falls is over sixty feet tall. A nearby boardwalk provides a clear view of the waterfall.

In the early nineteenth century, Peninsula was established on a peninsula formed by a horseshoe bend in the Cuyahoga River. Mill owners long ago rerouted the river for water power. In 1827, after the Ohio & Erie Canal opened, the village became much like a seaport town, sporting fourteen honky-tonk bars and five hotels. Today, commerce is limited to two restaurants, a bicycle store, and some antique shops and galleries. The town has retained its charm, and its location in the heart of the Cuyahoga Valley National Park makes for a nice cultural experience.

Fisher's Café and Pub has a better than average menu for a small town eatery. I can choose from wings, ribs, steaks, fish, shrimp, burgers, salads, and soups. I decide on the grilled chicken salad and sit on the outdoor patio to enjoy the warm clear day.

After eating, I head west on State Route 303 (SR303), climb a couple of blocks to the intersection with Riverview Road and turn north. Riverview Road runs along the hip of the hillside until Boston Mills Road. At one point, Riverview runs under the high bridge of the Ohio Turnpike, passing near the mighty stanchions that carry the span, and I look right to see the tracks, the river, and the trail.

By the time I cross Boston Mills Road, Riverview Road has returned to the floor of the valley. To my right is a station used by the Cuyahoga Valley Scenic Railroad and to my left is Boston Mills Ski Resort, with its runs arching up the hillside. Within the park, both Boston Mills and Brandywine ski resorts offer wintertime activities.

FISHER'S CAFÉ AND PUB
1607 Main Street, Peninsula, OH 44264
330-657-2651
Open year-round

HOURS
Summer
Monday–Friday: 11:00 A.M. to 11:00 P.M.
Saturday: 8:00 A.M. to 10:00 P.M.
Sunday: 8:00 A.M. to 9:00 P.M.

Winter
Monday–Friday: 11:00 A.M. to 10:00 P.M.
Saturday: 8:00 A.M. to 10:00 P.M.
Sunday: 8:00 A.M. to 9:00 P.M.

SPECIALTIES
Burgers

I pedal on Riverview Road until I come to Columbia Road and head off to the left. I turn onto Columbia and almost immediately start upward. This incline quickly gives me first-hand experience of how deep the Cuyahoga River has cut into the valley. I climb seriously for a mile and a half. (The upward grade continues still further west until I turn north on Barr Road.) On Columbia Road, I am still in the park with forest on both sides of the road. Once I pass the park boundaries, a few houses are scattered along the way, but the road retains a rural flavor. At Dewey Road, I turn right, and in less than half a mile, I cross from Summit County into Cuyahoga County.

I turn west onto Snowville Road, a climb that is not as severe as Columbia had been. Snowville is a residential road, and the whole time I am on it, I play leapfrog with a postal truck delivering mail to the homes along the way.

Snowville ends on State Route 21 (SR21) or Brecksville Road. This is a four-lane thoroughfare that can be congested during rush hour, but off hours, the road is only moderately traveled, and I pedal on it for a half mile. At the intersection with Miller Road, Brecksville Road has a turning lane down the middle of the street. I move into this lane and am aligned for the left turn when the traffic light changes. The first section of Miller is home to some administrative and office buildings and is moderately busy to the entrance ramp for Interstate 77 (I-77). Past the on ramp, Miller Road is residential and relatively quiet.

I turn right onto Barr Road, head north to Valley Parkway and turn right. I can finally leave the incline and all my huffing and puffing behind.

Valley Parkway is the primary road through the western half of the Cleveland Metroparks system. Valley Parkway begins in the Rocky River Reservation, runs south to Mill Stream Run Reservation, turns east, and then makes a straight run across southern Cuyahoga County to Brecksville Reservation. Although the section of Valley Parkway between Mill Stream Run and Brecksville is not on the land of either reservation, the road is administered by the Metroparks and is a park road. Properties on both sides of the road are wooded, and houses can be seen occasionally through the canopy.

I am not going steeply downhill, but am dropping gently back to the valley. After a mile and a half on the parkway, I cross Brecksville Road and enter Brecksville Reservation. Although the parkway continues into the reservation, I jump onto the paved multipurpose trail immediately adjacent to the parkway and roll downhill in earnest.

Valley Parkway ends within the reservation on Chippewa Creek Drive where I turn right and continue on the trail to Riverview Road. (Chippewa Creek Drive continues briefly beyond Riverview Road to the train station beside the Station Road Bridge. If you opt for the shortened ride, the Chippewa Road–

Riverview Road junction is where you would join the return leg.) I leave the trail, turn north onto Riverview Road, and climb for a short, but surprisingly steep, stretch to SR82. I cross at the traffic light and continue on Riverview Road for the next couple of miles. This section of the road is outside of park property, but I notice efforts have been made to ensure that the properties blend in with the natural environment.

Riverview, after reentering the park, ends at Brookside Road. I pedal a short distance to Pleasant Valley Road, a reasonably busy artery cutting across the park on an east–west line, and I use it to overpass the railroad, the river, and the trail. I take it to the access road just beyond the three, which takes me down to the trail, right beside Alexander's Mill and the remains of Lock 37. During the canal era, the mill used water from the lock's spillway to grind flour and later feed.

Crossing Canal Road, I use the short Fitzwater Bridge to get over the canal to the Towpath Trail, where I turn north and ride the final mile and a half to the Canal Visitor Center, completing this unique ride.

Ride 6
Western Reserve Roundabout

Route: Mantua to Burton loop
Counties: Portage, Geauga
Terrain: Relatively flat to rolling
Distance: 38 miles
Lunch: Joel's Italian-American Grille, Burton (440-834-9050)
Points of Interest: Century Village Museum in Burton, Hiram Rapids, Historic Mantua Glass Company site, John Johnson farm (Mormon historic site)
How to get there: This ride starts at the corner of Main Street (State Route 44) and Prospect Street in Mantua, Ohio. From the Ohio Turnpike (I-80), head north on State Route 44, which will lead directly into Mantua and become Main Street.

THE Western Reserve is the part of Northeast Ohio that once belonged to Connecticut. In 1662, when the colony of Connecticut received its charter from Charles II, the English king, its northern and southern boundaries were set by decree. Those borders, the charter said, extended westward to the "South Sea" (Pacific Ocean) although nobody knew how much land was included. Other colonies were also granted similar indefinite western borders, and in some cases, their western lands actually overlapped, leading to territorial disputes. After the original thirteen colonies became states, the Continental Congress proposed that the states cede their western lands to the Confederation to be made into additional states as population warranted. The former colonies agreed.

In 1786, Connecticut surrendered most land west of Pennsylvania, but retained a sizable piece along the southern shore of Lake Erie. (Today this area is approximately marked by Conneaut on the northeast, Port Clinton on the Northwest, Youngstown on the southeast, and Willard on the southwest.) Connecticut kept this area, in part, to compensate for the state's small size. Between 1786 and 1800, much of the area was given or sold to settlers from Connecticut, who brought with them New England style architecture and village layout. In 1800, Connecticut relinquished claim to the land, and the Western Reserve became part of the Ohio territory.

"Western Reserve" ceased to have any legal meaning, but the name continued to be used to describe the region and to identify the New England heritage of the area. The Western Reserve ambiance is reflected in Burton with its business district surrounding a central green.

I ride the loop between the two villages on a gray, chilly day in November. I wear a balaclava under my helmet, am clad in tights, three jersey layers, a windbreaker, and full gloves. I have a pair of woolen socks on under my bicycle shoes but I have forgotten to

Changing Gears

A balaclava is also called a ski mask. Usually, there is a single opening for the eyes, but a wide variety of styles can be found.

bring my neoprene overboots made expressly for winter riding. I am too far from home to drive back and get them.

I leave my truck in the parking lot of McDonald's in Mantua (pronounced MAN-a-way). A tidy village in Portage County on State Route 44 (SR44), Mantua has about one thousand residents and is located on the Cuyahoga River twenty-seven miles southeast of Cleveland. Despite the New England influence in the region, Mantua is named for a city in northern Italy, though nobody seems to know what the connection is.

I wheel the half block to the main crossroad of the community where I turn east on Prospect Street. Shortly before Prospect bends toward High Street, I pass a bike-and-hike path on my left called the Headwaters Trail. This cinder and gravel route is seven miles long and runs from Mantua to Garrettsville, Ohio. The Trail does parallel my intended route briefly, and I could have turned onto the path, but I would have been able to use it for only about a mile. Instead, I stay on the paved, village streets since they are not heavily traveled.

After leaving Mantua, I turn north on Peck Road, which lopes over a series of small hills. Peck ends at Pioneer Trail. I turn left, pedal through a dip, continue for a mile, and make a sharp right

Charter of 1662

And know yee further, That Wee, of our more abundant grace, certaine knowledge and meere mocion have given, Graunted and Confirmed, And by theis presents, for vs, our heirs and Successors, Doe give, Graunt and Confirme vnto the said Governer and Company and their successors, All that parte of our Dominions in Newe England in America bounded on the East by Norrogancett River, comonly called Norrogancett Bay, where the Said River falleth into the Sea, and on the North by the lyne of the Massachufets, Plantacon and on the South by the Sea, and in longitude as the lyne of the Massachufetts Colony, runinge from East to West.

From Charter of the Colony of Connecticut 1662,
Lockwood & Brainard Company, 1900

Changing Gears

The New England-style stonewall is built by stacking stones without the use of mortar.

onto Sheldon Road. I come quickly to a small clearing on the right with a sign from the Portage County Historical Society that marks the site of the Mantua Glass Company, a business having operated on the location from 1821–1829. Founded in a building that had been constructed as a tannery, the firm was started by David Ladd, who had moved to the area from Connecticut in 1816. It was the first glass manufactory in Portage County.

The factory is long gone and the site has been reclaimed by the forest. The sign indicates that some of the foundation remains. By matching the terrain with the drawing on the sign, I am able to make out a bit of the footprint of the former factory.

I mount up and continue on Sheldon Road and find myself in the middle of a New England scene. Stone walls extend along the fields on my left and homes on my right look like a rural Con-

James and Lucretia Garfield

Lucretia Rudolph Garfield was the daughter of Zebulon Rudolph, a farmer who resided near Garrettsville, Ohio. He was one of the founders of Hiram College. Her mother was the daughter of Elijah Mason of Lebanon, Connecticut, a descendant of General Nathaniel Greene. She first met her future husband, James A. Garfield, at the Geauga Seminary. They attended this school together until young Garfield entered Hiram College, of which institution he was a graduate. Not long after he entered the college he was called upon to take the place of one of the teachers because of illness. Into his classroom came his schoolgirl friend, Lucretia Rudolph, whom he considered one of his brightest pupils. She was especially apt in Latin and was so well instructed by Mr. Garfield that twenty years after she prepared her boy in Latin to enter college. After she graduated from Hiram College, she also became a teacher. When Mr. Garfield went to Williams College to finish his education she went to Cleveland to teach in one of the public schools. By that time they were lovers and both studied very hard, believing that there was a great future before James A. Garfield.

From The Part Taken by Women in American History,
Perry-Nalle Publishing, 1912

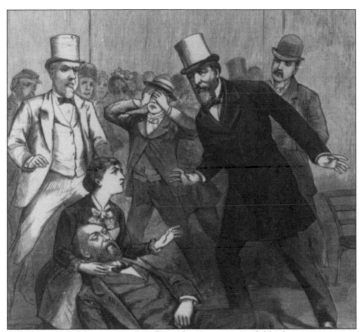

Depiction of the assasination of President James A. Garfield July 2, 1881.
Courtesy Library of Congress, Prints and Photographs Division.

necticut postcard. Even the newer homes are designed to blend in with the original construction. The Western Reserve settlers would have appreciated the care taken. The New England regional feel does not continue for long, though; I am soon passing rural homes that are more typical of Ohio.

At some unmarked point, but probably where I cross from Portage County into Geauga County, Sheldon Road becomes

New England Stone Walls

Stone walls are the sign of thrift, energy and patience; and they are a distinctive feature of New England farms. One of our late writers has well said: "If ever a coat-of-arms should be adopted for New England as a section of the United States, no more significant emblem could be incorporated in the device than an ordinary stone wall."

From The New England Magazine, *New England Magazine Co., 1901*

Entering Burton. Courtesy of Christina Getrost.

Fox Road. The stretch on the two back roads let me pedal quietly for five miles. Even when I continue north on Rapids Road, traffic is sparse giving me another two miles of serenity.

I do, however, meet two cyclists who are heading south on Rapids Road. I don't know either of the young men, but as is customary, we stop, chat, and exchange route information. Each rider is also swathed in neoprene and nylon layers to keep warm. One looks at my outfit and remarks, "I see you're a hard-core rider, too." I wish I had remembered my booties because my toes were starting to get cold. I leave the two and soldier on.

About four miles south of Burton, my lunch destination, I come to the entrance of Eldon Russell Park on the east side of Rapids Road. This 132-acre green area, part of the Geauga County Park District, stretches from Rapids Road to the Upper Cuyahoga River. The attractive expanse offers trails for hiking, tables, and a shelter for picnicking, and a launch area for putting boats into the river. I turn into the park and follow the park drive to the river. I talk briefly with a man who is launching a boat to go fishing. He comments that he appreciates that the county had taken measures to keep some areas, such as this park, free from development. We are apparently the only people in the park.

Changing Gears

Burton hosts several pancake events in the spring and fall. Check with the Burton Chamber of Commerce for a list of events.

www.burtonchamber ofcommerce.org

The park is located where dredging of the Cuyahoga River stopped following a boondoggle that came to be known as the "Onion Wars." In 1901, a Burton resident, Pace Latham, tried to set up a large-scale onion farming operation by attempting to deepen and straighten the river and make the surrounding areas available for planting. Unfortunately for Latham, folks down river at Hiram Rapids, where a natural rock dam stood, had no interest in freeing up the water flow. Twice Latham hired confederates to dynamite the dam, but on both occasions townspeople drove the mercenaries off with shotgun blasts of rock salt. Eventually, Latham abandoned his onion-farming scheme. Spoil heaps from the project still remain along the river.

Returning to Rapids Road, I continue my trek to Burton, with very cold feet. I enter Burton from the south. Burton has a village green typical of New England towns, but is also the site for the Burton Log Cabin, a working sugar house producing maple syrup every spring and making maple candy year-round. In 1973, Burton adopted the nickname "Pancake Town, U.S.A." Every Sunday in March, people come to Burton to enjoy pancakes drenched with real maple syrup.

The Village Green

A village green is almost always a subject for a painter who is fond of quiet home scenes, with its old, knotty, wide-spreading oak or elm or ash; its gray church-tower; its cottages scattered in pleasing disorder around, each looking out of its leafy nest. . . . It served for trapball [similar to cricket], for cricket, for manly humanizing amusements, in which the gentry and farmers might unite with the peasantry.

From Chamber's Cyclopaedia of English Literature, *J. B. Lippincott, 1904*

JOEL'S ITALIAN-AMERICAN GRILLE
14614 East Park Street, Burton, OH 44021
440-834-9050
Open year-round

Summer
Monday–Thursday: 11:00 A.M. to 9:00 P.M.
Friday–Saturday: 11:00 A.M. to 10:00 P.M.
Sunday: 2:00 P.M. to 9:00 P.M.

Winter
Monday–Saturday: 11:00 A.M. to 9:00 P.M.
Sunday: 2:00 P.M. to 9:00 P.M.

SPECIALTIES
Wraps, Pasta, Homemade Ice Cream

Not hungry for pancakes, I pull into Joel's Italian-American Grille on the east side of the square. I order a calzone, a baked turnover of pizza dough filled with vegetables, meat, and cheese.

During the meal, I slip my shoes off to let the heat get at my toes, and they gradually warm up. Wanting to keep them that way, I resort to a variation of a practice I have used before when the winds prove colder than expected: shoving my map inside my windbreaker to protect my chest, which always makes me

> **The Calzone**
>
> Calzone, while used today to describe an Italian dish, also was used to describe leggings or more properly trouser legs that had an apron which was generally folded up in front to serve as a handy pocket. HOT POCKETS® brand sandwiches, a calzone-like product, are marketing spin-offs of the trouser leg meaning.
>
> *Editor's Note*

warmer. So I ask the waitress for some extra napkins. In the restroom, I remove my socks, fold the napkins over my toes, and then put my socks and shoes back on. My feet stay sufficiently warm for the entire return trip.

After eating, I ride my bike on the street around the tidy square, noting the gift and antique shops, the impressive wood frame Burton Congregational Church, the library, and additional eateries.

Burton, founded in 1798, is the oldest settlement in Geauga County and home to the Century Village Museum, an authentic representation of a Western Reserve Village from 1798 to the turn of the nineteenth century. The museum boasts over twenty-two historically accurate buildings and over fifteen thousand museum artifacts that include original art from the 1800s, antiques, textiles, and more. Located in the heart of Geauga County, Ohio, Century Village Museum is the gateway to the Burton Historic District, an area named in the National Register of Historic Places. I had previously visited the Century Village on a family trip, so I don't stop, but I do recommend it.

Burton Library

Bill Kennedy, Gideon Finch, John Ford, Eleazer Hickcox, Uri Hickcox, Lyman Benton, Jedediah Beard, Selah Bradley, Andrew Durand, Simeon Rose, and others, were incorporated as the "Village Library Society of Burton," in the county of Geauga.

From A Manual of the Ohio School System, *H. W. Derby, 1857*

I leave town from the south end of the square, following State Route 700 (SR700) to its junction with State Route 168 (SR168), just south of town. These primary routes have more traffic than the back road I rode into town, but both roads are sufficiently wide to give me room to maneuver. I ride along SR168 for a couple of miles before veering right onto a low-traffic rural route called Jug Street.

The rural roads in Ohio are often named for the communities toward which they run (e.g., Hartville Road) or for a family that once lived on them (e.g., Miller Road). Jug Street didn't seem to fit. I haven't found any history on how this particular Jug Street came to be named, but I do know that in the medieval town of Saint-Denis in France, there was a street named the *Rue du Grand-Pichet* and another street named the *Rue du Petit-Pichet*—"Big Jug Street" and "Little Jug Street," respectively. The speculation is the French streets took their names from taverns located on them.

I start down Jug Street, rolling along between farms and rural homes, some clearly occupied by Amish families. This is obvious not only from the buggies in the yards, but also from the absence

The Burton Academy

The war of 1812 seriously interfered with the progress of Burton Academy, as it did with all things on the Reserve. In 1817 a new building was started on the east side of the square and completed two years afterward. In May, 1820, David L. Coe, a graduate of Williams College, Massachusetts, opened the new structure and continued in charge until 1824. The original charter of Burton Academy was then extended for ten years, and the Presbyterian and Congregational churches of the Western Reserve induced the old management to add a theological department to the curriculum, but the widespread fever epidemic which visited Burton and the vicinity during the years 1823 and 1824 induced those in control of the academy to consider a proposition to remove the institution to Hudson, Ohio, and for this purpose a charter was obtained February 7, 1826. This proposition, it is needless to say, was strongly opposed by Judge Hitchcock and others; and the success of the academy while located at Burton, as well as the health of the residents of the section in after years, proved that the fears as to the unsanitary condition of Burton was groundless. Notwithstanding, in 1830 the academy was removed to Hudson, and still later, to Cleveland, as the Western Reserve University.

From History of the Western Reserve, *Lewis Publishing Company, 1910*

Postal Boxes in the Century Village General Store. Courtesy of Anne M. Lape.

of electric wires running into the buildings, and from the simple, white curtains tied to one side in the windows of the houses. The area surrounding Burton is home to the second largest settlement of Amish people in Ohio.

If at one time Jug Street had rowdy taverns, I find instead nearly seven miles of quiet cruising before I come to Grove Road and turn west into Portage County. Grove Road becomes Allyn Road. I cross SR700, and after about another mile, I enter the tiny village of Hiram Rapids, the site of the natural stone dam at the heart of the Onion Wars.

Passing the village green, I turn onto Winchell Road to the river, where I stop to see the rapids. I don't see, however, anything resembling the natural rock dam that figured in the Onion Wars saga. I find a side road that parallels the stream and start down it. After about a mile, and seeing no dam, I notice an older man pulling letters out of his mailbox. I stop and ask him about the dam. He listens intently, but shakes his head and says, "I've lived here for more than forty years, so I'd know if there was one."

Since the Onion Wars took place over a century ago, it's likely the dam was eroded by the Cuyahoga's continuous action.

I exit Hiram Rapids heading south on Alpha Road, pedaling up an unexpected incline. I then jog east briefly on SR82, and at the western edge of Hiram, I turned south once more, this time on Ryder Road climbing uphill past farm fields to Pioneer Trail up on the ridge.

Shortly after turning right on Pioneer Trail, I see a large house and farm complex, the John Johnson Farm, which is a site of historic significance in the Church of Jesus Christ of Latter-day Saints, or Mormons. In 1831, Johnson and his wife Alice, a prosperous farming couple, became Mormon converts and welcomed the young Joseph Smith, the founder of the Mormon religion, into their home. Smith stayed for a year, during which time the farm became the church's headquarters until Smith moved on. Smith also reportedly received several significant revelations while lodged with the Johnsons. The Church of Jesus Christ of Latter-day Saints purchased the farm in 1956 and restored it, in 2001, to its original condition. The farm is open for tours.

Continuing beyond the farm, I come to a large Mormon church on the same side of the road. This structure is a part of the Church of Jesus Christ of Latter-day Saints' Seminaries and Institutes. The objective of religious education in these seminaries and institutes is to assist individuals, families, and priesthood leaders in accomplishing the mission of the church.

I turned south a mile later on Vaughn Road, pedal a mile to Mennonite Road, turn east, and a mile further enter Mantua.

Ride 7

Bicounty Byways

Route: Lodi to Wellington loop
Counties: Medina, Lorain
Terrain: Relatively flat
Distance: 40 miles
Lunch: Bread-N-Brew, Wellington (440-647-0082)
Points of Interest: Lowatha Statue in Lodi, Wellington square
How to get there: The Lodi Town Square sits at the
   intersection of State Route 421 (SR421) and State Route 83
   (SR83). Take Interstate 76 (I-76)/US Route 244 (US244). If
   you are heading west, take SR83 southeast to the Lodi town
   square. If you are heading east on I-76/US244, take SR421/
   US Route 42 southwest to the town square.

I HAVE named this ride Bicounty Byways because the ride winds through parts of two counties. The name doesn't fit perfectly because nothing on the route indicates the individual jurisdictions, and the communities on the loop are not seats of their counties. Aside from the two towns, the ride wends through rural Ohio. I could have called the route the "Rural Tour of This Part of Ohio," but that didn't seem very catchy. Anyway, Bicounty Byways has clever alliteration.

Bicounty Byways is a good route, has very little traffic, and is a nice trek for chatting and cycling at the same time. The joy of this ride comes from the freedom to pedal through open country with good friends.

I ride from the village of Lodi on a late winter day when the air temperature is expected to reach a high of about forty-two degrees with a wind chill of about freezing. I dress appropriately. The day is bright and clear, and after a gray week including a heavy snowfall, I feel pretty sunny.

The village of Lodi is the oldest settlement in Medina County and is home to just over three thousand people. Lodi was founded in 1811 and called Harrisville for Joseph Harris, the head of the founding family. In 1829, the townspeople wanted to change the name, but disagreed. One educated citizen, who thought the proceedings were like Napoleon's Battle of Lodi in Italy, offered up the name, which was adopted.

A prominent feature of the Lodi town square is the statue of an Indian named Lowatha. The statue was given in memory of Judge Joseph Harris and his wife by their daughter Elvira Ainsworth in 1888. Elvira, known for her charitable works, was married to Henry Ainsworth, a merchant in the community for many years.

I leave my truck on the public square, not far from Lowatha. (There are no time limitations and no parking meters, but overnight parking is not permitted.) I mount up and head southwest on Bank Street. As I proceed, I notice a hill as tall as a three-story building to my left. This structure is a man-made mound built to carry railroad tracks across the depression in which Lodi sits. The railroad embankment encompasses the south side of the village and proceeds for a few miles beyond it to the west. At a point where State Route 421 (SR421) leaves the town, an arch bridge spans a break in the mound, but the size and extent of the embankment gives this part of Lodi a sense of being walled in.

I leave town heading north on West Street, which becomes Richmond Road, and I find myself in a rural environment almost immediately. After crossing the four lanes of US Route 224 (US224)/US Route 42 (US42), I turn west on Sanford Road and then north on Congress Road. The land is devoted to two uses. The larger portion is primarily agricultural, although at this time of year, the spring planting has not yet begun. Also, along the stretch are many uniquely-designed, single-family homes. While some of the structures are older farmhouses, newer homes are interspersed along my route.

The pattern of fields and homes essentially describes the entire loop. The route is relatively flat, except for small dips, especially on Congress Road. In the depressions, streams often cross under the road, and in several places, they feed ponds on the properties adjacent to the roadway. Even on the level ground, a surprising number of ponds, several man-made, add to the landscape.

Congress Road eventually bends to the northwest and becomes Spencer Mills Road after crossing State Route 162 (SR162). River

---

Lodi Embankment

The old Chapman homestead was bought in 1905 by the Baltimore and Ohio Improvement Company from which the gravel and timber were taken to make the large fill on the Baltimore & Ohio Railroad double track through the incorporated town of Lodi.

From History of the Western Reserve, *Lewis Publishing Company, 1910*

Corners, a small hamlet, is located at the intersection of Spencer Mills and River Corners Road. Not far north of River Corners is Spencer Lake Wildlife Area, a popular place for fishing and hunting.

Spencer Mills turns due west, taking me past a blueberry farm. The fruit bushes are organized in straight rows much like a vineyard. If I were travelling in midsummer, the berries would no doubt be abundant.

Eventually, after a series of roads that jog both north and west, I roll into Wellington. This architecturally attractive village was organized in 1821. The town's name was originally to be Charlemont, since an early settler, Charles Sweet had been willing to chop out the most roadway to the town. Sweet's compatriots didn't like the moniker and offered to do the road-clearing job for him on the condition that he would surrender the right to name the spot. Sweet agreed, and the name Wellington was chosen to honor the Duke of Wellington and William T. Welling, one of the first settlers.

Wellington is also the town where Archibald M. Willard got his start. Willard is the celebrated painter of "The Spirit of '76." (See ride 1, page 14, for directions to Hugh Mosher's hometown of Perry, Ohio. Mosher was the fifer in the painting.) Willard came to Wellington in 1855 and returned there after the Civil War. He painted the exteriors of carriages for a local manufacturer. One of

River Corners

Phineas Davis kept an accommodation for travelers, not exactly a tavern, at the River Corners, at an early date. Shubael Smith built and kept the first regular public house in the township. This stood on the square at the center. The first saw-mill was built at the River Corners, on Black River, by Calvin Spencer, in 1833. It was a water-power. The dam was built about six months before the mill, and Mr. Spencer began to get out lumber to build a grist-mill soon after.

From History of Medina County and Ohio, *Baskin & Battey, 1881*

The Spirit of '76 *by A. M. Willard. Courtesy Library of Congress, Prints and Photographs Division.*

Willard's creative designs interested J. F. Ryder, a famous Cleveland photographer and publisher, and Ryder and Willard formed a long-lasting business partnership and friendship.

Wellington today, with about 4,500 people, offers an array of impressive buildings, the most notable of which is the red-brick town hall constructed in 1885 under the direction of Chicago architect, Oscar Cobb, who combined Byzantine, Greek, Gothic, and Spanish styles. Also along the village green are the United Methodist Church, an attractive public library, and a smaller brick building that looks like a former bank. Main Street boasts some large homes that are also architecturally significant, including residences built in the styles of Gothic Revival, Italianate, Second Empire, Queen Anne, Folk Victorian, Shingle Style, Colonial Revival, Greek Revival, and American Neoclassicism.

Wellington Town Hall. Courtesy of Rona Proudfoot.

I buy lunch at a little shop called Bread-N-Brew, a casual eatery located at the corner of Herrick and Main. The place features specialty coffees, soup, salads, and hot and cold sandwiches. I select a Reuben panini sandwich with chips and a pickle, all of which I chase down with an apple-cheese Danish.

While I was eating I couldn't help but notice the Herrick Memorial Library across the street. The library was built between 1902 and 1904 by former townsman Myron T. Herrick, who became governor-elect of Ohio while the construction was taking place and presented the deed to the township trustees shortly before taking office in Columbus. The spacious, new structure inspired the local library committee to appeal successfully to the state legislature for an amendment to the "township library law"

Myron T. Herrick, Republican candidate for governor. Courtesy
Library of Congress, Prints and Photographs Division.

allowing the committee to purchase books to match the size of
the library.

The Herrick Memorial Library was built on the site of the
Wadsworth's Hotel, a place with historical significance in the
abolitionist saga prior to the Civil War. John Price, a fugitive
slave from Kentucky, had been residing in Oberlin, Ohio. In September of 1858, he was apprehended by U.S. Marshals under the
Fugitive Slave Law and moved to the Wadsworth's Hotel with the
intent of returning him to his owners. Residents of Oberlin and
Wellington congregated at the hotel and after peaceful negotia-
tions failed, the group stormed the hotel and rescued Price, who
was later taken to freedom in Canada. Of the thirty-seven people
indicted for their action, only two went to trial and their pun-

BREAD-N-BREW
100 South Main Street, Wellington, OH 44090
440-647-0082
Open year-round

HOURS
Monday–Friday: 6:00 A.M. to 7:00 P.M.
Saturday: 8:00 A.M. to 4:00 P.M.
Sunday: 8:00 P.M. to 4:00 P.M.

SPECIALTIES
Coffee and Pastries

ishment was minimal. The Oberlin–Wellington Rescue Case was reported nationally and it became another sign for southern slave owners that the tide was turning.

After finishing my lunch, I head south on Main Street, riding slowly to look at the diverse buildings. Once beyond the village limits, I turn east on Cemetery Road to Hawley Road, which runs south.

The wind is becoming a problem. As I pedal a few miles due south, the wind hits me strongly at an oblique angle, sapping my energy, and slowing me to a crawl. I get a break eventually when I ride past the backside of Findley State Park, a large forest on my right, which serves as a windblock for almost one mile, but I am soon struggling against the strong breeze again. I know from my speedometer I am riding slower than usual, but my struggle against the wind is verified when an Amish horse and buggy passes me. The driver even asks if I am all right. I assure him, and myself, I am.

Changing Gears

Like bicycles, Amish buggies are treated as vehicles on the road. If you happen to pass a buggy, be sure to follow traffic laws and signal before passing.

My reprieve comes when I turn east and pedal in that direction for several miles. The wind is now aiding me and I speed down New London–Eastern Road into an area populated with

A sheet music cover illustrated with a portrait of prominent black abolitionist Frederick Douglass as a runaway slave. Courtesy Library of Congress, Prints and Photographs Division.

Amish people. I start to see few houses that have the distinctive curtain arrangements common to Amish homes. I also notice several fields with corn shocks bundled in the old-style harvest technique favored by Amish farmers. The Amish homes and farms create a new panorama for the inbound leg.

New London–Eastern Road ends at Pawnee Road where the town of Pawnee is located. I see a few homes gathered together and railroad tracks. At one time, I imagine the train stopped here, but now it looks like only about fifty people call Pawnee home.

I head south on Pawnee, again into the wind, but I was able to recover on the previous part of my journey so I am able to ride more strongly now. I turn on Sanford Road. After a mile, I am on the route I had taken out of Lodi. I roll back into that village and end my ride.

Lowatha had kept an eye on my truck the whole time.

Ride 8
Medina's Meander

Route: Medina to Hinckley loop
Counties: Medina
Terrain: Flat to hilly
Distance: 39 miles
Lunch: Foster's Tavern, Hinckley (330-278-2106)
Points of Interest: Hinckley Reservation, Medina Square
How to get there: From the north/south: US Route 42
   (US42)/ State Route 3 (SR3) runs through downtown
   Medina and is named Court Street within the Medina city
   limits. There is a municipal parking lot on South Court
   Street.
   From the east/west: State Route 18 (SR18) intersects with
   Court Street in downtown Medina. Head south on Court
   Street to find the municipal parking lot.

When a friend suggested I consider Medina, Ohio, as the starting and ending point for a ride, I was skeptical. Medina is an attractive city with a picturesque public square that is surrounded by Victorian-era buildings. But the square also serves as the crossing point for US Route 42 (us42), State Route 57 (sr57), State Route 3 (sr3) and State Route 18 (sr18), the latter having continuous truck traffic. East of Medina, Interstate-71 (I-71) has an interchange at sr18, adding to the traffic density. There are 275,000 people living within a fifteen-mile radius of Medina and 25,000 residents who live in Medina proper.

After taking a closer look at possible routes, I found, with a little trial and error, a loop that is practical and appealing for the cyclist. The route offers a variety of terrain and provides a stimulating workout. The first half of the ride is hilly, which is good for fresh legs, and the second half allows for recovery.

Medina is also a community that works hard at being visitor friendly. Free three-hour parking is available on the public square and adjoining streets. Since three hours is not long enough for cyclists pedaling Medina's Meander, I suggest parking at one of the three municipal lots—one is on South Court Street and the other two are on West Liberty Street—where parking is free for up to ten hours. Even though, at first glance, Medina's constant activity might dissuade you, the Medina Meander is an enjoyable trek.

Medina, Ohio

Medina, Ohio (pop. 2,734, alt. 1,086 ft.), the county seat of Medina county, is on the old stage road from Columbus to Cleveland. It was laid out in 1818 and was originally called Mecca and was so marked on the early maps of Ohio. It is noted for its extensive bee culture interests and for the manufacture of implements devoted to that industry.

From The Automobile Blue Book, *The Automobile Blue Book Publishing Company, 1918*

Downtown Medina. Courtesy of Robert D. Tompkins.

Although stories vary, it is likely that Medina was originally named Mecca by Elijah Boardman, an early Western Reserve
landowner who thought the place was the "end of the trail" for
many settlers from Connecticut. Unfortunately, the Postmaster general informed the locality that another town in Trumbull
County was already named Mecca. In 1825, Mecca became Medina. Medina incorporated as a village in 1835 and as a city some
years later.

I ride Medina's Meander on a bright day in early spring. I
do ride year-round, but my winter rides are fewer and shorter
because of the cold, snow, and early darkness. I am eager to get
on the road for a full journey. I park my truck in the municipal
lot on South Court Street and walk my bike to the city square.

On the street by the southeast corner of the square, I mount up, head one block south on Broadway Street, and turn left onto Smith Road to begin the eastbound section of the loop.

Smith Road is a city street lined with houses for several blocks. Eventually, the houses thin out and Smith takes me down a hill into River Styx Road. In Greek mythology, the Styx is the principal river of the underworld—the stream across which the souls of the dead are ferried to Hades. Styx comes from a Greek word that denotes both hatred and extreme cold. The road parallels the Styx River and there is also a River Styx Park in Medina County. The park is the summer home to neotropical songbirds of Central America.

Following county roads over hills and dales, I eventually come to State Route 162 (SR162), a relatively quiet byway on which I pedal one mile to Sharon Center. The town was originally called Mather for one of the early settlers, Samuel Mather, but when the township was organized in 1830, the name was changed to Sharon Center to reflect its Sharon, Connecticut, heritage. I continue on SR162 for one mile beyond Sharon Center and turn north on State Road.

Sharon Center

Sharon, a township of Medina county, situated immediately S. E. of Medina. It was first organized in 1830. It now contains 200 families, 1 church, 1 academy, 7 school houses, 175 voters, a post office called *Sharon Center,* and one tavern. It is 9 miles from the county seat, and 115 from Columbus.

From The Ohio Gazetteer, and Traveler's Guide, *Isaac N. Whiting, 1837*

Medina's Meander loop is more rectangular than circular. The entire eastern side, comprised of State Road, is closest to a continuous straight line, running from the southeastern corner of the loop to the northeastern tip. State Road also proves the most challenging leg of the ride because of its undulations and stiff climbs.

As I start north on State Road, the landscape on both sides of the road is wooded, with rustic suburban homes in small clearings. I expected to see more open cropland. The area I am trekking through was once heavily agricultural.

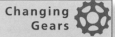

Changing Gears

The Hinckley Township website cites information that the buzzards came to the area long before the Hinckley Hunt.

Before Ohio was settled, it was virtually all forested. But by the late 1800s, many of those forests had been cut down, leaving the state with only 20 percent forest cover. In the early 1900s, the coverage had dropped to 10 percent. In 1916, the state forest system was initiated with the purchase of over 1,700 acres of land. Since the late 1920s, state nurseries have produced five hundred million seedlings that have been planted on more than one million acres of forested land.

State Road eventually crosses the heavily-trafficked SR18. I am relieved to find that the intersection has a traffic light. I cross easily when the light turns green.

North of SR18, State Road resumes its rural character and I pass some working farms, though a good bit of modern housing also is also evident. As I approach the northeastern corner of the loop, I pedal into the wooded Hinckley Reservation, a two thousand acre Cleveland Metropark. (See ride 4, page 44 for a full description of the Metropark system.) The reservation is also home to the annual spring return of the buzzards. Hinck-

The Hinckley Hunt

The amount of game killed was, about three hundred deer, twenty-one bear, and seventeen wolves that were killed in the ring; and it was estimated that about one hundred deer were killed while marching to the center. The night was spent merrily in singing songs, roasting meat, etc. [A quotation of Mr. Cogswell who was a participant in the Hinkley Hunt.]

From History of the Western Reserve, *Lewis Publishing Company, 1910*

Changing Gears

Every March 15 is Buzzard Day at the Hinkley Reservation.

The following Sunday is celebrated as Buzzard Sunday.

ley's flock of buzzards (turkey vultures) returns each March 15. According to legend, that's because in 1818 there was a big hunt for livestock predators. After the hunt, the animal carcasses froze, and the scavenger birds feasted on them during the mid-March thaw. I am too early in the year to see the vultures.

Coming to West Drive, a reservation road, I turn left into the park and wheel over onto the paved multi-use trail adjacent to the drive. West Drive and the trail end at the same place, but in the middle, the trail moves away from West Drive and leads to Hinckley Lake while the drive leads over a good-sized hill.

At Bellus Road, the northern boundary of Hinckley Reservation, I start the westward leg of the loop. Bellus Road soon brings me to State Route 94 (SR94) and I turn north for a short run up to the center of Hinckley township. At the intersection of SR94 and SR303 is Foster's Tavern. I park my bike and head in to lunch.

Foster's Tavern has a diverse menu. Part of the menu is the standard bar food, but many offerings are eclectic. Half of Foster's menu changes each day. The "standard" part of the menu features large burgers made from Black Angus beef, ground fresh daily, and served in a variety of ways and with an assortment of sides. There are also chicken dishes and even grilled bologna sandwiches. The daily specials include steaks, oysters, pierogies, lobster, crab cakes, shrimp, wings, scallops, pizza, and more. Food is served both at the bar and in the adjacent dining room. At the time I am there, the wait staff consists of one unruffled bartender who handles whatever is needed. I eat at the bar and down a bowl of potato and sausage soup.

After lunch, I return to Bellus Road, make a number of stair-step turns on local roads, and then turn onto Sleepy Hollow Road for the main part of the westbound leg. Sleepy Hollow Road has three distinct segments. The eastern end, where I start, is rustic

FOSTER'S TAVERN
1382 Ridge Road, Hinckley, OH 44233
330-278-2106
Open year-round

HOURS
Monday: 11:30 A.M. to 9:00 P.M.
Tuesday–Thursday: 11:30 A.M. to 10:00 P.M.
Friday and Saturday: 11:30 A.M. to 11:00 P.M.
Sunday: 11:30 A.M. to 5:00 P.M.

SPECIALTIES
Burgers and Fried Bologna

suburban, the middle section is suburban, and the western section is rural.

Sleepy Hollow Road ends on Muntz Road and I turn south. Muntz Road leads me into Abbeyville Road almost immediately, and I take Abbeyville Road back to Medina.

Of all the roads included in the Medina's Meander loop, Abbeyville Road is the one surrounded by the most farmland. Even as I ride along the stretch, however, I notice some new "crops" growing, including housing developments and a golf course. Abbeyville, Ohio, itself is basically a spot on the map marked by the Lagerheads BBQ Smokehouse, which appeared to be doing a brisk business.

Abbeyville Road brings me to the northwest edge of Medina and I hop onto SR18 for the last couple of miles into town. The busy part of SR18 is on the eastern side of Medina, so I relax on this stretch of SR18—a two-lane road with a wide, paved shoulder and a city speed limit. I roll into Medina and arrive at its Public Square.

Ride 9

Arsenal's Edge

Route: Ravenna to Craig Beach loop
Counties: Portage, Trumbull, Mahoning
Terrain: Relatively flat, with a couple of hills
Distance: 37 miles
Lunch: Olde Dutch Mill Restaurant, Craig Beach (330-654-4100)
Points of Interest: Covered bridge in Newton Falls, Ravenna Arsenal
How to get there: Havre's Woods is a park located in Ravenna, Ohio. From Interstate 76 (I-76), take the exit for State Route 44 North (SR44). Turn northwest (left) onto New Milford Road. Havre's Woods Park will be on your left.

East and slightly north of Ravenna is a large tract of land that on most maps, appears as a vast, empty space, uninterrupted by roads, bodies of water, or railroad tracks. Some county maps label the area as "Ravenna Ordinance Plant" without any explanation. Nonetheless, this large chunk of real estate, comprised of 21,427 acres and stretching twelve miles from east to west, is completely surrounded by chain-link fence and dominates the region.

Established in 1940 by the United States Army, the site was built at the beginning of World War II to assemble and load a variety of conventional ammunition, bombs, primers, fuses, and other explosive devices. Although initially split into two divisions—the Ravenna Ordinance Plant, for production, and the Portage Ordinance Depot, for storage—the facility was eventually combined and renamed the Ravenna Arsenal (RAP).

The Ravenna site was chosen because of its remote, non-coastal location, the accessible land, a ready workforce, ample water, and excellent rail connections. According to local lore, the site also was selected because the region has more cloudy days than anywhere else in the United States except for the Pacific Northwest, giving the arsenal protection against spies in the skies. Personally, I've never noticed that the area is cloudier than anywhere else in Ohio.

During WWII, the facility employed some fourteen thousand people. From 1942 to 1945, workers at the Ravenna Arsenal produced more weapons for the war effort than at any other plant in the United States. After WWII, the place stopped pro-

The Ravenna Arsenal Construction Statistics

10,000,000 common brick used.
300,000 cubic yards of concrete.
63 miles of fences built.
25,000,000 board feet of lumber used.
1,000,000 rivets and bolts used.

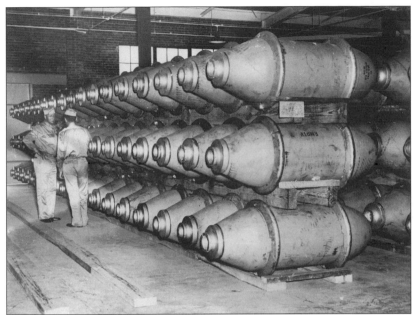

Two workers in a storage facility at the Ravenna Arsenal, circa 1944.
Courtesy of Hiram College Archives.

duction but remained a weapons storage facility. RAP was reactivated during the Korean War and the Vietnam conflict. Today, the facility is largely mothballed, though the National Guard uses a small portion of the land for training.

The public is seldom allowed into the plant and its 1,371 buildings. This is understandable since almost two-thirds of the acreage has been declared environmentally contaminated from the munitions work that went on there. Cleanup efforts are ongoing and sporadic.

The once-frenetic area is no longer a source of employment. Unfortunately, roads that once crossed the region now stop at the facility's gates. People who live north or south of the arsenal have to drive well out of their way to get around the sealed off land. Besides the fences, trees and a few buildings at the entry points, there isn't even much to see from outside. The site sits if the need arises again.

President Warren G. Harding and his personal secretary, George B. Christian, on horseback, circa 1921. Courtesy Library of Congress, Prints and Photographs Division.

Arsenal's Edge begins in Ravenna, travels along the southern boundary of the arsenal; passes though the small community of Charlestown, a community that had its northern access completely eliminated when the arsenal took over the land above the town; continues to the village of Newton Falls, known for its easy to remember ZIP code (44444); includes a lunch stop in Craig Beach, a lakeside community; and then heads back to Ravenna on roads that zigzag their way below the Michael J. Kirwan Reservoir and West Branch State Park.

For this ride, my brother Scott, a fellow cyclist, joins me. We had agreed to start the ride from Havre's Woods, a park belonging to the city of Ravenna. Since Scott lives in Ravenna, he pedals his bike to our rendezvous. I park my truck in the park's lot.

Ravenna was founded in 1799 and is the county seat of Portage County. The community is the birthplace of the Quaker Oats Company, founded in 1877. Ravenna was also the former home to the Riddle Coach and Hearse Company, a business known for its finely crafted horse-drawn vehicles. Presidents William McKinley and Warren Harding were both carried to their grave sites in Riddle Hearses. The company closed in 1926, but in 1998, when the popular cowboy star Roy Rogers died, he was wheeled to his burial place in a restored Riddle Hearse.

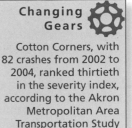

Changing Gears

Cotton Corners, with 82 crashes from 2002 to 2004, ranked thirtieth in the severity index, according to the Akron Metropolitan Area Transportation Study traffic crash report.

We begin our ride by heading north on New Milford Road. Scott, in the lead, reminds me to exercise caution once we reach Main Street because it is a four-lane highway with constant traffic. We travel about half a mile on Main Street, but to make our next turn, we need to move from the curb lane to the passing lane, and then, at the five-points intersection (known locally as Cotton Corners possibly because it was the name of a small locality in the early 1800s) with the traffic light, move into left-turn lane. We have no difficulty, but be sure to watch the traffic carefully and signal clearly as you maneuver. This short stretch is the only section of the entire Arsenal's Edge route where you actually ride in a busy traffic stream. When we have the right of way, we turn slightly left onto Newton Falls Road and leave the high traffic area behind. Most of the traffic is headed for one of the three state routes that intersect at the light. Newton Falls Road, by contrast, is a county byway heading into a lightly populated area. Except when approached by the occasional car, Scott and I ride side by side and converse about family news and recent happenings in our lives.

About a mile and a half later, we pass Garrett Road on our left. This road changes its name a few times as it heads north, but it marks the western boundary of the RAP, our silent companion for several miles as we continue east on Newton Falls Road.

Scott and I chat as we ride until we near Charlestown. The only two hills worthy of the name on this ride are on the approach to this small community. At the long hill leading to the town's single crossroad, Scott and I break off our conversation and climb the hill, each at our own pace and stride. We have ridden together so often we naturally understood that we'd rendezvous at the summit. I reach the top barely ahead of Scott, who is a couple of strokes behind.

Charlestown is little more than a fire station, a community building, a church, and a sprinkling of houses situated near the crossing of two county roads. Although our route continues straight east, we decide to make a quick detour north to check out one of the arsenal's gates that chopped off the northern arm of the little town. Prior to construction of the RAP, property owners, some of whose farms had been in family hands since the early 1800s, were required to sell their properties and evacuate.

A small park sits on the town's side of the fence, but other than the park and a house across the street from it, there is no reason for vehicles to venture this way. In fact, we notice a boy of about ten riding in the middle of the street on his all-terrain vehicle. He didn't expect to see much traffic as he practiced at becoming the next Dale Earnhart.

We return to the main intersection, head east out of town, and glide down a hill about as steep as the one we had climbed to reach the place. Over the next few miles, we encounter a few climbs, but each becomes less steep. We are back on level ground for the rest of the trip when we reach State Route 5 (SR5).

State Route 5 is a moderately busy thoroughfare, but its wide, paved shoulder accommodates bicycles. We ride single file for a

Timbers from Charlestown, Ohio

In 1834 the timbers and planks for the brig "John Jacob Astor" [supplied the early outposts along Lake Superior and was wrecked in 1844] were fashioned at Charlestown, Ohio, and the next spring they were carried to the Soo on the schooner "Bridget."

From Proceedings of the State Historical Society of Wisconsin, *Democrat Printing Company, 1892*

little more than a mile. On the way, we pass one of the arsenal's main entrances.

We turn south onto Wayland Road taking us away from the arsenal. The arsenal continues east for several miles, but we have seen the last of the property. Wayland Road leaves SR5 and immediately travels under a railroad overpass. The proximity of this railroad influenced the committee that chose the RAP location.

We stay on Wayland Road for a brief stint and turn east back onto Newton Falls Road. Previously, this section of Newton Falls Road was part of a continuous route from Charlestown. The two sections of Newton Falls Road are on the same latitude. The construction of SR5 and of the railroad, both of which transect the area on a northeast-southwest axis, chopped Newton Falls Road into two pieces.

We make steady progress toward the small city for which the road is named. On the way, we go through Paris, a rural intersection with a boarded-up old school building and a tavern. As we pass by the tavern, Scott says, "Wait a minute," brakes to a stop, and dismounts. I follow suit. He picks up a man's wallet he has spotted. Inside, we find a driver's license and a couple of dollars. Assuming a guest of the tavern likely dropped the wallet, Scott attempts to enter the bar, but finds it closed. However, we hear a sound around back and find the bar owner, who recognizes the

Charlestown, Ohio

Charles Curtiss came to Portage county about 1809. He secured a tract of wild land in what is now Charlestown township, and there set to himself the arduous task of reclaiming a farm from the wilderness. The township of Charlestown was named in his honor, as derived from his Christian name, and it is a matter of historical record that a barrel of whiskey was donated to assist in the erection of a new church in the locality, on consideration of the name of Charlestown being applied to the newly organized township.

From History of the Western Reserve, *Lewis Publishing Company, 1910*

man pictured on the license. We leave the wallet with him and resume our trek.

Finding items along the road is not uncommon. One ride, I spotted what appeared to be a shiny pen and a zippered leather case about five inches square lying side by side on the edge of the road. When I stopped to pick them up, the shiny object turned out to be a high-intensity flashlight, in perfect working order. The case contained a complete set of lock-picking tools that I was careful not to touch, though I took the items with me.

When I got home, I telephoned the police department and described my find to an officer. He showed little interest. He mentioned that there was no law against owning lock-pick equipment, there were no recent cases of unlawful entry, and I had already handled the items. I told him I had made sure not to touch the tools, but he seemed to indicate that I had been watching too much *CSI (Crime Scene Investigation)*. I've never found a use for the tools or the case, but the penlight with its bright, focused beam is a great addition to my gear on extended bicycle journeys when I camp out.

Eventually, the road Scott and I are on ends at a point where the name changes to McClintocksburg Road to the south, but continues as Newton Falls Road to the north, which is the direction we take. As we continue to Newton Falls, Newton Falls Road becomes Ravenna Road—as if we are nearing the community from which we started the ride—and Church Street when we enter the village limits. Actually, the ride into Newton Falls is not very complicated because once we turn at the McClintocksville Road–Newton Falls Road juncture, we simply follow that

Paris, Ohio

Paris, Ohio, was founded about 1810 and named for a town in New York State. The Ravenna Arsenal absorbed the town and its land.

Editor's Note

Newton Falls

Judson Canfield, owner of the lands about the small falls in the Mahoning River in Newton Township, proposed a settlement at this point, and in 1806 a town plat was surveyed for him by Ezekiel Hover. John Lane became the first settler at this place and shortly afterwards Bildad Hine and family arrived. In 1808, Mr. Canfield built a sawmill at the falls and two or three years later erected a grist mill. Additional settlers came, larger mills were erected and in 1813 a distinct improvement was made with the building of a bridge across the west branch of the river. Later a woolen mill and foundry were put up and Newton Falls became the trade center of Newton Township. The advent of the railroad made it still more important.

From History of Youngstown and the Mahoning Valley, Ohio, *American Historical Society, 1921*

pavement into Newton Falls. Still, the naming schemes must have taken some time for the local mail carriers to sort out.

Newton Falls is a city of about five thousand people that was named for the two sets of falls within the city, each on different branches of the Mahoning River. When we arrive at the main street of Newton Falls—called Broad Street, not Main Street—the West Branch of the Mahoning River is a few hundred yards to our left. However, we turn right down Broad Street toward the East Branch of the river. Before turning south to follow the river, we pedal north a block to see an old covered bridge. Constructed in 1831, the bridge is the second oldest covered bridge in the state and last one in Trumbull County. Its one lane still supports auto traffic.

We turn around, cross Broad Street, and take River Street south. River Street becomes River Road and ambles along the East Branch of the Mahoning, which we see infrequently. We travel through an area of rural homes and farms with very little traffic.

At County Line Road, we turn west. County Line Road bisects Trumbull and Mahoning counties. We stay on this road to Grandview Road, the first cutoff. We are now in Mahoning

County, entering the community of Craig Beach, and with a few strokes of the pedals, we arrive at the Olde Dutch Mill Restaurant and Golf Course, our lunch stop.

We enter the small restaurant that also serves as the clubhouse for the golfers. In the pleasant little dining room, we select food from the menu that features soup, sandwiches, salads, and sides. I have a sandwich called the "Shark," a huge portion of battered fish on a hoagie bun. The meal is enjoyable and filling.

South of the golf course is the dam on the Mahoning River that formed Lake Milton Reservoir. The dam was completed in 1913, and Craig Beach was developed as an amusement park with a swimming beach, roller coaster, and midway. Today, the area encompasses a small community park but is mostly homes. Employees at the Ravenna Arsenal seeking housing accelerated growth in residential dwellings, resulting in the decline of the amusement park.

After lunch, Scott and I peddle down the main street to see the town. We could continue south, taking us out of our way, but we turn around instead. Soon, we are back on County Line Road, heading west. For the next several miles, this road, called Cable Line Road once we reenter Portage County, rolls through a rural and flat landscape. Scott and I pass the time in desultory conversation until we come to the entrance of West Branch State Park. This park was built around the Michael J. Kirwan Reservoir, named for a sixteen-term congressman from the

Dean Martin

Dean Martin, a member of the fabled "Rat Pack," was born in Steubenville, Ohio, in 1917. He got his start at the Craig Beach amusement park in the early 1930s. Among the crooner's hits were "Memories Are Made of This" (#1, 1955), "That's Amore" (#2, 1953), "Powder Your Face with Sunshine" (#10, 1949), and "You Belong to Me" (#12, 1952).

Editor's Note

OLDE DUTCH MILL
2745 Grandview Road, Craig Beach, OH 44429
330 654 4100
Open year-round

HOURS
Summer: 6:30 A.M. to 1:00 A.M.
Winter: 8:00 A.M. to 10:00 P.M.

SPECIALTIES
The Olde Dutch Burger

Youngstown area. The reservoir is the result of the damming of the West Branch of the Mahoning River, which was completed in 1965 to aid in flood protection. Though we can't see the lake from where we are, Cable Line Road is stopped by the reservoir. Shortly after we pass the park entrance, we swing south and follow a series of crossroads until we are able to turn back north and resume travel on the western segment of Cable Line Road.

I seldom mention the condition of the roads, largely because any information I provide would change due to weathering and construction. However, the final stretch of Cable Line Road is in bad condition. When I talked to a park ranger about the road's condition (this section of Cable Line Road is within the boundary of the state park) she indicated that there are no plans to repave it partly because the road is not a major access route into the park and the only house on the road is occupied by a park employee. I would suggest another route, but this two-mile stretch of Cable Line Road is essential to the Arsenal's Edge circuit. Alternative roads add more distance or lead you into high-traffic areas. So grin, bear it, and watch out for the impediments.

Changing Gears

West Branch State Park has several trails that are open to mountain biking.

Shadow on the pavement. Courtesy of Robert D. Tompkins.

Cable Line Road brings us to State Route 14 (SR14), a busy road with a passable, paved shoulder. We travel it for about half a mile before taking a wide left onto Hayes Road. Hayes takes us quickly to New Milford Road. We turn north and are soon back at Havre's Woods Park, comfortably tired, and glad to have pedaled Arsenal's Edge.

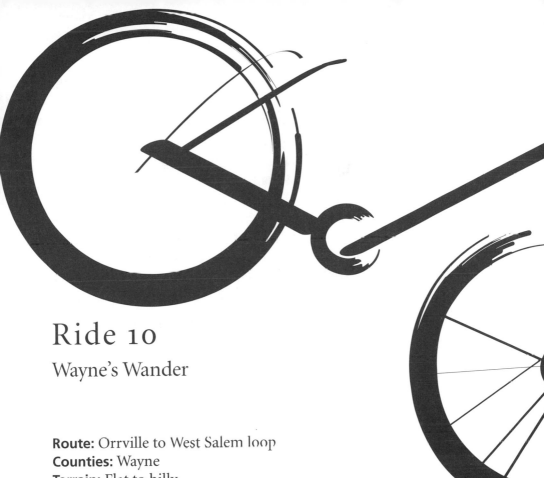

Ride 10

Wayne's Wander

Route: Orrville to West Salem loop
Counties: Wayne
Terrain: Flat to hilly
Distance: 53 miles
Lunch: The Village Cornerstone, West Salem (419-853-4885)
Points of Interest: Ohio scenery, Smithville Pioneer Village
How to get there: The Orrville Railroad Heritage Museum is at the intersection of Market Street and Depot Street. Take State Route 57 (SR57) into Orrville. State Route 57 becomes Main Street within the Orrville city limits. Turn west onto Market Street. Depot Street and the museum will be on your left.

A
t fifty-three miles, this ride gives you a good tour of the
northern half of Wayne County. The landscape is mostly rural. On the way, you'll see many farms and small
villages, conquer some challenging climbs, and have plenty of
opportunities to pedal flat out on low-traffic country roads.

Orrville is the start of the trek. The settlement of what was
to become Orrville began 1814, and the area grew rapidly with
the arrival of the Pittsburgh and Fort Wayne Railroad (later
becoming the Pittsburgh, Fort Wayne, and Chicago Railroad)
in 1851. When the railroad's plan to lay track through the area
was first announced, one landowner in town, Christian Horst,
did not welcome it. This provided an opening for a more vision-
ary townsman, Smith Orr, who immediately purchased Horst's
eighty acres, as well as the property of David Rudy and Peter Per-
rine. When the railroad did arrive, Orr persuaded its owners to
erect a water tower in town to replenish its steam engines. And,
since the locomotives would need to take on fuel at the same
time, Orr, in partnership with another man, started a sawmill so
they could be the suppliers of the wood to feed the trains' boilers.

Thomas Shreve of Wayne County

Thomas Shreve . . . visited Wayne county in 1817, and April 21, 1821,
settled in Clinton township with his father, his wife (Mary Wigle)
and five children, five more being born to him in Ohio. He was a
miller by occupation, and immediately bought the mill now owned
by George W. England, and cleared land, farmed and ran the mill. In
time he became highly prosperous, owning at one time 1,400 acres
of land in Wayne and Holmes counties. He held many public offices—was Justice of the Peace; member of the Legislature in 1839–
40; in 1841 was a candidate for State Senate, but beaten by Charles
Wolcott of Wooster; was delegate frequently to State conventions;
held nearly all the township offices; and was President of the convention held in Wooster to take action on the construction of the
P[ittsburgh], Ft. W[ayne] & C[hicago] Railway through the county.
He died July 4, 1858.

From History of Wayne County, Ohio, *Robert Douglass, 1878*

Orrville City Hall. Courtesy of The Ohio Historical Society.

I've found no record of what the community was called at the time, but eventually it was named Orrville in honor of Smith Orr, who, in addition to his entrepreneurial enterprises, was also a land surveyor and a Common Pleas court judge.

Orrville incorporated as a village in 1864, which is probably when the name was officially adopted. Judge Orr died the next year, but the town continued to grow and prosper, in part because a second railroad built lines through the community. All of this caused Ben Douglass, a historian of that day, to write of Orrville in such gushing terms that today we'd suspect him of being on the payroll of the community's economic development corporation. Here how he described the town in 1878:

> *Orrville, a creation and product of the railroad, and the inevitable genius which surrounds and pursues such corporations, is fast approaching the proportions of cityhood. Concerning her enterprise, sagacity, foresight and quick identity with what best promotes her welfare, we need distill no pen-praise or eulogy. She has two railroads—one more than Wooster—and has petitioners for other ones. . . . Her people are wide-awake, gritty, self-reliant, and full of life. Despoil her of her energy, if you please, and her situation renders her existence and success compulsory. A junction, crossway and point of distribution of railways, she must thrive. With communication direct to Cleveland, and her proximity to the coal regions, both east and south, she combines the elements that insure her permanence and stability and impart to her the qualities of a rival.*
>
> *Surrounded by excellent farms, carefully cultivated by the most frugal and industrious farmers in Wayne County, she is girt with a zone of wealth, the central figure of which she is to stand.*
>
> *Her commercial population is progressive, alert and enterprising. Her massive and beautiful business blocks will challenge comparison with any town of its age and size in the State. Her churches are solid and substantial structures, and some of them, in point of design are architectural beauties. Her hotels are commodious and in their appointments surpass those of older villages. Her school building is a capacious and costly edifice. . . . In general manufactures she has taken the lead of Wooster, and in the course of twenty-five years, estimating from her past rapid growth, she will rival the county-seat in population and in trade. (Ben Douglass,* History of Wayne County, Ohio: From the Day of the Pioneers and First Settlers to the Present Time, *Robert Douglass, Publisher, 1878, p. 686)*

Douglass' bullish prediction was only half right. Orrville did continue to grow, enough that it incorporated as a city in 1950. And today, it is the home of the J. M. Smucker Company, a major player in the jelly and jam market. But its growth does not rival that of Wooster, the county seat. At the 2000 census, Orrville had 8,551 people and Wooster had 24,811.

The smaller population, however, means Orrville is bicycle friendly. I drive to Orrville on a bright day in late autumn and find parking for my pickup in the lot of the Heritage Museum on Market Street. The weather is not quite warm enough to commit to short sleeves but not quite cold enough to put on three layers of clothing. I wear tights, but don a short-sleeve jersey and arm warmers that can be easily removed if the temperature warms—or I do. Before embarking, I am still a little chilly, so at the last minute, I put on my windbreaker jacket.

I head west on Market Street and work my way through the turns that take me out of town. I am soon on Smucker Road heading to Smithville. The pedaling warms me up, and I remove my windbreaker, fold it up, and tuck it under the bungee cords on my bike's rear rack. I won't need the jacket again.

On Smucker Road, I move quickly through farm country and look for the "frugal and industrious farmers" Douglass raved about in 1878. I see a few farmers operating large farm machinery and bringing in the last of the harvest. The farmers look pretty industrious. I don't know if they are frugal, but if they are financing their equipment, they probably have to be quite thrifty.

Soon enough, I arrive in Smithville, Ohio. Smucker Road becomes Center Street in Smithville, a village of about 1,300 people with several actively-used, nineteenth-century buildings on the main street. Smithville is also home to a pioneer village that includes a

Changing Gears

A former downtown Orrville landmark, The National House was operated by Peter Everly as a hotel and hosted notable guests including former presidents Rutherford B. Hayes and William McKinley. The building was demolished in 1914.

www.orrville.com/ history.htm

Changing Gears

Smithville holds a Heritage Days festival in mid-July. The festival includes crafts, dancing, and an ox roast.

www.smithvilleohio.org

Wooster University, circa 1910. Courtesy Library of Congress, Prints and Photographs Division.

log cabin, log house, carriage barn, blacksmith shop, barn exhibit, the historic Church of God, and the Mishler weaving mill. The weaving mill was built in 1887 by John Mishler, who had come to America from Switzerland. During its heyday, the mill manufactured rugs, carpets, cloth for fruit presses, dishcloths, and towels, and was the only producer of cheesecloth in the United States for the Swiss cheese industry.

I intend to pick up Smithville–Western Road after leaving the village. If you extend a horizontal line directly west from Smucker Road, the line connects with Smithville–Western Road. I find, however, the connection is not "straight forward" and jog northwest and then southwest through town. The southwest part is on Smithville's Main Street (sr585), which carries a good deal of traffic. I get a good view of part of the village along Main Street, but don't stay on the route for long.

Chief Killbuck

Killbuck's Town. A former Delaware town on the E. side of Killbuck cr., about 10 m. s. of Wooster, Wayne co., Ohio; occupied as early as 1746 by a chief named Killbuck, from whom it received the name.

From Handbook of American Indians North of Mexico, *G.P.O., 1907*

Although Smithville–Western Road bisects farm land, the road is a primary artery enabling drivers to cross the center section of the county without driving through Wooster, the largest community in the county. Smithville–Western carries a little more traffic than I prefer, but no other alternatives are available and the traffic does not hinder my travel. The trek from Orrville, including the first mile or so of Smithville–Western Road, is fairly flat. Now, the road is more rolling as I pedal across the countryside.

After I cross State Route 83 (SR83), the traffic almost disappears and the road has that rural feel again. The terrain changes from rolling to hilly, and I pedal up some surprisingly steep grades and plunge down their declines. The climbing warms me sufficiently and I remove my arm warmers.

I sail down another dramatic descent surrounded by woods, roll out onto a valley floor, and cross over Killbuck Creek (for information on Chief Killbuck, see inset and also ride 15). At this point, Smithville–Western appears to end at Overton Road. The continuation isn't obvious because Smithville–Western Road jogs slightly to the right, bounds sharply uphill on an angled road, and then resumes its westward course.

In fact, after I turn right and travel a few hundred yards north on Overton Road, two ladies in a car slow down beside me and ask "What's happened to Smithville–Western Road?" As I give them directions, I notice both women are wearing purple dresses and red hats, and I guess out loud that they are heading to a meeting of the Red Hat Society. They say they are and seem delighted I know about the social organization.

The Red Hat Society

An organization for woman who are aged fifty or over and promise to attend functions in full regalia—red hats and purple outfits.

Editor's Note

THE VILLAGE CORNERSTONE
180 East Buckeye Street, West Salem, OH 44287
419-853-4885
Open year-round

HOURS
Monday–Thursday: 7:00 A.M. to 7:00 P.M.
Friday and Saturday: 7:00 A.M. to 8:00 P.M.
Sunday: 8:00 A.M. to 2:00 P.M.

SPECIALTIES
Specials Change Daily

I am now in Overton, too small to be called a village, with its cluster of houses where Overton Road, like the handle of a fork, splits into three irregular tines. I turn onto the left tine, Cedar Valley Road. The road is a winding byway, slithering through a narrow, wooded valley beside Cedar Run Creek, a tributary of Killbuck Creek. The scenery is rustic, with homes scattered here and there along the valley. Cedar Run Creek flows south as I ride north. I climb gradually out of the valley and eventually head uphill in earnest.

At the top of the valley, I am again in agricultural Ohio. The expanse of fields here and elsewhere on the ride is impressive. I continue north, passing farm after farm, come to Pleasant Home Road, and turn west on Congress Road. The road swings north and I am soon in the village for which the road is named.

Congress, Ohio, is a small settlement that was laid out in 1827 and has a population of about two hundred people. Originally called Waynesburg, the name was changed in 1838 to avoid conflict with another Waynesburg in Stark County (see ride 20). I turn west in Congress, then northwest off of Oak Street, putting me on a beeline for West Salem. West Salem is on the path of US Route 42 (US42), a federal highway that, in Ohio, runs from

Cleveland to Cincinnati, roughly paralleling Interstate 71 (I-71). While most through travelers now use I-71, US42 brings a good bit of traffic to the village of 1,500 residents. Another larger road, State Route 301 (SR301) also crosses through the main intersection, but the village still maintains a small-town atmosphere. I quickly find my lunch destination, The Village Cornerstone. Its menu offers an assortment of sandwiches and full meals. I select the open-faced roast beef sandwich, with mashed potatoes, gravy, coleslaw, and a dinner roll. I had worked up a good appetite and eat every morsel of the tasty dish.

West Salem, established in 1834 by Peter and John Rickel, was incorporated in 1864. John Rickel moved onto the land in 1819 and Peter followed in 1822.

After lunch, I hoist myself back onto my bicycle, turn onto a side street adjacent to the restaurant, and bear east on Britton Road. I stop after a couple of moments and put my arm warmers on because the temperature has dropped a bit and, while eating, I cooled down.

The initial stretch of Britton Road is relatively flat followed by a series of fairly steep hills. I pass Overton Road, make one more climb, and pedal along rolling-to-flat terrain for the rest of the journey. At Canaan Center Road, I turn south and ride through the tiny settlement of Canaan, the center of the township of the same name. From there, I follow a string of country roads that jog south and east back to Orrville. I arrive tired but glad for the day on the road.

Ride 11
The Seven Hills

Route: Clinton to Sterling loop
Counties: Summit, Wayne
Terrain: Flat to hilly
Distance: 34 miles
Lunch: Bradley's Restaurant, Sterling (330-939-4531)
Points of Interest: Rogues' Hollow
How to get there: This ride starts at the trailhead for the
   Ohio & Erie Canalway Towpath Trail located at 2749 North
   Street in Clinton, Ohio. From Interstate 76 (I-76) take the
   exit for State Route 21 (SR21) south. Turn southeast (left)
   onto Clinton Road. From Clinton Road, turn south (right)
   onto Cleveland Massillon Road. At the next intersection,
   turn left onto Main Street. Immediately after the bridge on
   Main Street, turn left onto North Street.

A ncient Rome, so the story goes, was constructed on seven hills, but it wasn't built in a day. On this ride, you can do even better. The first half of the ride lets you conquer seven hills. The second half lets you recover on flatter ground.

The route begins in Clinton, a village of about 1,300 souls in the southwest corner of Summit County. In 1825, it was named for DeWitt Clinton, who as governor of New York was a champion of that state's Erie Canal, and of canals in general. The Ohio & Erie Canal was built through the area that is now Clinton. Construction on the canal started in 1825 and was completed in 1832.

The canal was a boon to the village; the town became a major transportation and business center serving surrounding counties. Standing on the hamlet's short main street today, it is hard to believe that Clinton once rivaled Akron as an up-and-coming metropolis.

The Towpath Trail now makes Clinton a recognized spot for cyclists. The trail, completed through Clinton within the last decade, is a linear park on the path of the old Ohio & Erie Canal towpath. Constructed 175 years ago, the towpath was a simple dirt track for the animals pulling canal boats. When the economically unprofitable canal finally ceased operation after the 1913 flood, parts of the towpath survived as a silent witness to an earlier era. The Towpath Trail, when completed, will extend from downtown Cleveland to New Philadelphia, Ohio. The finished segments receive a lot of cycle and foot traffic on good weather days.

My interest in Clinton is as a starting point for a road ride. I leave my truck in the parking lot that is an entry point for the Towpath Trail, but instead of rolling my bike onto the path, I mount up and wheel out of the parking lot, turning west on North Street. I quickly pedal through town and, without time to warm up, I find myself on hill number one on Clin-

Changing Gears

Towpath at Clinton:

2.6-mile section

Supports an abundance of wildflowers from spring to fall that attract a variety of insects, including many butterflies

A number of tree species can be found along the trail, especially hackberry, elm, silver maple, and swamp white oak

www.summit metroparks.org

Ohio and Erie Towpath Trail at North Clinton, Ohio. Courtesy of Tom Bower.

ton Road. I rate this climb, as Ohio hills go, about a three out of five, steep enough and long enough to keep me focused on turning the pedals in my lowest gear, but not bad enough to make me rethink the wisdom of my route choice. Knowing that six more hills lay ahead, I make sure to conserve energy.

Before reaching the crest, I cross into Wayne County. I carefully cross State Route 21 (SR21), a four-lane expressway at the hill's summit. I pump along a quiet continuation of Clinton Road until it plunges down a heavily wooded hillside, propelling

The Seven Hills of Rome

The seven hills upon which Rome is built are the Aventine, Capitoline, Coelian, Esquiline, Palatine, Quirinal and Viminal. Their altitude above the Tiber is only about one hundred and fifty feet.

From The Western Rural Year Book, *a Cyclopedia of Reference, M. George, 1886*

Starting Point at Clinton, Ohio. Courtesy of Tom Bower.

me onto Hametown Road in a narrow valley known locally as Rogues' Hollow.

Today, the area is simply a unique and somewhat cloistered place to live. However, in the nineteenth century, especially in the 1860s and 1870s, the place was known and feared as a hangout for rascals and scoundrels. There were at least three coal mines in the valley. Local miners who lived in cabins and huts there and canal men from Clinton and Canal Fulton spent their earnings in the seven saloons in the hollow (I'm told that two of the tavern buildings live on as present-day residences). Once the miners and canal hands exhausted their wages in the saloons, some, so the story goes, were not above surrounding hapless farmers, who came to the area to trade at the two grist mills, and demanding that the farmers buy a round of drinks. Fearing their well-being, the farmers usually obliged.

Changing Gears

The Rogues' Hollow Festival: An annual event that takes place the first Friday and Saturday of August

www.doylestown.com

These incidents prompted farmers to rearrange their schedules to avoid the drunken masses. Word spread, and as old-timers remember, most travelers heading to and from nearby Doylestown bypassed Rogues' Hollow. Even the sheriff avoided the location.

The coal mines are closed now, but the industry left its stamp on the area. Two nearby roads are called Coal Bank Road and Black Diamond Road.

I climb out of Rogues' Hollow to Doylestown on hill two, the severest of the seven. Along its two miles, I bound upward in three leaps, leveling off a bit in between, but never really finding flat terrain. The middle upgrade is the meanest, with one pitch that nearly forces my bike to a standstill. My determination keeps me moving, though I am continually gasping for air.

Finally, I enter Doylestown, a village of about 2,800 people. One of the first things I see as I approach Portage Street is a statue of a World War I infantryman on a stone pedestal—a memorial to men from the town and surrounding area who fought in that "great war." The doughboy on the pedestal looks down Portage Street to the small business district, and I do too. I have more hills to climb, so I pedal on, heading west out of town on Doylestown Road and gunning for hill three.

Truth be told, this hill is a pussycat, not more than a two. I climb it easily. The adventure comes on its backside—a very steep decline, or if you are going in the opposite direction, a serious climb. I *have* ridden up this slope, heading east, and found the hill so memorable that I wrote about it in my book, *Roll Around Heaven All Day*.

> *This particular hill is deceptive, because the first sight of it comes while wheeling down a spectacular decline that allows a substantial speed buildup. But, like an armed camp surrounded with land mines to deplete any force moving against it, this hill guards itself with speed-sapping topography.*

First, the entrance downgrade concludes with a tight S-curve that forces me to slow down so as not to careen off the edge of the road. Then the road ascends a short but steep foothill; I'm standing on the pedals by the time I top that.

But the real killer—the final approach to the hill proper—looks like a gentle downgrade. Actually, that's an optical illusion that led me, when meeting it for the first time, to relax and try coasting. Not only does this stretch not drop at all; it actually climbs. If I stop pedaling, I lose ground. I've yet to figure out how such a significant incline can look like a down-slope, but the result is that when I finally reach the real hill, I've lost absolutely all momentum.

It's in that tired, near standstill state that I tackle the final grade, a struggle of downshifting, grunting, and copious perspiration. (Stan Purdum, Roll Around Heaven All Day: A Piecemeal Journey Across America by Bicycle, *Communication Resources, 1997)*

I head *down* the monster and get a jolly-fast descent into a scenic farm valley. I pedal into the S-curve at the bottom and use it as an entrance ramp onto hill four. I tap my pedals steadily on this climb, a three, and enjoy the trees that line both sides of the road.

Near the top, I cross State Route 94 (SR94) and finish the ascent. I then enjoy a downhill run of more than a mile through a suburban housing area that ends after crossing State Route 57 (SR57), at the edge of Rittman—a city of about 6,400 residents.

Rittman is at least the fifth name given to this community. The original settlement, platted in the early 1800s, was called Shinersburg, though that name was in local use only and had no official standing. The spot was later named Trenton, a tribute to a local man who had been a hero in the Battle of Trenton during the Revolutionary War. When a post office was established in 1836, the Trenton name was rejected because there was a post office elsewhere in Ohio with that moniker. The town was renamed New Prospect. When the railroad came to the area, the depot was dubbed Milton Station, but a nearby intersection was called Milton Crossing. Finally, in 1881, the exasperated rail company named the community Rittman, after one of its officials, Fred Rittman. At least they didn't use his first name.

Rittman straddles two counties, Wayne and Medina, but my route keeps me in Wayne County. I proceed toward the center of Rittman and soon find myself on hill five. This upslope is short—the equivalent of a couple of city blocks or so. I might not have included the incline, but I have to stand on my pedals to get to the top. (Also, "Six Hills" just doesn't have the same ring, does it?)

Completing the climb, I roll down to a city street junction, wait for the traffic light to change, and start up hill six, a climb entirely within the city limits, with houses on both sides of the broad street. Beyond Rittman, the land levels off briefly and becomes rural. I wheel along, still riding west, beside fields filled with growing crops.

Hill seven pops up in this rural stretch—an ascent of medium difficulty—and not overly long. I pump up it, cruise along its ridge for a spell, and then follow the road downhill and out onto a plain, eventually intersecting Seville Road.

I turn south, and after about a half mile, I enter Sterling, an unincorporated community that stretches out on both sides of Seville Road. The town name was chosen in 1880, by Joseph Ross, a silversmith, who selected "Sterling" while thinking of fine sil-

---

Shinersburg

This village got its name in this way: Michael Hatfield bought the first lot in what is now Shinersburg, from Philip Fritz, and built a house on it, starting a grocery, selling drugs, beer, whisky, etc. One day Michael, Noah-like, got drunk, and in one of his more ecstatic moods was heard exclaiming, "When I get to heaven I will shine as bright as anybody;" hence *Shine*-rsburg. Lancetown, called after the Lances, exists only as a memory.

From History of Wayne County, Ohio, from the Days of the Pioneers and First Settlers to the Present Time, *Robert Douglass, 1878*

BRADLEY'S
14004 Kaufman Avenue, Sterling, OH 44276
330-939-4531
Open year-round

HOURS
Monday–Friday: 11:00 A.M. to 10:00 P.M.
Saturday: 6:00 A.M. to 10:00 P.M.

SPECIALTIES
Bradley Burger (sirloin), Bradley Fries,
Fish Fry Friday (all you can eat)

verware (what connection he was making to the location, I don't know). Prior to that, the place had been called Amwell, named by a woman who had just survived a serious illness, but, according to folklore, could now say of her condition, "I am well."

Several more strokes of the pedals delivers me to Bradley's Restaurant, a tavern-restaurant combo, which, as far I could tell, is the only place in Sterling to get a hot meal. I order the Friday "all-you-can-eat fish" dinner and find it quite delicious. The initial serving is plenteous. Though the waitress offers me more, the first plateful is sufficient.

The big hills are done, and the next part of my route, from Sterling to Marshallville, is mostly flat and entirely through farmland. Riding the hills was my outbound challenge, and the wind is my faithful opponent now. Like a sailboat tacking, I work my way south and east for about ten miles to Marshallville. The prevailing wind in this part of Ohio is usually from the west or southwest. The wind today, however, is blowing briskly from the south, and I am confronted with a headwind each time I turn south and a crosswind when I ride east.

Eventually I come to Marshallville, a small village of 825 residents. Platted in 1817, it was named Bristol by its founder, whose

Remains of old canal locks at Canal Fulton, Ohio. Courtesy of Tom Bower.

last name was Marshall (so you can see where this name story is going), and became Marshallville when it was incorporated in 1866. The town's heyday started in 1832 when the Ohio & Erie Canal opened. The nearest landing on the canal was seven and a half miles away at Canal Fulton. With many transient boat crews and little permanent law, Canal Fulton was a rough place. Farmers bringing goods from the west to ship on the canal often stopped at Marshallville for the night, rather than take their chances in Canal Fulton. Marshallville prospered until the railroad arrived in the region in the 1850s. With its coming, shippers moved their business to the trains, the canal boats stopped running, and the overnight sanctuary for travelers near the canal was no longer needed.

Today, the town is a quiet place of a few blocks. It has a tiny business district, a grade school, a few churches, a meat-packing

Changing Gears

Clinton has a "Sports School," a "Belly Dancing School," and in the very near future, a Veterans Memorial Park, all within a few hundred feet of each other

www.clintonohio historicalsociety.org

plant, and a park with softball diamonds, community buildings, and pavilions.

I bike through the village and continue east on rural Fulton Road. There is some rise and fall to the land, though nothing as hilly as on the outbound journey. At the intersection where Fulton Road (now also identified as Marshallville Road) crosses Deerfield Avenue, I turn left and pedal the final three easy miles into Clinton.

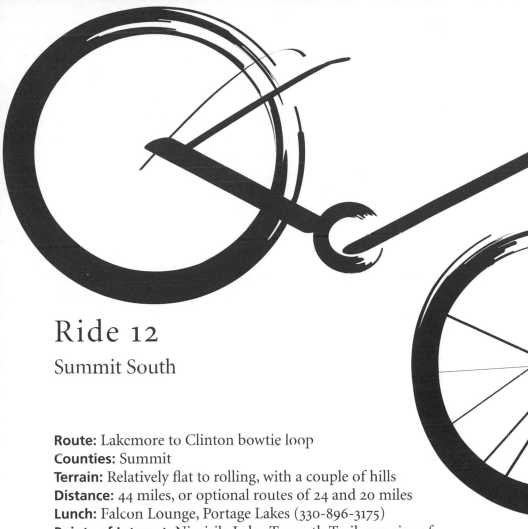

Ride 12

Summit South

Route: Lakemore to Clinton bowtie loop
Counties: Summit
Terrain: Relatively flat to rolling, with a couple of hills
Distance: 44 miles, or optional routes of 24 and 20 miles
Lunch: Falcon Lounge, Portage Lakes (330-896-3175)
Points of Interest: Nimisila Lake, Towpath Trail, remains of old canal and locks, Lime Lakes
How to get there: The Nimisila Campground is located in the Portage Lakes State Park on Nimisila Road. To get to the park, take Interstate 77 (I-77) to the Arlington Road exit. Head south on Arlington road until you reach Nimisila Road. Turn west (right) on Nimisila Road.

A lthough Lakemore and Clinton, Ohio, mark the east and west extremes of this loop ride, the middle point, Nimisila Campground, is the starting and ending point for the trek. The ride takes a bow tie path, emanating outward in opposite directions from the "knot" in the middle, making it easy to split the ride into two shorter excursions of twenty-four miles eastward and twenty miles westward. Since lunch is at the knot of the bow tie, getting a bite is convenient for a partial or complete jaunt.

Nimisila Campground is part of Portage Lakes State Park and is situated on a peninsula that extends into Nimisila Reservoir. The reservoir is the southernmost of a string of lakes that together are called Portage Lakes. Some of the Portage Lakes were initially scooped out by glaciers and filled as kettle holes when the ice retreated. The East, West, and New Reservoirs were created in the 1820s by damming the Tuscarawas in order to maintain the Ohio & Erie Canal's water level in times of drought. The Nimisila Reservoir was built in 1936 to support the water needs of the area's growing industries.

The Portage Lakes occupy one of the higher points in Ohio. The lakes are named for the eight-mile path from the Cuyahoga River to the Tuscarawas River on which native inhabitants por-

Portage Lakes and the Flood of 1913

A good deal of damage was done at Akron, Summit County, on the Little Cuyahoga River by the breaking of the banks of the largest of a string of artificial lakes known as the Portage Lakes. It is called the East Reservoir, and the bank was cut where the feeder from the Tuscarawas River enters. The power equipment and storerooms of the Goodyear tire and rubber plant were flooded, causing a loss estimated at from $50,000 to $100,000; one of the city playgrounds was damaged to the extent of $12,000; bridges were carried away; and 15 to 30 houses were demolished.

From Department of Agriculture Weather Bureau Bulletin, *Government Printing Office, 1916*

Section of the Portage Lakes State Park in Akron, Ohio.
Courtesy of Ohio Department of Natural Resources.

taged their canoes to traverse from Lake Erie to the Ohio River. The Portage Lakes area now offers visitors a variety of outdoor recreational experiences including boating, swimming, and fishing.

I park my truck in the parking lot on the peninsula just outside the campground gate. Once on my bike, I pedal out the entrance drive to Christman Road, which runs north and south along the east side of the lake. I turn south and enjoy several sweeping views of the lake as I wheel along.

Beyond the lake, I pass, on the opposite side of the road, a dam that creates a much smaller lake for Camp Y-Noah. A facility of the YMCA, Camp Y-Noah is an outdoor adventure camp for those aged six to seventeen. After a few more strokes of the pedals, I turn right onto Stoner Road. (The Stoner Road sign is on a high light pole on the left side of Christman Road.)

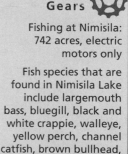

Changing Gears

Fishing at Nimisila: 742 acres, electric motors only

Fish species that are found in Nimisila Lake include largemouth bass, bluegill, black and white crappie, walleye, yellow perch, channel catfish, brown bullhead, and redear sunfish

www.dnr.state.oh.us

The Portage Princess, one of the many attractions at Portage Lakes State Park.
Courtesy of Ohio Department of Natural Resources.

Stoner Road runs through a wooded hollow where several people have built homes without destroying the natural look of the area. The road ascends out of the hollow, an enjoyable climb, and connects with Comet Road. I turn left at that junction and take a moment to glance at the building on the near left corner. The first time I rode past this spot, a few years earlier, a white-frame church was on the location with a sign in front identifying the congregation. On a later trip, I noticed that the sign was gone. I now see that the building has been converted into someone's home. The owners have retained the character of the structure despite the conversion to a living space.

Comet Road has a number of houses along its length, but I hesitate to label it a "residential" street, as that implies houses lined up in tidy rows. The homes are unique and not crowded together. As I jog on Man-

Changing Gears

Education at Camp Y-Noah: Children learn about amazing animals, archeology, archery, canoeing, creepy crawlies, ecosystems, fishing, nature art, orienteering, outdoor cooking, pond life, water rocketry, and survival.

www.akronymca.com

A scene on the beautiful Tuscarawas River (1905). Courtesy Library of Congress, Prints and Photographs Division.

chester Road to the western section of Comet, I notice many of the older homes have been tastefully restored and expanded. The newer structures retain the rural feel. Several farms on the western end of the road enhance the pleasant variety of structures.

Comet Road ends in the village of Clinton (see ride 11, page 118 for a description of the town), the southwest corner of the ride. Clinton is a village of about 1,300 people and was an important stop on the Ohio & Erie Canal. From North Street, I turn right onto the Ohio & Erie Towpath Trail, part of the linear park that runs on the former canal towpath from Cleveland to New Philadelphia, Ohio. The trail, heading north, is paved with asphalt for about a mile and then with finely crushed stone. The surface supports bicycles well. I stop to study the remains of the old locks (Locks 2 and 3) along the trail.

As I press on, I see to my left the canal bed and railroad tracks, and to my right the Tuscarawas River. When I first learned about

Tuscarawas River on Vanderhoof. Courtesy of Tom Bower.

canals in my grade school history classes, I always pictured them as filling the lowest ground in any given location. When I became familiar with engineering principles, I understood that canals would not always follow the lowest ground. From the vantage point I have on the trail, even though there is no water in the canal depression, I see that the canal had been constructed at a higher elevation than the river.

At the Vanderhoof Road trailhead, I leave the trail and take the road east. After a short trek, I glance to the north and notice

Lime Lakes Today

Wildlife: Today, we find the following species living peacefully in these areas: Tiger swallowtail, red-tailed hawk, painted turtles, white-tailed deer, ring-necked pheasant.

Plant Life: Grasses, trees and wildflowers planted not only support wildlife, but absorb rainwater, preventing water from picking up chlorides (salt) before entering groundwater and nearby surface water.

Courtesy of PPG Industries Inc.

the land is fenced off. In 1899, the Pittsburgh Plate Glass Company (PPG) built a factory in nearby Barberton to produce synthetic soda ash for glassmaking. For more than seventy years, production waste—totaling more than thirty million metric tons, mostly in the form of limewater slurry—was pumped into six

Changing Gears

In the early 1900s, PPG controlled over 75 percent of the plate glass output in the United States

ponds, referred to as Lime Lakes, an environmental graveyard. Recently, PPG Industries Inc. has reclaimed much of the land and turned it into a model natural wildlife habitat. In 2001, The Garden Club of America awarded PPG Industries Inc. a national medal in recognition of the great strides the company had made in reclaiming the land. PPG Industries expects the entire project to be completed by 2015. The Lime Lake sites are not open to public use; only the adjacent bike and hike trail is.

I turn right from Vanderhoof Road onto Grove Road and face a surprisingly hefty hill. I climb, huffing and puffing. I turn east onto Johns Road and find another hill.

Canal Engineering

In laying out a line of canal the engineer is more restricted than in forming the route of a road or railway, where gradients can be introduced to suit the undulating surface of the country. A canal, on the contrary, must follow rigidly the bases of hills and windings of valleys, to preserve a uniform level, accommodation being made for the road traffic by erecting suitable "fixed" and "movable" bridges. It is important, as already stated, to lay out the work in long level reaches, and to overcome elevations *in cumulo* by groups of locks at places where it can be most advantageously done. This leads to a saving of attendance and expense working the canal, and causes fewer stoppages to the traffic. But to prevent waste of water the locks must be placed sufficiently far apart, say 100 yards, or an intervening pond or increased width of canal must be formed, so that a descending boat does not let off more water than the area below will receive without raising its surface so much as to lose the surplus water over the waste-weirs.

From New Werner Twentieth Century Edition of the Encyclopaedia Britannica, *Werner Company, 1907*

FALCON LOUNGE
246 East Caston Road, Akron, OH 44319
330-896-3175
Open year-round

HOURS
Monday–Thursday: 11:00 A.M. to 9:30 P.M.
Friday–Saturday: 11:00 A.M. to 10:30 P.M.

SPECIALTIES
Falcon Burger, Prime Rib, and Steak

All roads, from the start of the ride to this point, were lightly trafficked. As I continue along Johns Road to my lunch stop, the roads are busier because they pass through more densely populated areas. I move along easily, arrive at the north end of Nimisila Reservoir, and complete the western half of the bow tie. Falcon Lounge is located where Christman Road ends at East Caston Road.

Falcon Lounge has a split identity. For the dinner crowd, the restaurant is a full-blown steak, chicken, and seafood eatery, featuring filet mignon, lobster tails, and similar fare. During the hours most cyclists would patronize the establishment, the menu features a nice soup, salad, and sandwich selection. I order and enjoy a battered fish sandwich with fresh, homemade potato chips.

After lunch, I begin the eastern section of the ride. I wheel south on Christman Road, turn east onto East Nimisila Road, and climb a modest hill. At Greensburg Road, I jog briefly left and turn right onto King Drive, a residential street. The next few streets carry more traffic than the western wing of the bow tie. I suspect the traffic would increase during rush hour but since I am riding the stretch in the early afternoon, I have no problem.

RIDE THE
INTERURBAN
Hourly Limited
Service between
Akron—Canton
Cleveland.

No Dirt
No Dust
No Cinders

Comfortable
Courteous
Service

THE NORTHERN OHIO TRACTION & LIGHT CO.

The Interurban Line made stops at Lakemore so passengers could go to the Springfield Lake Amusement Park. Courtesy Special Collections, Cleveland State University Library.

After several jogs, I turn north onto Kreighbaum Road. This is the easternmost boundary of the ride; I leave most of that traffic behind and have a quiet five-mile jaunt all the way to Lakemore, Ohio (except when I intersect a couple of busier roads).

Lakemore—a community of about 2,500 residents—is at the northeast corner of the ride and sits on the south shore of a spring-fed lake called Springfield. The area became a popular summer destination around 1914 with the development of an amusement park that featured two roller coasters, a merry-go-round, a dance hall, and water activities. People who enjoyed the park began constructing summer cottages around the lake. The area grew further in 1915 when the Springfield Lake Sanitarium (for tuberculosis patients) opened. More streets and year-round homes followed. The village of Lakemore was incorporated in 1921.

The Great Depression adversely affected the amusement park, but the final blow was the 1930 crash of the park's largest roller coaster, the Blue Streak, in which eleven people were injured. The resulting lawsuits bankrupted the park, led to the dismantling of the roller coaster, and the disposal of other park assets.

Springfield Lake Sanitarium is now the Edwin Shaw Rehab Hospital. As a part of Akron General Hospital, the center is the region's oldest and largest accredited rehabilitation facility. After I turn onto Flickinger Road, Edwin Shaw is on my right. The terrain makes it hard to get glimpses of the buildings.

I continue through a string of Lakemore village streets and end up on Lakeside Drive, which follows along the shore of the lake. Lakeside Drive becomes Lake Road, and I pedal away from the water and out of the village. I travel through a series of neighborhood and through streets and return to Nimisila Lake and pass the Falcon Lounge for the second time. I ride back down Christman Road one more time to the campground and my waiting truck.

I glossed over the route from Lakemore back to the Nimisila Lake because the section is essentially suburban and has few notable landmarks. Residential, however, doesn't mean level. While there are no big hills, plenty of small climbs add up to a substantial altitude gain.

The very last stretch of the ride is back along the shore of Nimisila Lake, and the view of the water makes for a fitting and scenic finale. The ride is quite satisfying, and I feel good about my accomplishment.

Ride 13
Heartland Hike

Route: Hartville to Atwater loop
Counties: Stark, Portage
Terrain: Relatively flat to rolling
Distance: 34 miles
Lunch: Kinsey's Korner, Atwater (330-947-2288)
Points of Interest: Quail Hollow State Park, Our Lady of
   Lourdes Grotto
How to get there: This ride starts at a shopping plaza in
   Hartville, Ohio, on the south side of State Route 619
   (SR619). The shopping plaza is located west of the junction
   of SR619 and the northbound section of State Route 43
   (SR43).

The Heartland Hike—Hartville to Atwater and back—is a good, challenging ride without long and steep hills. The terrain between the two communities is mostly flat with several modest climbs that, coupled with the distance (about thirty-four miles), provides a good workout.

While the ride is through fairly plain territory, part of what makes the ride memorable and rewarding are the various everyday activities. Since this ride is not far from where I live, I have pedaled this route and the surrounding roads many times, and haven't become bored.

The Heartland Hike begins in Hartville. For a village with a population of only about 2,200 people, Hartville is a hopping place. On a good-weather Saturday when the huge Hartville Marketplace and Flea Market is open, traffic inches along State Route 619 (SR619). Hungry shoppers stand in line that snakes around the large parlor of the Hartville Kitchen—the massive Amish-style restaurant near the flea market—and wait for a table. The nearby Hartville Hardware store is one of the best stocked and busiest in the state, and the employees are friendly and knowledgeable.

As bustling as the community can be, Hartville is a surprisingly easy place to get around on a bicycle. Most of the activity and businesses in the town are found along SR619 (Edison Street), the primary east–west path through town. The Heartland Hike route starts in a parking lot off of SR619, keeps you on low traffic streets, and quickly sends you out into the country to avoid the congestion.

I park my truck in the parking lot of a shopping plaza with a Big Lots store on the south side of SR619. Hartville was platted in 1851 and incorporated a hundred years later. The town was named for two early settlers—John Morehart and John Willis, whose last name was a Pennsylvania Dutch version of "ville."

I exit the lot, turning south onto Grand Trunk Avenue. Despite its name, Grand Trunk is a side street and only two

Quail Hollow State Park in Hartville, Ohio. Courtesy of Ohio Department of Natural Resources.

blocks long. I ride along this street to the first intersection and turn east on Sunnyside Street, which parallels SR619 but is far less busy. Sunnyside Street ends on Prospect Street where I turn north and proceed across SR619 at the traffic light. Prospect Street quickly becomes Congress Lake Avenue. Congress Lake Club, a golf course and exclusive housing complex that blends with the rural nature of the road, is on my left.

I come swiftly to the entrance road to Quail Hollow State Park. This public facility was once the estate of Harry Stewart, who became president of the Akron, Canton, and Youngstown Railroad in 1912. The railroad was a financial success, allowing Stewart to acquire the 750 acres and build his forty-room home on the property. The building and grounds were acquired by the State of Ohio in 1975. Today, the park

Changing Gears

Mountain biking at Quail Hollow State Park offers a scenic and challenging four-mile loop trail through forest, meadows, and pine woods, which is easy to moderate in difficulty. This trail was built and is maintained by the Cleveland Area Mountain Bike Association.

www.quailhollow.org

The Manor House, a popular tourist destination at Quail Hollow State Park.
Courtesy of Ohio Department of Natural Resources.

is a striking combination of meadows, marshes, and forests that surround the manor house, which is open to the public for special events only. The park offers nineteen miles of hiking trails, five miles of bridle trails, and four miles of mountain bike trails.

I turn into the park and follow the main road to the manor house. While the same road leads into and out of the park, the little detour stretches over a couple of modest hills, which allows me to pump up briskly, warming me up early in the ride. After viewing the impressive manor house with its Greek revival and Federal architectural influences, I turn around, retrace my route to Congress Lake Avenue, and resume my northward trek.

I next turn right onto Pontius Road, which runs along the northern boundary of Quail Hollow. The right side of the road is heavily forested. In one spot where the land dips down, I notice a beaver pond on the park side of the road. I glance toward the pond in time to see five white-tailed deer making their way across the shallow end of the water.

I turn north onto Griggy Road and wheel along between farm fields filled with maturing crops. Griggy Road is an odd name for a byway, but a more oddly named road—Steffy Road—tees into it. Houses occupy the north and south corners of this junction, and I wonder if those homeowners can tell people they live "on the corner of Steffy and Griggy" without feeling a little foolish.

While on Griggy Road, I spot one of the Goodyear blimps in the sky a few miles to the west. The Goodyear Tire and Rubber Company maintains a blimp hangar at its Wingfoot Lake Airship facility in Suffield, Ohio, about four miles west of Griggy Road. I see the blimp in the air about every other time I pedal this route.

Griggy Road eventually funnels me east onto Waterloo Road and after a short distance, I enter a small community named

> **Changing Gears**
>
> The Goodyear Blimp: Today, these graceful giants travel more than 100,000 miles across the United States per year as Goodyear's "Aerial Ambassadors."
>
> During World War II many of the Goodyear-built airships provided the U.S. Navy with a unique aerial surveillance capability.
>
> *www.goodyearblimp.com*

The Goodyear Tire and Rubber Company (1919)

The Goodyear Tire and Rubber Company of Akron, Ohio, was the most extensive aerostatic exhibit of the show. The outstanding feature of the booth was the dirigible pusher-car, completely equipped, of a type which has many sisters in service. A 35,000-cubic-foot type "R" military kite-balloon is suspended and equipped complete. Attractive models of the twin-engine navy dirigible and a transcontinental passenger dirigible car are on display. These models are complete in every detail, including full set of instruments and controls, lockers, and upholstery.

A full-sized dirigible car equipped with dual control, indicating devices, including manometers, tachometers, air-speed indicators, incidence and bank indicator, clock, driven by an 8-cylinder OX-2 Curtiss motor, of the type used on the FC training dirigible, having a cubic capacity of 85,000 feet, form an interesting part of the Goodyear exhibit. Models of "R" type kite-balloon, military free balloons, and of the U dirigible are also on display.

From Aircraft: Its Development in War and Peace and Its Commercial Future, *C. Scribner's Sons, 1919*

The Goodyear Blimp. Courtesy of Jamie Newhall.

St. Joseph. I'm not sure "community" is the right term. Several homes are in close proximity along the highway, but the focal point of the area is a tall-steepled, brick Catholic Church. A cemetery stretches up the hill behind it, along with a rectory, a Catholic school next door, and a parish house beside the school. The spot seems to be an oasis, an impression that deepens when I visit the grotto I spot through a gap between the buildings. I park

Our Lady of Lourdes Grotto at St. Joseph's Church, Ohio

On August 14, 1927, the eve of the Feast of the Assumption, Bishop Schrembs solemnly dedicated the completed Grotto. It was reported that five thousand people witnessed this dedication. Although the weather was inclement, the moment the statue of Our Lady was unveiled, the sun pierced through the darkened skies. This was a scene never to be forgotten.

From The St. Joseph's Church website (www.stjosephrandolph.org)

my bike and walk to the structure. The grotto is a cave built into the hill with an altar and candles and a statute above the altar of a lady, hands folded in prayer.

(After the ride, I learned the shrine is a faithful replica of the Lourdes Grotto in Southern France. Our Lady of Lourdes Grotto at St. Joseph's Church, Ohio, attracts visitors who come to pray. The spot has a quiet, comfortable feel, and though no one else was there during my visit, I could imagine people gathered in prayer. I also learned that in the summer, Saturday evening Mass is held outside the grotto, weather permitting.)

Although I do not need to leave Waterloo Road for the approximately eight miles to Atwater, Ohio—my lunch stop, I cross nearby US Route 224 (US224) twice. Waterloo Road is old US224. Several years ago, a modern highway was built parallel to and a quarter of a mile north of Waterloo Road, but the new route was laid out so that a short distance east of St. Joseph, Waterloo Road and US224 cross each other. Waterloo Road becomes the northern road until after the village of Randolph, Ohio. A couple of miles beyond Randolph, the old and new roads swap places again.

Randolph is a small, unincorporated community. The area includes a village green with a gazebo, three white-steepled churches, a gas station, a bank, a home-furnishing store, a couple of restaurants, two car dealerships, a barbershop, a convenience store, other small businesses, and a number of homes.

In Ohio, when a community is unincorporated, a larger township usually governs the smaller entity. In this case, the township

---

Randolph, Ohio

Randolph—Township 1, range 8; settled in 1797. Previous to its settlement it was owned by Col. Lemuel Storrs, of Connecticut, and it was named for his son, Henry Randolph Storrs.

From History of the Western Reserve, *Lewis Publishing Company, 1910*

Congregational Church, Atwater, Portage County, Ohio, 1934.
Courtesy Library of Congress, Prints and Photographs Division.

is also named Randolph. Figures for Randolph Township indicate that no municipalities exist. I don't know how the local people feel but frankly, Randolph (not the township) seemed like a village to me, incorporated or not.

I pedal on, re-cross US224 and progress toward Atwater. After I pass through a five-point intersection, I spot a business that

Atwater, Ohio

The second settlement was made at Atwater early in 1799. The party was lead by Capt. Caleb Atwater, the land was surveyed, and the men returned to the east with the exception of Asa Hall, who with his wife stayed through the winter. They were the only people in the township for two years.

From History of the Western Reserve, *Lewis Publishing Company, 1910*

reminds me of the agricultural nature of the region. Several rows of used tractors are in the lot of a farm supply store.

A few more miles on Waterloo Road brings me to Atwater, another unincorporated settlement that has all the elements of a proper community, though I am not certain where Atwater starts. On the mileage list, I mark the start of Atwater at mile 15.5, even though I don't notice a village sign at that point. That's simply where I started noticing houses built close together. The remainder of Atwater stretches out for about a mile to a point at which State Route 183 (SR183) intersects Waterloo Road.

About three-quarters of a mile before getting to SR183, in what seems to be the former town center, railroad tracks cross Waterloo Road and four side streets parallel the tracks. The closest side street is called Bank Street, and the brick building on that corner looks like it might have once been a bank. On the opposite side of Waterloo Road sits a tidy two-story brick building with display windows on the first floor and a sign that indicates the place was once called "Long's Automobile Emporium." The building is antiquated and probably has not housed a business for several decades. The ground floor of this old Chevy dealership is vacant, but someone may well have been living on the second floor.

Atwater has in effect moved itself. The busiest area is now at the junction of SR183 and Waterloo Road—a location with a

The Atwater Congregational Church, Designed by Simeon Porter

Simeon C. Porter (1807–1871), an architect active in Cleveland from 1848–1871, was born in Waterbury, Conn. to Lemuel and Margatana Welton Porter. His father was a woodworker and joiner. The family moved to Tallmadge, Ohio, in 1818, and later to Hudson. Porter erected several buildings of Western Reserve College (now Western Reserve Academy) and many Hudson houses before moving to Cleveland in 1848. Later, he designed many structures in Akron, Brecksville, Kent, Hudson, and Alliance. When Porter died in 1871, he was buried in the new Lake View Cemetery in Cleveland.

From The Encyclopedia of Cleveland History *(www.ech.cwru.edu)*

gas station-convenience store combination doing brisk business, and a restaurant in an old, large house—which is my lunch stop. I pedal around back to the eatery's entrance and dismount.

Kinsey's Korner is a combination of a pizzeria and a family restaurant with a large selection of dishes. I have a satisfactory meatloaf dinner that is reasonably priced and served promptly. Before leaving, I talk to the owner and ask him about the variegated menu. He explains that he had been operating a pizza shop on the opposite corner, but when this location, a family restaurant, became available, he essentially moved his pizza shop to the family restaurant and combined the two menus.

When I exit Kinsey's Korner, I notice the tall white church just to the south. The Atwater Congregational Church was built in 1841 in Greek and Gothic Revival styles. The church features a tall-domed steeple and six two-story columns supporting the full-width overhang above its front door. The building is listed in the National Register of Historic Places, but is an ongoing church as well.

After eating, I head west on Waterloo Road. At the five-points crossing, I pedal straight onto Eberly Road. Eberly Road is about four miles long and I wheel its entire length, which runs through farmland and several rural housing areas, and ends at Hartville Road.

Tuscarawas River

Tuscarawas river, the main branch of Muskingum river, above the town of Coshocton, is frequently called by this name. It rises in the southwestern quarter of Portage county, whence it runs a south by east direction 50 miles across Stark into the interior part of Tuscarawas county, to the mouth of Stillwater creek, and from thence 30 miles further in a southwestwardly direction to Coshocton, where it receives the Walhonding river from the northwest; and the joint stream, thus united, is called Muskingum river.

From The Ohio Gazetteer, and Traveler's Guide, *I. N. Whiting, 1839*

KINSEY'S KORNER
1281 State Route 183, Atwater, OH 44201
330-947-3005
Open year-round

HOURS
Sunday–Thursday: 7:00 A.M. to 8:30 P.M.
Friday–Saturday: 7:00 A.M. to 9:00 P.M.

SPECIALTIES
Burgers, Pizza, Wings, Chicken

I turn southwest on Hartville Road. Oddly, when I near Hartville, the road crosses Pontius Road and becomes Duquette Road. Again, I have forest to my right since Duquette Road forms the eastern boundary of the Quail Hollow State Park.

Part way down Duquette Road, on the opposite side of the road, I come to a cluster of old, white travel trailers, and a short distance farther, a colony of small, white-frame buildings that look like camp cabins. These dwellings are temporary housing for approximately 375 migrant workers who have harvested the vegetables—since the 1940s—grown in the rich, jet-black soil of the fields stretching off to the east. A bit further, I come to the colorfully frescoed building that houses the Hartville Migrant Ministry, a nonprofit Christian group providing welcome kits, household items, medical services, and educational programs for migrant families.

I soon reach the junction where Duquette Road ends on Edison Street. I turn west on Edison for half a mile, turn south on William Penn Avenue, and pedal beside a golf course and rural homes. I turn right onto Smith Kramer Road, bringing me to a point directly south of Hartville. I turn north on Geib Road—a route through an area in the process of moving from farming to residential. While a couple of working farms still dot the road, the newer houses suggested that the days of working the land are numbered. Geib Road takes me to the vicinity of a small stream where the Tuscarawas River begins—a landmark I wish were visible from the road. Getting to the river's source, about one–tenth of a mile away, requires crossing private property, and the spot is not accessible by bicycle in any case (for further information on the Tuscarawas River, see ride 19, page 222). Occasionally I've found articles indicating that the river rises in Summit County. However, the true source of the river is in northern Stark County.

At the edge of Hartville, Geib Road becomes Crestmont Avenue, leading me to Menlo Park Street. The street name, coupled with Edison Street—the town's main drag—brings the inventor Thomas Alva Edison to mind. Edison never resided in Hartville, but he did live for a time with his second wife's relatives in nearby Greentown while working on his phonograph.

A quick jog on Menlo Part Street brings me to Grand Trunk Avenue and back to the parking lot where I started my ride.

Mrs. Thomas Edison

Mrs. Edison met the inventor in Akron, Ohio, the home of her father, and it is generally believed to have been a case of love at first sight. They were married within a year of the meeting. Mrs. Edison takes considerable interest in her husband's work, and she has watched the development of many of his inventions with considerable pride. She frequently goes down to the laboratory and has even assisted at an occasional experiment, much to the inventor's amusement. [The distance from Greentown, Ohio, to Akron, Ohio, is approximately 17 miles.]

From Thomas Alva Edison: Sixty Years of an Inventor's Life, *Hodder and Stoughton, 1908*

Ride 14
Reservoir Roundabout

Route: Walborn Reservoir to Lake Milton loop
Counties: Stark, Mahoning, Portage
Terrain: Relatively flat
Distance: 39 miles
Lunch: The Sand Trap, Lake Milton (330-654-3445)
Points of Interest: The four reservoirs, Noah's Lost Ark
How to get there: This ride starts at the parking lot for the
   Walborn Reservoir Marina located in Stark County, Ohio.
   Take US Route 244 (us244) to State Route 183 (sr183). Turn
   south on sr183. Follow sr183 into Limaville and turn west
   (right) on Price Street. The marina will be on the south
   (left) side of the road before you reach the water.

R eservoir Roundabout includes four lakes created expressly as water sources for Ohio communities. The ride provides several scenic views of open water. In terms of physical geography, the route is one of the flatter ones in my riding area. In northeast Ohio, "flat" is a relative term. The ride never required me to use the low "granny" gear on my bike and it includes no memorable climbs, but there are frequent rises and falls to the land. The small grades do not come in series, however, so the terrain is not rolling.

Changing Gears

Walborn & Deer Creek Reservoir Activities: biking, bird watching, boating, canoeing, equestrian trails, fishing, hiking, hunting, kayaking, picnicking

www.ohiodnr.com

My ride starts in the parking lot of Dale Walborn Reservoir, a narrow body of water about four miles long. It is located mostly in northeast Stark County, except for the reservoir's northern extremity, which pushes into Portage County. Created by the damming of local creeks, the reservoir is a water source for the city of Alliance, Ohio, but is managed by the Stark County Park District for the purpose of public recreation. Price Street, actually a rural road, spans the center of the lake. The Park District has built a marina including a boat-launch ramp, a fishing pier, public restrooms, and an outlet selling food and bait and managing boat rentals.

I roll out of the marina parking lot, turn east on Price Street, and immediately pedal out of the shallow valley on a modest incline. The sparsely settled byway brings me to Limaville, which has about 193 residents (in 1880, there were 164 folks). In the 1850s, the Cleveland and Pittsburgh Railroad was completed through Limaville, and the Limaville Terra Cotta and Stoneware Works opened shortly thereafter. As I pedal along, I see a build-

Dale Walborn Reservoir

The reservoir was named for Dale Walborn, the mayor of Alliance from 1963–1971, who initiated its construction.

Editor's Note

Beautiful Walborn Reservoir. Photography provided by the Stark County Park District.

ing that looked like it had been a store, and another structure that had obviously been a church. Both are vacant. As far as I can tell, the only public services currently available are the post office, housed in a house trailer, and an auto-repair garage.

I continue on Price Street, cross State Route 183 (SR183), a double set of railroad tracks, and roll down a road bounded by woods that eventually takes me to the shores of Deer Creek Reservoir. Deer Creek Reservoir, larger than Walborn Reservoir, is also a water source for Alliance, and is managed for recreation by the Stark County Park District. Deer Creek Reservoir features an accessible fishing pier, boat ramp for electric motors only, pic-

---

Limaville Churches

Limaville had three churches in 1880, the Methodist, United Brethren, and Disciples. . . . Of the original group of churches the Methodist is the only one left.

From The Stark County Bicentennial Story, 1776–1976, *Stark County Bicentennial Story Committee, 1979*

The Deer Creek Reservoir. Photography provided by the
Stark County Park District.

nic tables, and grills. Price Street hugs the northern shore of the
lake, and often provides fine views of blue water surrounded by
continuous woodlands.

Price Street terminates at State Route 225 (SR225), a highway
that runs north from Alliance. I jog north on SR225 for two–
tenths of a mile, and in that short distance no fewer than four
semis roar by me. I am glad to arrive at Lowe Road and turn
right, leaving the big rigs behind. I proceed up the road and catch
glimpses of another wing of Deer Creek Lake to my left. After
entering Mahoning County on Lowe Road, I angle right onto
North Benton West Road.

Most of the Reservoir Roundabout is on back roads that are
either wooded or "rural residential"—my term for housing on

Shores of the Deer Creek Reservoir. Photography provided by the Stark County Park District.

country lots interspersed occasionally by farms. The stretches along North Benton West Road fit the latter definition. I notice a curious mix of dwellings; I ride past aging mobile homes and untidy frame houses. Perhaps these folks want to live off the beaten track without the burden of zoning laws or the pressure to "keep up with the Joneses." In contrast, I also pedal by a majority of homes that are well kept, and a few are even quite grand. The region allows people to march to the beat of their own drummer. Personally, I keep my yard mowed, but the thought of spending evenings and weekends edging the yard, weed-whacking around every tree and bush, or otherwise cleaning the grounds around my house leaves me cold. I do what's necessary to keep my place from becoming the neighborhood eyesore, but when free days come, I prefer to go out with my wife or ride my bike.

North Benton West Road takes me to Miller Airport, a paved runway on the north side of the road. The small airport building, about the size of a house, includes a café that is open on weekends. The landing field accommodates small aircraft and a glider group.

North Benton West Road ends at Twelfth Street, so named because the road is an extension of Twelfth Street in the community of Sebring, a few miles to the south. I turn left and immediately enter the community of North Benton, named for the forceful orator and United States Senator, Thomas Hart Benton. In 1880, the population of North Benton was about 250 people, but by 1940, the number was only about 150. That number seems to have remained steady. The town has its own post office and a Presbyterian Church, but not much otherwise. I park my bike and go into the post office, where I ask the woman behind the counter, Doris Tolley, about the building.

"Yes, it was an old schoolhouse," she says, "and what's more, I was a student in it." She continues, "It's a strong old building. I've ridden out many storms in here and always felt perfectly safe."

I also ask Doris about the location of the Chester Bedell gravesite. Bedell was the village agnostic who hated superstition and ignorance. Before he died in 1908 at the age of eighty-two, he

Churches and Schools near North Benton, Ohio

Smith township has four churches. The first erected was in 1829 by the Friends on section thirty-four. This building was also used for a school, taught by Hannah Courtney. A Methodist Episcopal church was erected at North Benton in 1840. A Presbyterian congregation formed in Deerfield, Portage county, moved to Smith, and elected a church near North Benton in 1851. A union church was built in 1859 on section twenty-six, but was sold to the Presbyterian society in 1870.

The first school of the township was taught in an old log-house on the site of North Benton, but by whom is not known. Margaret Davis taught the school at a very early day. The township was originally divided into four districts, but now comprises ten. The annual cost of the maintenance of schools is about $2,500.

From History of Trumbull and Mahoning Counties, *H. S. Williams, 1882*

Thomas Hart Benton, the United States Senator, 1858.
Courtesy Library of Congress, Prints and Photographs Division.

commissioned a life-sized, bronze statue to be placed on a tall pedestal on his gravesite. The figure's left foot rests on a stone scroll inscribed with the word "superstition," and his right hand holds a bronze scroll the reads, "universal mental freedom." Legend has it that, on his deathbed, Bedell said, "If there is a God or any truth in the Bible, let my body be inhabited by snakes."

Sebring, Ohio

Sebring, Ohio was founded by the Sebring family from East Liverpool, Ohio. They owned and operated many pottery businesses.

From Sebring Ohio Historical Society
(www.sebringohiohistoricalsociety.org)

Bedell's gravediggers supposedly had to contend with snakes in such quantity that they entangled the digging tools, and another snake had to be removed from the grave before the coffin was lowered. The local sexton reportedly said he never saw a snake at any other grave. Some versions of this story claim snakes still slither in and out of Bedell's grave.

Bedell's resting place, Hartzell Cemetery is a little over a mile north of the North Benton. Bedell's descendents have removed the statue because it became a target for repeated vandalism. The statue is now on display at the Weidenmier House in Berlin Center, which is about four miles from North Benton.

"What about the snakes?" I ask.

"Well," Doris says, "my grandparents are buried in that cemetery, and I've never seen any snakes there. I think some local people used to drop snakes off there just to keep the story alive."

I leave the post office, pedal along a few village streets, cross State Route 14 (SR14), and turn east onto Western Reserve Road. Before long, I pass Beloit-Snodes Road, intersecting Western Reserve Road from the south. Route J, one of the several lengthy bicycle routes marked out by the Ohio Department of Transportation on various roads throughout the state, joins Western Reserve Road from Beloit-Snodes Road at this junction.

Moments later, I turn north on Bedell Road, presumably named for Chester Bedell or his family. Route J coincides with my route and would do so until my lunch stop in Lake Milton.

Ohio Cross State Bicycle Routes

Nine bike routes. All routes are on low-traffic-volume paved roads. Route J–Marietta to Conneaut. A north-south route in the eastern part of the state. Very hilly and scenic in south, rolling in the middle, flat in the north. The north 100 miles is signed, but signs may be missing: southern section is mapped only. State routes are used in south because all alternates are gravel.

From Ohio Department of Transportation website (www.dot.state.oh.us)

I soon come to Noah's Lost Ark, Inc., a nonprofit shelter for exotic and endangered animals. The facility provides a safe haven for abandoned, unwanted, and abused tigers, wolves, and other creatures. Noah's Lost Ark also offers guided educational tours that enable visitors to view these exotic species. The Ark's daily feeding bills are huge, and tour fees and donations keep the place, no pun intended, afloat.

Changing Gears

Noah's Lost Ark is home to over 125 exotic animals and over 60 big cats.

www.noahslostark.org

Next I wheel past Mill Creek Campground along the shores of Berlin Lake. This third reservoir on my route covers nearly eight thousand acres, making it bigger than the other two. The Mill Creek Recreational Area is close by and offers camping, fishing, boating, and hunting in posted areas. The Army Corps of Engineers completed the lake's dam in 1943 as a flood control project. Draining almost 250 square miles, Berlin Lake is estimated to have prevented flood damages amounting to nearly one billion dollars. The reservoir also provides water for several

Berlin Township, Ohio

The early settlers of Berlin Township numbered many of German blood and it was one of these, Matthias Glass, who gave it its name. Previous to that it was known as "Hart and Mather's" after its original owners. Glass was the original miller of the township, having erected a grist mill and sawmill on Turkey Broth Creek in 1825. Later a second grist mill was built on the same site by Isaac Wilson. The first store was started at the Center by Joseph Edwards about 1833, while Peter Musser kept the first tavern, this being in the northern part of the township. Dr. James W. Hughes, practicing physician at the Center from 1834 to 1869, was the first resident doctor. In 1828 a post office was opened at Amity, where Musser's tavern was located, and in 1833 Berlin Center was made a post office station. Berlin Center is the one village in the township. Schilling's Mills, site of the first mill in the township, attained the dignity of a village name under the title of Belvidere.

From History of Youngstown and the Mahoning Valley, Ohio, *American Historical Society, 1921.*

communities downstream. Although Bedell Road edges along Berlin Lake for about five miles, the lake is only occasionally visible from the road.

I cross US Route 224 (US224) and continue on Bedell Road until I reach Shillings Mill, a small stop marked by a few houses, Shillings Mill Tavern, and a modern bridge crossing the East Branch of the Mahoning River. At Shillings Mill, as if taking a break from being dammed up and filling lakes, the waters of the Mahoning River flow freely.

The first mill at Belvidere (which would become Schillings Mill) was built by Matthias Glass in 1825. A few years later, the mill burned down and Isaac Wilson built a new one. In 1856, George Shilling purchased the second mill and the location became known as Shillings Mill. The mill continued to operate and produce an output of flour until 1915. The building no longer exists.

The structure that sits beside the river today is the tavern. The sign on the tavern advertises its amenities: "Sandwiches–Pool–Liquor." A landing behind the bar makes it possible for boaters to stop by to partake of all three.

I turn left, pedal across the bridge, and turn right onto Mill Road. Mill Road takes me to Ellsworth Road, where I turn right and pedal back across the water to the south end of Lake Milton. Cruising across the bridge I have an expansive view of the lake. On the east side of the water, I turn left onto River Road, but the lake is not visible from the road for most of the trek. After I pass the Lakeside Golf Course, I see the lake again.

I pedal several more strokes and come to Mahoning Avenue, the main street of the community of Lake Milton. Bicycle Route J jogs briefly to the right and then continues on the northern stretch of River Road. I, however, turn left and cross the midsection of the lake on the Mahoning Avenue Bridge. Mahoning Avenue is an extension of Mahoning Avenue in Youngstown, Ohio. Youngstown, a major Ohio city with a population of about eighty-two thousand people, is about a dozen miles to the east, but has a strong tie to Lake Milton. In 1910, Youngstown acquired the land expressly for the construction of a reservoir as a water supply for the city. The 2,800-foot dam was completed in 1913, impounding 1,640 acres on the Mahoning River. In the early days, the land around the lake included a small amusement park at Craig Beach (for more on Craig Beach, see ride 9, page 104). The lake and the surrounding area were officially dedicated as a state park in 1988. Activities include boating, water sports, fishing, swimming, picnicking, and hunting.

I wheel across the Mahoning Avenue Bridge and can see to my right speeding vehicles crossing over the lake, less than a mile away, on the Interstate 76 (I-76) bridge. The traffic, however, bypasses the small town of Lake Milton, where I now stop for lunch at the Sand Trap, a restaurant situated on Lake Milton's main street. The golfing theme is evident since the inside is decorated with course and player pictures and other golf paraphernalia. The menu and atmosphere is that of a small-town diner, which is why I select it. The structure itself appears to have once been a convenience store.

The Sand Trap offers breakfast all day, as well as lunch and dinner. I order an omelet. The service is friendly and efficient, and the prices are reasonable. Other eating options are available along Lake Milton's main street, including a Mexican restaurant and a pizzeria.

Fredericksburg, Ohio

Even more tragic was the fate of Fredericksburg, once a flourishing village on the Mahoning River above Pricetown. Once a stage-stop on the Cleveland–Pittsburgh route and a place of taverns, stores and mills, Fredericksburg is now buried beneath the waters of Lake Milton. Today there is not a post office or even sizeable village in Milton Township.

From History of Youngstown and the Mahoning Valley, Ohio, *American Historical Society, 1921.*

THE SANDTRAP
17653 Mahoning Avenue, Lake Milton, OH 44429
330-654-3445
Open year-round

HOURS
Monday–Saturday: 8:00 A.M. to 8:00 P.M.
Sunday: 8:00 A.M. to 2:00 P.M.

SPECIALTIES
Fried Fish, Burgers

Pleasantly full, I get back on the bike, continue a little farther on Mahoning Avenue to Mahoning Road, and turn south. Mahoning, also the name of the county in which Lake Milton sits, is a popular name. Mahoning is derived either from the Native American word *Mahoni,* signifying "a lick," or from *Mahonink,* "at the lick." Mahoning Road marks the boundary between Mahoning and Portage counties. (Note: Don't be confused by the signage at this intersection where Mahoning *Avenue* becomes Tallmadge Road. Turning left puts you on Mahoning *Road.* If you had turned right, however, you would end up on Milton–Newton Road. When I last traveled the route, all four roads were marked correctly.)

Having seen all four reservoirs, I pedal the return route knowing I won't pass any large bodies of water except at the very end of my trek. I am content to travel along low-traffic rural roads. The first, a right turn off of Mahoning Road, is Yale Road, on which I amble due west for about six miles. The scenery is typical for rural northeast Ohio.

About a mile before Yale Road ends, I come to a six-point roadway junction identified on some current maps as Yale, Ohio. I notice a few houses, as well as a construction and landscape business. Yale was probably named by a graduate of the New Haven, Connecticut, institution, and the area once had a Methodist Episcopal Church. Yale Road crosses Alliance Road and State Route 14 (SR14) at this point. At one time SR14 was a primary route from Pittsburgh to Cleveland.

State Route 14 is still a busy highway, and I wait for a good opening before hurrying across. I pedal the last mile of Yale Road through thick woods and some houses on both sides.

Yale Road ends without drama, making a ninety-degree left turn to become Porter Road, which heads straight south. I head down Porter Road. The first mile and a half offers an interesting contrast on the opposite sides of the road. To the right, the land is mostly cleared, with houses built near the road and farm fields behind. To the left, the land is thickly forested, and the few houses sit on clearings cut out of the woods. I wheel farther south and watch as the woods recede. I cross US Route 224 (US224), continuing south on Porter Road.

Porter Road ends on German Church Road. An old, freshly-mown cemetery (Dutch-Old German Church Cemetery), unfenced and having no identification sign, is at this junction. The few graves have tombstones dating from the early 1800s to 2005. The level site, directly next to the cemetery, is probably where a church once stood.

German Church Road is the boundary line between Portage and Stark counties. Heading west on the road, I eventually cross the double railroad tracks and SR183, about a mile north of where I crossed them on my outbound ride. I continue on German Church Road and pass through a "tunnel" formed by the hardwood branches extending from the trees growing on both sides of the road.

German Church Road brings me to a crossroad with Strope Road, to the right, in Portage County, and McCallum Avenue, to the left, in Stark County. On the southwest corner is Deer Creek Quaker Cemetery, an old burial lot that is mowed but not oth-

Deer Creek Quaker Cemetery. Courtesy of D. J. Reiser.

erwise kept up. Many of the stones are broken, fallen, or sinking into the ground. A historical marker at the roadside tells the story.

> *Deer Creek Quaker Cemetery was established on land donated by Isaac Coates, who brought his family from Chester County, Pennsylvania to settle in Lexington Township in 1820. The name Deer Creek comes from the nearby stream and it signifies the numerous deer that have abounded in the vicinity. The cemetery sits across from the former Deer Creek Quaker Meeting House. Isaac Coates is among the pioneers laid to rest here.*

A private home that looks to be about the size of an old church stands on the southeast corner of the intersection.

Many of the early Quakers who came to Ohio were either immigrants from Germany, often by way of Pennsylvania, or the children of German immigrants, of which many still spoke German. Quite possibly, the road might have been first informally called "the German Church road" simply because the church, where worship was probably conducted in German, was on it. Descendants of the first German immigrants were sometimes called "Pennsylvania Dutch," an anglicization of the word "Deutsch," (Deutschland) that means "German."

Heading south on McCallum, I come to Price Road. I turn right, and in a short while, am back at the Walborn Marina.

Pennsylvania Dutch or Pennsylvania German

The language spoken by the Germans who immigrated to Pennsylvania between 1683, when Pastorius settled in Germantown, and the middle of the eighteenth century. During this time, some 100,000 settled principally in the southeastern counties of the state such as Lancaster, York, Franklin, Cumberland, Berks, Schuylkill and Lehigh. The emigration was due partly to the ravages of the armies of Louis XIV and partly to religious persecution. The settlers came principally from the Rhineland-Palatine, Württemberg and Switzerland with a sprinkling from the Lower Rhine, Bavaria, Alsace, and Saxony.

From New International Encyclopedia, *Dodd, Mead and Company, 1903*

Ride 15
Amish Country

Route: Brewster to Shreve loop
Counties: Stark, Wayne, Holmes
Terrain: Rolling to hilly
Distance: 58 miles, or optional routes of 23 and 35 miles
Lunch: Des Dutch Essenhaus, Shreve (330-567-2212)
Points of Interest: Through the heart of the largest Amish settlement in the United States
How to get there: This ride starts from the intersection of State Route 93 (SR93) and Main Street in Brewster Ohio. Curbside parking is available on side streets. Take Interstate 77 (I-77) to US Route 30 (US30). Head west on US30 and then turn southwest (left) onto State Route 241 (SR241). From SR241, turn south (left) onto SR93. State Route 93 becomes Wabash Avenue in Brewster.

The largest concentration of Amish people in the world can be found in Wayne and Holmes counties in Ohio. This ride passes through the heart of Amish country. You will likely see fields being worked by men driving draft-horse teams, or depending on the season, stacks of corn-shocks in the meadows or piles of loose hay being heaped on wagons. You will ride by one-room school houses where children in Amish garb might be playing or leaving, carrying lunch pails, for their walks home. You will pass buggies steadily pulled along by sleek horses, and pedal through communities where hitching rails are as common as parking spaces for cars.

Tidy Amish farmhouses without electricity, but with laundry lines bearing the day's wash, bountiful gardens, and birdhouses on tall columns will provide pleasant backdrops. In addition, you will ride through lush countryside, see some grand vistas, get a terrific workout from many ups and downs on the route, and have a great lunch at a restaurant featuring Amish-style cooking.

Amish Country is a hearty figure-eight trek of fifty-eight miles. The route can be split into two shorter rides of thirty-five and twenty-three miles. If you choose one of the alternative treks, you can pedal to lunch in either Fredericksburg or Brewster. (I've provided detailed directions for both the eastern and western shorter loops.)

Most of this route traverses Wayne and Holmes counties, but I begin in southwestern Stark County where there is a growing Amish presence. Brewster, a village of about 2,300 people, is my starting point. Brewster was incorporated in 1910, but was actu-

In 2008, there were 52 Amish settlements in Ohio with a population of 55,620 people.

From Young Center for Anabaptist & Pietist Studies,
Elizabethtown College, Elizabethtown, PA

Down through the Amish heartland in Holmes County, Ohio. Courtesy of Holmes County Chamber of Commerce and Tourism Bureau.

ally "birthed" a few years earlier as the result of the Wheeling & Lake Erie Railway (WLER) construction. An early route of the WLER included a steep grade in Massillon, requiring the power of three locomotives and separate crews to reach the summit. The railroad purchased two hundred acres in the Brewster area and laid twenty-five miles of track to enable trains to bypass Massillon. In 1908, a fire destroyed the WLER shops in Norwalk, Ohio, and the main offices of the company were rebuilt in Brewster.

I drive into Brewster from the north and pass under a railroad bridge. A refurbished caboose is parked permanently on a site on the west side of the street. Directly across the street is the large headquarters of WLER. Even the main street itself, State Route 93 (SR93), has a railroad name—Wabash Avenue. (The WLER was a subsidiary of the Wabash Railroad.) In addition to the railroad, two other industries provide employment in Brewster. Shearer

*Amish children riding in a buggy. Courtesy of Holmes County
Chamber of Commerce and Tourism Bureau.*

Foods is a snack food manufacturer, and Brewster Dairy is a well-known producer of Swiss cheese.

I find a place to leave my truck on a side street where curbside parking is permitted. The quiet street is a couple of blocks west of Wabash Avenue. I unload my bicycle and mount up.

I start south on Wabash Avenue and turn west on 7th Street, which becomes Mt. Eaton Road at the village limits. I cross from Stark into Wayne County after about three miles, and the road name changes to Harrison Road. This stretch from Brewster to

Mount Eaton, Ohio

Mount Eaton, a small post town, (post office same name,) in Paint township, Wayne county, 15 miles southeast from Wooster, and 104 northeast from Columbus. It was called Paintville, until 4th Feb. 1830, when the legislature changed its name to Mount Eaton. At the census of 1830, it contained 214 inhabitants.

From The Ohio Gazetteer, and Traveler's Guide, *Isaac N. Whiting, 1837*

Farming in Amish country. Courtesy of Holmes County
Chamber of Commerce and Tourism Bureau.

Mt. Eaton is very challenging because it includes a couple of the tougher hills on the ride. By the time I reach Mt. Eaton, I am thoroughly warmed up and have already had more exercise than many longer but flatter rides provide.

The community of Mt. Eaton, as the name suggests, is at the top of a hill and is the crossing point for several roads. The town has a population of only 250 folks, but sustains a restaurant, gas station-convenience store combo, a grocery store, and a few other businesses. Undoubtedly, the traffic on the multiple routes, US Route 250 (US250), State Route 241 (SR241), State Route 94 (SR94), and four smaller roads that pass through or into Mt. Eaton provide plenty of commerce for the area.

I pedal through Mt. Eaton without much danger or difficulty. I leave town on the northwest leg of US250, which is heavily traveled by semis, but US250 has sufficiently wide paved shoulders to give me a clear path for the half-mile I travel to the contin-

*Line of buggies waiting for their passengers. Courtesy of
Holmes County Chamber of Commerce and Tourism Bureau.*

uation of Harrison Road. This momentary ballet with traffic in
Mt. Eaton and a brief stint on State Route 93 (SR93) near the end
of the trek are the only times I don't pedal on low-traffic roads.

This portion of Harrison Road has a strong Amish presence.
On farm after farm, I see men in straw hats and teams of horses working fields. I pass two Amish schools with outhouses. At
several places, sawmills—a common Amish industry—
are in operation, as well as shops selling handcrafted
furniture, cabinets, and wood flooring. The houses are
distinctly Amish, always painted white with curtains
pulled to one side of the window.

When I enter Maysville, a very small settlement, I
see a fabric store with several buggies parked outside.
Maysville is also the site of a one-room school. The
building is a couple of doors north of Harrison Road on

**Changing
Gears**

Amish art is largely
three-dimensional,
using materials like
fabric, pewter, clay,
wood, and stone.

*Courtesy of Holmes
County Chamber of
Commerce and
Tourism Bureau*

*Sign signaling the slower pace of the Amish buggies. Courtesy of
Holmes County Chamber of Commerce and Tourism Bureau.*

Mt. Hope Road. While the other schools were built of wood, this
one is built of yellow brick with a short tower above the front
door.

I return to Harrison Road and start climbing the hill out of
Maysville, passing a boy in Amish garb trudging up the grade.
As I pass him, he says, "How about pulling me up the hill?" and
laughs good-naturedly. I ride on through the luxuriant scenery and up and down the hills. A flat ride would not provide the
many good vantage points and spectacular views.

Harrison Road enters Fredericksburg, Ohio, on a steep downgrade, requiring me to brake frequently, since the village's sole
traffic light is at the bottom of the hill in the center of town.
Fredericksburg, with a population of about five hundred, is in
the heart of Ohio's Amish settlement. The community is a blend
of the two cultures, Amish and English. I notice a sign in front of

what appears to be a car wash that reads "Car and Buggy Wash." The town has a traditional pizzeria, Lem's, and the Ashery Country Store, the "Grandma of the Bulk Food Stores." There is also a bank, a library, and a True Value hardware store.

What goes down must go back up. Harrison Road takes me out of Fredericksburg and I climb sharply. When I get to the summit, I know more hills—and more countryside—await me.

I pedal a while before I cruise down a hill that bottoms out where Harrison Road crosses SR84. At this junction I cross into Holmes County for a brief spell. Harrison Road becomes County Road 1 (CR1) for several miles, before straightening out to run along the boundary of Wayne and Holmes counties as Centerville Road. Homes to the north of Centerville Road are in Wayne County, while those to the south are in Holmes County.

When I cross SR84, I enter the Killbuck Creek wetlands area. I will cross the creek farther on, but at this point, I notice that the terrain around me has a distinctly different appearance. The land is obviously low country, a flood plain on which no houses are built. In places, I see standing water, and at times, mud trails across the blacktop.

Killbuck Creek, which begins several miles north, is a tributary of the Walhonding River. The Walhonding waterway joins the Tuscarawas River at Coshocton to form the Muskingum River. The Muskingum flows into the Ohio River, and the Ohio

The Amish and English Mesh?

In one instance, Amish are installing solar panels from The Lighthouse of Ohio Distribution of Fredericksburg, Ohio. In the same community, Mrs. Miller's Homemade Noodles, celebrating over thirty years in business in the midst of Amish Country, uses Grandma's recipe to bring old fashioned goodness to their egg noodle, no-yolk, and vegetable pastas. *Witness,* a 1985 film starring Harrison Ford and Kelly McGillis, provided a Hollywood slant on the differences in the two cultures.

Editor's Note

flows into the Mississippi River. In a circuitous way, Killbuck Creek is part of the watershed of Old Man River.

The wetlands of Killbuck Creek valley, which sit in Wayne, Holmes, and Coshocton counties, are the largest complex of Ohio wetlands inland from Lake Erie. Development and other man-made changes have reduced Ohio's wetlands by 90 percent. To protect the Killbuck wetlands, part of the region has been declared a Wildlife Area under the Division of Wildlife of the Ohio Department of Natural Resources, and more of the wetlands are being included as funds become available.

The origin of the name "Killbuck" is not clear. A few years ago, I stopped at the Killbuck Valley Museum in the village of Killbuck to find out the true story while cycling the length of US Route 62 (US62) from Niagara Falls, New York, to El Paso, Texas. US62 goes right by Killbuck.

> *I asked [the museum curator] how Killbuck got its name. "It depends on what you want to believe," she said. "Some say it was because of a big deer shot near here. Others say it was for an Indian named Killbuck." She hauled out a book of local history and let me see the pages regarding the town. Naming the place after a deer kill sounded like a spurious tale to me, but sure enough, it was repeated in the book.*
>
> *As to the other possibility, there was not one Indian, but three and maybe even four. No birth dates were given, but the first Killbuck's father died in 1776. Killbuck, the son, was a Delaware chief. His sons, Killbuck II and Killbuck III were also chiefs. These two later assumed the names John Henry and Charles Henry, out of respect for the patriot Patrick Henry. Regrettably, the book didn't explain that connection. These two sons of Killbuck I, along with one Francis Henry, signed a 1798 agreement between the U.S. government and the Society of United Brethren allowing the latter group to "assume 12,000 acres for the propagation of the Gospel," though what that much land has to do with missionary work eludes me completely. In any case, it's*

possible that Francis Henry was Killbuck IV, a brother to II and III. (From Playing in Traffic: America from the River Niagara to the Rio Grande by Bicycle, *Stan Purdum, Expanded edition, CSS Publishing, 2004.)*

Continuing, I climb a long hill out of Killbuck Valley, turn a wide right off of Harrison Road onto Shreve-Eastern Road, and return to Wayne County. After several miles, I enter the village of Shreve, home to about 1,600 people. Des Dutch Essenhaus—my lunch destination—is on the town's main drag, North Market Street.

Changing Gears

Ohio Cheese
Guggisberg Cheese, near Charm, invented Baby Swiss.
Heini's Cheese Chalet, in Berlin, invented Yogurt Cheese.
Alpine Cheese Company, in Winesburg, is the only U.S. producer of Jarlsberg Cheese.

Courtesy of Holmes County Chamber of Commerce and Tourism Bureau

Des Dutch Essenhaus is a restaurant featuring Amish cooking. Though, many similar establishments are often referred to as "Amish restaurants," seldom, if ever, are such locales actually owned by the Amish. Most of these establishments serve traditional Amish dishes (slow, home-cooked, comfort food made from fresh ingredients) and they frequently employ Amish people. Both traits apply at Des Dutch Essenhaus, which literally means "The (Pennsylvania) Dutch Eating Place." The restaurant is not owned by an Amish family, but the Amish recipes used in the restaurant date back several generations, and most employees are from Amish households.

I order the pan-fried chicken dinner and fill a plate from the salad bar before my meal arrives. The meal is wonderful. The pies look excellent, too, but I pass on the sweets since I don't want to undo the calorie burn from the ride to Des Dutch Essenhaus.

Walhonding River

A river of Ohio, called also the Mohican and White Woman River, uniting with the Tuscarawas, at Coshocton, to form the Muskingum.

From The Life and Times of David Zeisberger,
J. B. Lippincott & Company, 1870

DES DUTCH ESSENHAUS
176 North Market Street, Shreve, OH 44676
330-567-2212
Open year-round

HOURS
Monday–Thursday: 8:00 A.M. to 8:00 P.M.
Friday: 8:00 A.M. to 9:00 P.M.
Saturday: 7:00 A.M. to 9:00 P.M.
Closed Sunday

SPECIALTIES
Meat and Potatoes, Soup and Salad Wagon
(Salad Bar), Baked Goods

Similar to Brewster, Shreve owes its beginning to another railroad, the Pittsburgh, Fort Wayne, and Chicago Railroad. The company needed a suitable place to service locomotives with water and fuel, and Shreve was chosen because it had a large spring—known as Stouts Spring—and an abundance of wood nearby. In 1852, the railroad placed a station there, and the community of Shreve, initially called Clinton Station, was born. However, another community in Ohio had the same name and this caused confusion for shipping and mail agents. A vote was

Shreve, Ohio, Train Accident

An accident occurred February 15, 1892, near Shreve, Ohio, a station on the Pittsburgh, Fort Wayne & Chicago Railroad, in which the railway post office car was crushed and totally destroyed by fire; the bodies of four of the clerks at work in it were incinerated, nothing remaining but ashes.

From A Life Span and Reminiscences of Railway
Mail Service, *Deemer & Jaisohn, 1910*

A classic rural American white country church. Courtesy of Tom Bower.

taken to rename the town for either Thomas Shreve, who headed the convention to back the railroad's expansion, or D. K. Jones, an early developer of the area. By the margin of a single vote, Clinton Station became Shreve, Ohio. The railroad still runs through Shreve, and the community is home to several businesses.

After lunch, I maneuver through a couple of turns and head south out of Shreve to Centerville Road. I jog briefly east, turn south again, and enter Holmes County on County Road 318 (CR318). Unlike in Wayne County, the byways in Holmes County

RIDE FIFTEEN: AMISH COUNTRY

are unnamed but identified by route numbers. (Holmesville and Holmes County, Ohio, were named for Major Holmes; see insert.)

County Road 318 brings me to County Road 329 (CR329), where I turn east. After a few miles, CR329 ends at a stop sign, where it connects with CR320, though the route number change isn't immediately apparent. The road I am on makes a sweeping bend to the southwest and appears to be CR329 continuing. After stopping for the sign, I start around the turn but at the last minute, I notice that the side road, coming in from the left, is CR320. My map shows that at the bend, the road I am on becomes CR320, and the side road is CR320 in the other direction. A bit confusing, so watch for the stop sign. I turn around, wheel onto the part of CR320 heading east, cross Killbuck Creek, and soon roll into Holmesville, a town of 386 people.

The War of 1812 and Major Holmes

In 1814, the only portion of our Territory remaining in the possession of the British was this Island of Mackinac. . . . In July, 1814, an expedition under Col. Croghan and Commodore Sinclair proceeded from Detroit to reduce the Island. Davenport was along, dealing out stores, and to act as guide. At Drummond's Island they destroyed some fortifications, and Major Holmes was sent up to the Sault Ste. Marie. Before his return, Colonel Croghan proceeded to Mackinac, and there remained with the fleet, opposite "Dousman's farm," fifteen days, waiting Major Holmes's return from the "Soo." During this fatal delay, the British commander increased his forces, and threw up Fort George. . . . On the arrival of Holmes, it was resolved to land the American forces (about 2,000) at the British Landing, and to proceed across the Island and attack the Fort. The landing was easily made, and the army proceeded towards the Fort. The British were ready for them, having their cannon and men upon the upper side of Dousman's farm, and the Indian allies posted in ambush. The Americans entered the clearing on the lower side, and the British opened upon them a deadly fire. Col. Croghan, standing upon an elevated mound, directed his troops, who stood their ground with desperate valor. The gallant Holmes, in attempting to flank the British, was shot down.

From Pioneer Collections, *Michigan State Historical Society, 1886*

The Kidron Valley near Jerusalem (for which Kidron, Ohio, is named)

Among the important references to the Kidron are the following. When David fled from Absalom, he is credited with having crossed it; Absalom forbade Shimei to cross it; there Asa burned the idol which his mother had erected; and there Josiah also burned the ashera which had been taken from the temple; and there Hezekiah is said to have thrown into the Kidron the altars found in Jerusalem. Kidron is now a vast burial place and has been so for many years for both Mohammedans and Jews, because of the belief that this spot is to witness the last judgment; the territory has been divided up between the two creeds, the Mohammedans occupying the side toward the temple, that is to the west, while the Jews occupy that part toward the Mount of Olives, that is to the east. To the Christians, the Valley of Kidron is of especial historical interest because, according to the account of John, Jesus visited a garden therein, in company with his disciples, shortly before his betrayal, judgment and crucifixion.

From The Encyclopedia Americana, *Encyclopedia Americana Corporation, 1919*

State Route 83 runs through Holmesville from north to south, and the main retail business is a gas station-convenience store combination directly on the highway. A cluster of homes and a few businesses are located east of SR83, and the Holmesville Elementary School is situated north of the convenience store. The traffic that travels on SR83 does not seem to be providing a great deal of added revenue for the town.

I pedal down Jackson Street, a street running east from SR83 between the convenience store and the school. After a few blocks on Jackson, I turn north onto the Holmes County Trail, a bike-and-hike path built on the right-of-way of the old Cleveland and Pittsburgh Railroad. The trail, created through the efforts of the Holmes County Rails-to-Trails Coalition, runs from Killbuck to Fredericksburg. I will use the Holmesville-to-Fredericksburg leg.

For much of its length, the Holmes County Trail is two lanes wide and paved with asphalt. One lane is restricted to Amish buggy traffic, providing a path on which these conveyances can travel and not encounter motor vehicles. By restricting the buggies to one lane, walkers, runners, skaters, and cyclists don't have to spend their time dodging horse droppings, either. I am grateful for the layout as I pedal the trail.

Between Holmesville and Fredericksburg, the trail runs through woodlands and pastures, and a gurgling stream parallels the trail. As I pedal north, I meet no fewer than five horse-drawn vehicles with Amish drivers. I also pass three other cyclists and a couple walking a large dog.

The trail roughly parallels County Road 192 (CR192), a road I could have used, but the trail offers an interesting change of pace from road riding and is almost flat, providing a welcome break from the hills.

I soon return to Fredericksburg and start to encounter routes with plenty of rises and drops. I am also back in Wayne County. Rather than retracing my path back to Brewster on Harrison Road, I pedal out northeast on Henry Street to Carr Road. The route leads me through more breathtaking rural Ohio scenery.

I continue along Carr Road, cross US Route 250 (US250), and turn east on Emerson Road. The first stretch has a few houses closer together, seemingly indicating I am approaching a village. However, when I crest another hill, I look out on a broad valley with Amish farms and a sawmill.

I pedal though the valley, climb out on Emerson Road, and reach Kidron, Ohio, a crossroads community. Kidron is the home of Lehman's Hardware Store, a merchandiser of the usual items, as well as Americana objects, and fixtures the Amish use, including non-electric appliances, oil lamps, gas refrigerators, and horse-drawn farm equipment. Lehman's has also become an important supplier to homesteaders, environmentalists, missionaries, doctors in developing nations, and others living in areas where there is no power or unreliable power. Not surprisingly, Lehman's is also a major destination for tourists looking for everything from sewing awls to wooden toys.

Changing Gears

Annual Amish country events include Ohio Mennonite Relief Sale & Auction, Thunder Over Walnut Creek Festival, Holmes County Fair, Holmes County Antique Festival, Apple Dumpling Festival & Antique Engine Show.

Courtesy of Holmes County Chamber of Commerce and Tourism Bureau

Lehman's is packed when I arrive. Across the street, ice cream is being made with a machine driven by a small steam-powered generator. I decide to sample the wares since I now have burned up many more calories trekking the hills leading to Kidron.

After finishing my ice cream, I cross the town's intersection on Emerson Road and bear right onto Jericho Road. Jericho Road adds another enjoyable leg to an already enjoyable journey. At State Route 241 (SR241), I jog south to Elton Road, and continue east. I see farms on this road too, but they do not appear to be Amish. I roll through a little crossroads spot identified on my map as Elton, which I assume gives the road its name. A few houses are clustered near the intersection, but there is little evidence of any past community.

I arrive at Manchester Road/SR93 shortly, turn right, and enter the outskirts of Brewster. I pedal for another mile into downtown Brewster.

Elton, Ohio

In the late nineteenth and early twentieth-centuries the area around Elton, Ohio, had some mining and farming operations.

Editor's Note

Ride 16
Stark Reality

Route: East Canton to Navarre loop
Counties: Stark
Terrain: Rolling to very hilly
Distance: 39 miles
Lunch: Kiki's Cafe, Navarre (330-879-5025)
Points of Interest: Ohio Scenery
How to get there: The East Canton Village Park is on Werley Road in East Canton, Ohio. From Interstate 77 (I-77), take US Route 30 (US30) east. US Route 30 will jog north on Trump Avenue. U.S. 30 will then continue east (right) as part of Lincoln Street. U.S. 30 will continue into East Canton and intersect with Werley Road. Turn north (left) onto Werley Road. The park will be on the east (right) side of the road.

I originally thought of titling this ride "Wicked Streets, Wild Avenues and Winding Drives." That's because some quirk of naming in this southern part of Stark County ended up attaching the terms "street," "avenue," or "drive" to most of the rural byways of this route. Since those urban-bred designations make the ride sound easier than it is, I thought to counterbalance them with my alliterative adjectives. But, rather than exaggerate the difficulty, let me simply state the stark reality: this ride traverses challenging country roads that include several tough climbs. They will give you a good workout over an interesting landscape where you will see many farms, loads of country residences, and lots of woodland. Yet because the terrain is varied, the scenery is constantly new.

Changing Gears

The Stark County Bicycle Club primarily features on-road cycling, however, trail and towpath rides are offered as well. The club also offers safety classes for youngsters and volunteers at community events.

www.bikescbc.com

The ride begins in East Canton, a village of about 1,600 people, founded in 1805. Originally called Osnaburg, the town was the first seat of Stark County. During World War I, due to anti-German sentiments, the town was renamed East Canton.

I drive to East Canton on a spring day and leave my truck in the village park on Werley Road. I wend my way through the village and cycle southwest, out of town, on Berger Road. I jog right on Orchardview Drive, continue southwest on Argyle Road

East Canton, Ohio, Manufacturer

The F. E. Kohler Company, 1006 Tuscarawas Street, East, Canton, Ohio. Anti-rattlers, dandelion spud, post hole diggers, steel door pulls; malleable D tops, garden, potato and weeding hoes; rotary hand planters, lawn rakes, steel garden rakes, sidewalk scrapers, kettle scrapers, wall scrapers, shovels, scoops, spades, snow shovels, soldering copper handles, turf edgers; garden trowels, plastering, brick and pointing trowels; weed extractor. Foreign agents, Hugo Lazar & Co., Johannesburg, South Africa. Cable address, "Kohlerco," Canton.

From American Trade Index, *American Association of Manufacturers, 1917*

and climb steeply up to Waynesburg Drive before turning south. After one long downgrade, I cross Zwallen Way/State Route 43 (SR43) and encounter a couple of substantial climbs as I start west on Baum Street. I pump up the hills vigorously since I still have a lot of energy. I also realize the climbs are harbingers of more challenging terrain ahead.

The immediate reward for my hard work is a long plunge into North Industry. The village is part of a district known unofficially as Canton South—an area of Canton Township. At one time, North Industry was a manufacturing area, and the village's main street, Ridge Avenue, was part of the north–south highway leading from Canton to points south. When State Route 800 (SR800) was constructed, bypassing North Industry, the impact was felt by the community. The school closed and Holy Cross Orthodox Church locks its parking lot between services. A boarded-up hardware store, across from where Baum Street ends on Ridge Avenue, seems to reflect North Industry's fortunes. The village is not run-down, but has become a bedroom community for the surrounding area.

I enter North Industry on a steep descent and exit with a stiff climb, beginning on 53rd Street. The grade increases rapidly on Fohl Street (pronounced "fall"). At the top of the climb, I jog right on Dueber Avenue and left onto the continuation of Fohl Street—a segment that begins downhill and then rises again. I

Canton Bicycle Club (1892)

Once at Canton you are safe. Here you will find the Canton Bicycle Club, whose clubhouse is located on Fourth Street, just east of North Market; here you will find the latchstring out to all L. A. W. [League of American Wheelman] tourists every evening and Sundays, and it goes without saying that you can get more pointers here regarding roads, directions, etc., to the square inch, than you can get any place in the county.

From The Handbook of the Ohio Division L. A. W., *C. H. Thomson, 1892*

cross over Interstate 77 (177), continue on Fohl Street, and settle down for a rolling run through open country all the way to Navarre, Ohio. At Navarre, Fohl Street becomes Wooster Street.

Navarre was named by the French-speaking wife of the community's founder, James Duncan, in honor of Henry IV, King of France and Navarre—a kingdom located mostly within the Pyrenees Mountains. Today's Navarre is the consolidation of three communities—Bethlehem, established in 1806; Rochester, established in 1833; and Navarre, established in 1834. The three were united in 1872.

Navarre now has a population of about 1,400 people. As I pedal through the town, I am surrounded by the smell of fresh-baked bread coming from Nickles Bakery plant.

I turn south onto Main Street and pedal to the intersection with Canal Street. I hang a left and arrive at a little bar called Kiki's Café—my lunch stop. Housed in an old building with original tin-paneled ceiling and walls, the establishment is unpretentious and friendly. I like the place immediately and take a seat at the bar where I can see into the adjacent kitchen. The menu features burgers and other sandwiches, salads, wings, and a host of deep-fried sides. I have the "Falcon Philly" basket, served with a mound of freshly-cut french fries.

North Industry, Ohio

North Industry, a new post town of Canton township, Stark county, 4 miles south from the town of Canton, on the road to New Philadelphia. It contains about 70 inhabitants, 12 dwelling houses, 1 store, 1 blacksmith shop, two cooper shops, 1 tavern, 1 distillery, 1 shoe makers shop, one weavers shop, 1 saw mill, and a large merchant grist mill, with 5 run of burrs, and 1 pair of chopping stones, in which there can be manufactured from 80 to 100 bbls. flour per day. It is situated on Nimishillen creek; 4 miles from Canton, 10 from Massilon, 8 from Bethlehem, 9 from Bolivar, 10 from Zoar, 8 from Sandyville, 7 from Waynesburg, and 120 from Columbus.

From The Ohio Gazetteer, and Traveler's Guide, *I. N. Whiting, 1839*

KIKI'S CAFE
19 Canal Street East, Navarre, OH 44662
330-879-5025
Open year-round

HOURS
Tuesday–Thursday: 2:00 P.M. to 1:00 A.M.
Friday: 11:00 A.M. to 1:00 A.M.
Saturday: 2:00 P.M. to 1:00 A.M.
Closed Sunday and Monday

SPECIALTIES
Falcon Philly (A Philly steak sandwich)

After lunch, I head east out of town on Canal Street and pass a building on the northeast corner of Canal and Market Streets, identified as the "Loew & DeFine Grocery Store and Home." John Loew bought the property in 1860 at a time when Navarre was a major commercial center on the Ohio & Erie Canal. From 1860 until the early 1900s, the building was known as Loew and Son Grocery. In early twentieth century, James DeFine bought

Henry of Navarre, Ohio

Navarre, Ohio, is a real town, even though it had no place on the literary map until Holworthy Hall put it there in his *Henry of Navarre, Ohio*. Thereby hangs a tale. When the book was about to begin its serial publication in a certain weekly, an agent was sent to the village saying that the periodical in question was about to print a story about Navarre. Everybody subscribed, everyone in Bethlehem, Rochester, and Navarre (like ancient Gaul, the place is divided into three parts, the combined population being about a thousand), and waited expectantly for the appearance of the story that would make their home spot famous. But when it did appear indignation ran high, for Holworthy Hall, it seemed, had not told the truth about them.

From The Bookman, *Dodd, Mead and Company, 1917*

the store. The building was placed on the National Register of Historic Place in 1979.

Canal Street becomes Hudson Drive and I pass alongside Craig Pittman Memorial Park—a green space through which the Ohio & Erie Towpath Trail runs. The trail is a 101-mile recreational path (of which about eighty miles are currently useable) that runs from Cleveland to New Philadelphia, Ohio, on the bed of old canal's towpath. (Ride 5, page 56, and ride 12, page 131, use parts of the trail.) I am able to see the vestiges of the canal channel and of a canal lock.

Craig Pittman Memorial Park

The Park was named for Craig Pittman who drowned in 1996 at the age of 28. Local business owners put out glass jars and collected enough money to remember the young man by building a pavilion and naming a park in his honor.

Editor's Note

Soon, I veer left onto Brinker Street and immediately start a stiff climb. Brinker Street goes up and down a lot, and I actually lose track of how many times I climb. Two of the ascents require significant effort, and the others are not easy either.

I turn south on Dueber Avenue, a flat stretch, and after a little over a mile, make a left onto Battlesburg Street, a winding eastward trek through valleys, over hills and around curves. The vistas are impressive. The terrain helps me burn off the plateful of french fries I had for lunch.

Battlesburg Road passes through the tiny settlement of Battlesburg, Ohio. The town is at the intersection of Battlesburg Street and Ridge Avenue. Aside from a few houses, the only other structure, to the north on Ridge Avenue, is the Asbury United Methodist Church, which looks like it clings to the side of a hill.

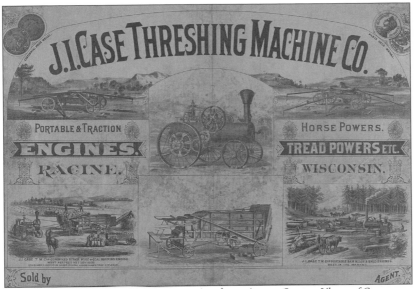

J. I. Case Threshing Machine Company promotion, date unknown. Courtesy Library of Congress, Prints and Photographs Division.

I turn off of Battlesburg Street onto Willowdale Avenue heading north. I continue on Waynesburg Drive, turn right onto Westfall Street and pedal over an incline that seems like an enormous hill at this point. I pedal onto Indian Run Avenue, another visually appealing rural route, jog left on Orchard View Drive and then turn right onto Wood Avenue for the final run into East Canton. I climb two more hills before I finish.

Threshermen

The first and second "Field Days" held by the Stark County Thresher-men's Association were at the F. E. Slutz farm near the little crossroads community of Battlesburg in Stark County, Ohio. These reunions harkened the era of the late 1800s to the 1930s when the custom steam thresherman brought his steam traction engine and his separator to the farm to do the threshing. Farm families paid the thresherman a set rate per bushel of threshed grain and fed the workers.

Editor's Note

Ride 17
High Fortress

Route: North Georgetown to Lisbon loop
Counties: Columbiana
Terrain: Rolling to hilly
Distance: 36 miles
Lunch: Spread Eagle Tavern & Inn, Hanoverton (330-223-1583) or Earl & Jackie's Steel Trolley Diner, Lisbon (330-424-3663)
Points of Interest: Plymouth Street in Hanoverton, Dungannon, Teegarden covered bridge
How to get there: The Old Stage Coach Inn is located on Main Street in North Georgetown, Ohio. From US Route 62 (us62), head south on Westville Lake Road. Turn east (left) onto Center Road. Center Road will curve south and merge with Georgetown-Damascus Road (State Route 716). Georgetown-Damascus Road will intersect with Main Street in North Georgetown. The Old Stage Coach Inn will be to the east (left).

H igh Fortress is a great ride, but not for the faint-hearted. Except for a short stretch on a multi-use trail, the terrain is either truly hilly or vigorously rolling. You'll get a good workout.

The route has many highlights. In Hanoverton, Ohio, you'll ride down a street that looks like it did more than 150 years ago. If you choose to eat at the Spread Eagle Tavern & Inn, you'll enjoy a fine meal in a building built as an inn in 1837. Dungannon, Ohio, is a location that was once important to Native American tribes, and later, as a point on the Sandy & Beaver Canal. Lisbon, Ohio, is the home to one of the few remaining steel trolley diners. You'll travel along some byways far removed from the hustle of every-day life and pedal on part of the scenic Greenway Trail.

(*A word about the route*: I advise you to stay on the route I have indicated, especially in the areas south and east of North Georgetown. Many of the roads I did not choose are paved only with gravel. I explored and backtracked quite a bit before settling on the route. Even at that, I had to choose a few roads that are not well-maintained, but they are paved and suitable for cycling.)

I start in North Georgetown, a small, unincorporated community in northwestern Columbiana County. In this little burg you'll find the Old Stage Coach Inn. Originally called the Western Inn, the establishment occupies a building dating from the early 1800s that actually served as a stagecoach stop on the route from Pittsburgh, Pennsylvania to Massillon, Ohio. I park my truck in back of The Old Stage Coach Inn, mount up, and head south on Rochester Road.

Old Stage Coach Inn

The Inn is now a restaurant, specializing in chicken and fish. Lunch and dinner are served daily, with breakfast served on weekends. A dairy-ette has been opened in the back, serving ice cream and carry-out.

Editor's Note

The Old Stage Coach Inn, Hanoverton, Ohio. Courtesy of Rob Matheny.

Other rides in the book have taken me through rural areas changing over to mixed use, residential areas interspersed with farms, but High Fortress runs through agricultural Ohio. The farmers do not have much flat land to plow, however. Much of the terrain is rolling.

I leave Rochester Road and turn left, working my way east and south on a series of back roads. I pedal over a couple of good hills on my route to Hanoverton, Ohio.

The Legend of Olivina Nicholas

The daughter of the Spread Eagle Tavern's second owner, Olivina, fell in love with a traveling actor from New York. When he left, she stayed in Hanoverton, never leaving the Tavern House for twenty years. One day, she tied a rope to a rafter in an upstairs bedroom and hung herself—some say by doing a swan-dive out of a nearby window. Her spirit continues to haunt the Tavern to this day.

Courtesy of Spread Eagle Tavern and Inn

Hanoverton, called simply Hanover in the early days (not to be confused with Hanover, Ohio, in Licking County, originally

Changing Gears

Legend has it that Abraham Lincoln once made a stopover at the Spread Eagle

called Fleming), saw its heyday with the construction of the Sandy & Beaver Canal in 1834. The area was home to two thousand people, at one point, but only four hundred folks live there now. The town was established in 1813 by a Quaker abolitionist, James Craig, and became a station on the Underground Railroad.

I ride down Plymouth Street, on which a cluster of ten National Historic Trust buildings and other Federalist style homes make up "Brick Row"—an area built by the nouveau riche of the canal days. The area has retained its historical atmosphere. One of the buildings, the Spread Eagle Tavern, a restored 1837 establishment, offers formal-to-casual dining. I didn't stop for lunch but would have been welcome in the rugged environs of the log "barn room."

Beneath Plymouth Street are remnants of an underground passage that connects some of the brick row houses to Dr. Robertson's house across the street. Runaway slaves used the tunnel because the doctor's house had a secret upstairs hideaway. At nightfall, the fugitives were then transported to their next safe-haven.

I wheel out of Hanoverton, and cross US Route 30 (US30), an artery in Ohio that has replaced the original Lincoln Highway—America's first transcontinental route. The highway was the idea of Carl Graham Fisher, who built the Indianapolis Motor Speedway in 1909, and said the country should have a "Coast-to-Coast

Lincoln Highway Association

The Goodyear Tire & Rubber Company's founder and president, Frank A. Seiberling, was president of the Lincoln Highway Association for many years.

Editor's Note

Spread Eagle Tavern along Plymouth Street. Courtesy of Rob Matheny.

Rock Highway" from Times Square in New York City to Lincoln
Park in San Francisco. Henry Joy, president of the Packard Motor
Company, supported Fisher and proposed to name the highway
in memory of President Abraham Lincoln.

In 1913, Fisher and Joy formed the Lincoln Highway Association to publicize the idea, and to see if private money could build
the route. A substantial amount of cash was raised from indus-
trialists, but a notable exception was Henry Ford, who thought
Federal funds should be used to finance the project. The Lincoln Highway began as a miscellaneous collection of downtown
streets, country lanes, and old trails marked with signs showing
an "L," rectangular, graphic, and emblazoned in red, white, and
blue. While the confusing and haphazardly maintained condition of the early Lincoln Highway illustrated the long-neglected
nature of the American roads inherited by the automobile, by

SPREAD EAGLE TAVERN & INN
10150 Plymouth Street, Hanoverton, OH 44423
330-223-1583
Open year-round

HOURS
Monday–Thursday: 11:30 P.M. to 2:00 P.M., 5:00 P.M. to 8:00 P.M.
Friday–Saturday: 11:30 P.M. to 2:00 P.M., 5:00 P.M. to 10:00 P.M.
Sunday: 11:30 P.M. to 8:00 P.M.

SPECIALTIES
American Cuisine, Crab Cakes, Steak

the 1920s, it had become the nation's premier cross-country thoroughfare, and a testing ground for new road and bridge-building techniques.

The Lincoln Highway, as an entity, came to an end in 1926 when the national system of route numbering was imposed. Much of the highway, from Pennsylvania into Utah, became

The Sandy & Beaver Canal

The Sandy & Beaver Canal, from Bolivar, on the Ohio Canal, to the mouth of the Little Beaver, on the boundary between Ohio and Pennsylvania. This canal was built by a private company incorporated January 11, 1828. Its length was 73 miles. Its lockage, from the Ohio Canal to the summit, was 205 feet; from the summit to the Ohio River, 464 feet; in all, 669 feet. Its dimensions were nearly the same as those of the Ohio Canal. It passed through a tunnel at the summit. The canal company failed before the work was fairly complete, and the canal was all abandoned except about six miles next to the Ohio Canal, which was adopted by the State in 1856. A branch of this canal, called the Nimishillen Canal, extended from Sandyville to the city of Canton, a distance of about 12 miles. Total length of the Sandy & Beaver system, 85 miles.

From Report of the Chief of Engineers U.S. Army,
Government Printing Office, 1896

Along the side of the Lincoln Highway, US30, is Morgan Mercantile, Ohio's oldest brick building, built in 1803. Courtesy of Rob Matheny.

US30, but the remaining sections were given other numbers, or became state or local routes. Today, US30 is a coast-to-coast road stretching from Atlantic City, New Jersey to Astoria, Oregon.

After crossing US30, I proceed along back roads to Dungannon—a place of a hundred residents that is not found on every Ohio map.

Though small, Dungannon is a well-hidden trove of Ohio history. The location was called Painted Post by Native Americans, because several trees bore marks inscribed by warriors to detail their prowess in battle. The area was also the junction of three major trails, and was a portage point for canoe travel into the Tuscarawas Valley. Dungannon was the first home of Catholicism in northern Ohio, and the first church was built in the area in 1820. During the canal-building era, Dungannon was the geographic summit of the Sandy & Beaver Canal, and was the location of the only tunnels on the whole waterway. In 1863, General John Morgan and Confederate troops, after they had crossed the Ohio River, rode through Dungannon. At Salineville, Ohio, Union Cavalry, under the command of Major W. B. Way and Major G. W. Rue, surrounded Morgan's Raiders and succeeded in capturing Morgan and most of his command. Morgan's incursion was the northernmost point reached by Southern troops during the war.

As I pedal to Dungannon, I see a church spire rising above the green canopy. St. Philip Neri Catholic Church—a towering edifice—stands on the highest ground around. A log cabin sits near the church. Originally located about a mile to the south, the cabin—Andrew McAlllister's house—was the place where the missionary priest, Father Edward J. Fenwick, the "Pioneer Apos-

Morgan's Raid

Relating to the collection of damages by John Morgan's raid.
Whereas, Commissioners duly appointed under the laws of Ohio, to examine and investigate claims growing out of the Morgan raid, so called, in 1863, have investigated and allowed claims for damages sustained by citizens of the state of Ohio, to the amount of four hundred and thirty-nine thousand and sixty-nine dollars, for property taken and destroyed by the rebel forces (the most of which said property was afterwards recaptured by the union forces and retained for the use of the United States), one hundred and forty-three thousand six hundred and eleven dollars for property taken, damaged and destroyed by the union forces, and six thousand two hundred and fifty-seven dollars for property taken, damaged and destroyed by the forces under the command of officers of the state of Ohio (the most of which property was afterwards recaptured and retained for the use of the United States); therefore
Resolved by the General Assembly of the State of Ohio, That the senators in congress from the said state of Ohio be and they hereby are instructed, and the representatives in congress from said state be and they hereby are requested to institute, have and maintain such action and proceedings as will, if possible, secure the payment of said claims, mentioned in the foregoing preamble, from the government of the United States. *Adopted April 18, 1874.*

From Acts of the State of Ohio, *N. Willis, 1874*

Father Fenwick, blessing settlers who are gathered, some on bended knee, near a log church or cabin on the frontier. Courtesy Library of Congress, Prints and Photographs Division.

tle of Ohio," celebrated the region's first mass in 1817. Three years later, St. Paul's Church was erected as the first Catholic church in northern Ohio. St. Philip Neri was constructed in 1849 at a cost of fifteen thousand dollars, a sum donated by Philip Ehrhardt.

A century and a half later the cabin was dismantled, moved to its present location, rebuilt, and rededicated in May of 1967 as the "Log Cabin Shrine of Dungannon." Riding through Dungannon, I discover the log cabin has now been enclosed within a garage-type structure. Obviously, preserving the log cabin is an issue, but, in order to see the monument, someone will have to open the building.

In 1833, George Sloan learned of the planned route for the Sandy & Beaver Canal, purchased twenty-six acres on the route, and named the location Dungannon after his home in County Tyrone, Ireland. In Gaelic, Dungannon means "Geanann's fort" or "Geanann's high fortress."

The heyday of Dungannon came during the construction of the ill-fated Sandy & Beaver Canal (see page 194 for history of the project). A few years before today's ride, I visited the area with my friend Wayne Vinson, a canal buff. Wayne had made contact with a Dungannon resident, Jerry Walker. A bear of a man, sporting a long gray beard and a camouflage cap, Jerry lives near the church and his house sits right in what was once the canal bed. Jerry drove us around and pointed out where the tunnels had been and where the line of the canal embankment could still be seen. Without this knowledgeable guidance, finding remnants of the canal would have been difficult.

I also asked Jerry where the Painted Post junction had been, and he nodded south of town. "No one knows for sure," Jerry said, "but when I was a kid, I used to walk an area over there with an old man who had a talent for spotting arrowheads. He'd point them out and I'd pick them up for him. And I heard someone found a bushel of arrowheads stored in a sandy bank along there. A lot of people think that's where the trail ran."

(To find where the canal once ran, face the Log Cabin Shrine of Dungannon, turn around and look across the street to the right. The former towpath line should be visible behind the houses.)

I leave Dungannon, heading northeast on Lisbon–Dungannon Road. Though the name of the road is auspicious, the road is not a major thoroughfare. I pass through areas so lightly populated that in places I travel down single lanes and wheel from

Sandy & Beaver Canal Tunnels

[A]bout 200 yards from the highway [State Route 172] is the western entrance to a Sandy & Beaver Canal Tunnel, closed by landslides and erosion. This and an adjacent tunnel were built by 150 men who labored from dawn to dark for $15 or $20 a month and daily "jiggers" of whiskey. One tunnel was a mile in length, the other a quarter mile; in places they ran 100 feet below the surface of the hill.

From The Ohio Guide, *Oxford University Press, 1940*

pavement to gravel. I am taking the most direct route to Lisbon, but I must walk my bike through the occasional graveled stretches. When the environment seems to be as remote from civilization as possible, the Lisbon–Dungannon Road jogs right on Trinity Church Road and then left again under its own name. The road is little more than an asphalted lane here. True to the map, I pedal onto Wayne Bridge Road, which delivers me to US30 for a very brief downhill stretch into Lisbon.

Lisbon (initially named New Lisbon) was founded in 1803 and is one of the older towns in Ohio. The seat of Columbiana County, it is rich with history. The main street, Lincoln Way, was part of the old Lincoln Highway and is lined with aging, but still majestic, Victorian homes. The small downtown retains an early twentieth-century look, reflected in the two-story stone courthouse that was erected in 1871.

Two prominent Ohioans and national figures were born in Lisbon. One was Marcus A. Hanna (1837–1904) [see inset, page 201], who became a well-respected Cleveland businessman and campaign manager for President William McKinley. The other local resident who gained national attention was Clement L.

Father Fenwick

As heretofore stated, Father Fenwick came to Northern Ohio for the first time in 1817, visiting among other places in Columbiana and Stark counties, the few Catholic families settled near the present village of Dungannon. Here also, under his direction, in 1820, was built the first church in Northern Ohio. It was a small brick building, dedicated to St. Paul the Apostle, and served its purpose till 1849, when the present church in Dungannon was erected. Three years later the Catholics in Canton also built a brick church, dedicated to St. John the Evangelist. It was replaced in 1872 by the present very beautiful church. Until 1829, the above were the only two churches in Northern Ohio, when a third was built at Chippewa, near the present village of Doylestown.

From The Church in Northern Ohio and in the
Diocese of Cleveland, *Short & Forman, 1890*

Earl & Jackie's Street Trolley Dinner in Lisbon, Ohio. Courtesy of Rob Matheny.

Vallandigham (1820–71), a congressman and member of the Copperheads, northern Democrats who opposed the Civil War.

Lisbon is also the place where the drinking straw was supposedly invented, patented, and first manufactured, made of "pure white manila paper . . . raw to finish state, untouched by human hands."

I choose an historic spot for lunch—Earl & Jackie's Steel Trolley Diner, one of the only nineteen authentic steel and neon diners still operating in Ohio. Earl & Jackie's menu features twenty varieties of the hamburger, including Bing's Gut Buster, "fifties style" sandwiches, hand-cut fries, milk shakes, and breakfast choices to satisfy everyone. The diner is open twenty-four hours a day and seven days a week. I order and thoroughly enjoy the Rodeo Burger with a side of fries.

After lunch, three past presidents lead me out of town. I turn south on Jefferson Street to Washington Street to Lincoln Avenue (not to be confused with Lincoln Way). On the southeast

STEEL TROLLEY DINER
140 East Lincoln Way, Lisbon, OH 44432
330-424-3663
Open year-round

HOURS
Open 24 hours a day, 7 days a week

SPECIALTIES
Fries, Chili, Burgers, Milkshakes

edge of the town, I turn off of Lincoln Avenue onto the Little Beaver Creek Greenway Trail, a blacktop surface on the former roadbed of the Erie–Lackawanna Railroad. (Ride 3, page 36, uses part of the same trail.) Currently, this section of the trail runs for twelve miles from Lisbon to Leetonia, to the north.

Marcus Hanna

Marcus A. Hanna (1837–1904) was born at Lisbon, Ohio, September 24, 1837. He amassed large wealth in the coal and iron business at Cleveland and elsewhere, and in the carrying-trade of the Great Lakes. In 1884, 1888, and 1896 he was a delegate to the Republican national conventions. In 1896 he was elected chairman of the Republican national committee, directed the McKinley campaigns of that year and 1900, and in 1896 was largely responsible for McKinley's election. The elaborate organization of the Republican campaign machinery and the collection and expenditure of large sums of money for campaign expenses, were the distinguishing features of his policy. In 1897 he was elected United States Senator from Ohio, and held that office until his death. On the formation of the National Civic Federation, in 1901, he was chosen its president. He died at Washington, February 15, 1904.

From Cyclopedia of American Government,
D. Appleton and Company, 1914

Teegarden Centennial Covered Bridge. Courtesy of Rob Matheny.

The trail is scenic and a relatively flat ride, and essentially follows the Middle Fork of Little Beaver Creek. In the early stages of the trail, I cross a narrow backroad called St. Jacobs Logtown Road several times. I pedal through what appears to be the backyards of small houses, and for a half-mile stretch, the trail route moves onto Logtown Road. When the Little Beaver Creek and Logtown Road diverge, the trail follows the creek and I pedal through a forested valley. After I pass by mile marker five, I turn left onto Eagleton Road and glide downhill into a wooded glen.

At the bottom of the road, I see the Teegarden Centennial Covered Bridge, built in 1875 and restored in 2003. At one time, two hundred and fifty covered bridges, including sixteen railroad bridges, were located in Columbiana County, but only five remain. The Teegarden Bridge was used until 1992.

This quiet wooded glen, with the river running through it, was once the site of a village called Teegarden, founded by Prussian immigrants, and named for one of the early families. I see no evidence that the village ever existed. The location is now a parking lot for users of the trail.

Eagleton Road ends at Teegarden Road, but no sign identifies the change. I turn left on Teegarden Road and right onto Yates Road, climbing out of the valley in the process. About a mile later, I bear left at a fork onto Winona Road and start the final leg of the ride. I am still nine miles from North Georgetown, but the intervening distance is almost entirely farmland, with the single interruption of a tiny crossroad community named Winona, which I wheel through in less than a minute. Turning on back roads, I proceed in a stair-step fashion, north and west, and arrive back in North Georgetown.

William Teegarden

William Teegarden was a native of Pennsylvania, and settled in Columbiana county, Ohio, in 1804, which State was at that time considered the "wilds of the far West." At that time his family consisted of a wife and two children. Civilization had made such slow progress, that the comforts of life were not thought of without suggesting the idea of a journey to procure them; and Mr. Teegarden was obliged to transport salt and provisions for his family across the mountains on horseback. He was a man of generous heart and kind disposition, and a friend of the red men of the forest. Their camp-fires often blazed near the door of his cabin. In this wilderness he cleared a large farm, raised a family of twelve children, lived to see them all married and advantageously settled in life; and then, at the ripe age of 84 years, peacefully passed to another state of existence.

From Biographical Sketches of the Members of the Forty-first General Assembly of the State of Indiana, *Indianapolis Journal Company, 1861*

Ride 18

Eye Candy

Route: Strasburg to Baltic loop
Counties: Tuscarawas, Holmes
Terrain: Relatively flat to hilly
Distance: 39 miles
Lunch: Miller's Dutch Kitch'n, Baltic (330-897-5481)
Points of Interest: Stunning Ohio scenery, Breitenbach Wine
   Cellars, Ragersville Cheese Factory, Broad Run Cheese
   House
How to get there: This ride starts at a Hardee's restaurant on
   US.Route 250 (US250) in Strasburg, Ohio. From Interstate
   77 (I-77), take the exit for US250 towards Strasburg.

E ye Candy" is one of my favorite routes because the ride is a scenic delight. The trek goes by working farms set against rolling hills, passes through quaint little villages and has many breathtaking vistas. Ride "Eye Candy" on a bright, sunny day, and you'll know why this state's official song is *Beautiful Ohio*.

On just such a midsummer day, I drive to Strasburg, Ohio. In 1828, a group of Germans led by Jonathan Folck settled at Strasburg, naming the town for the city in Germany. Strasburg is a small town of about two thousand residents, but thirteen thousand vehicles pass through the village each day due to its location at the junction of US Route 250 (us250) and Interstate 77 (I77).

I park my pickup in the lot of Hardee's fast-food restaurant on sr250—Strasburg's main street. I leave the lot; turn right on 9th Street, and left onto Race Road. In less than a minute, I leave the flurry of traffic behind and wheel down a quiet country lane that meanders through pleasant countryside, passing woods, fields and occasional homes.

Race Road ends at Schneiders Crossing Road; I turn right, and pedal to Winfield, Ohio—a tiny unincorporated community, marked by a brick United Methodist Church and a small cluster of homes along State Route 516 (sr516). I pedal across sr516 and onto Broad Run Dairy Road—a scenic path leading past farms and country homes.

I pedal a few miles to the intersection of Broad Run Dairy Road and Old Ohio Route 39 (or39). The Broad Run Cheese

Beautiful Ohio

Beautiful Ohio, where the golden grain
Dwarf the lovely flowers in the summer rain....
Beautiful Ohio, thy wonders are in view,
Land where my dreams all come true!

From the 1989 updated version

At the entrance of Broad Run Cheese House. Courtesy of Rob Matheny.

House, established in 1933, is on the corner. I turn left and after a few hundred yards, I pass the Breitenbach Wine Cellars. At Schilling Hill Road, I turn right, climb to, and cross over State Route 39 (SR39). I continue climbing to the top of Schilling Hill Road, glide down to Crooked Run Road, and turn west.

Crooked Run Road offers plenty of rustic beauty and two significant climbs requiring considerable labor. I manage the first climb, but barely get up the second one that has a short, very steep pitch near the top. After that, I climb one more small incline to the top. An abandoned tower without identification is at this high point with its unobstructed sight lines.

I make a rapid and easy descent and continue on Crooked Run Road into Ragersville, Ohio, founded in 1830 by Conrad Rager. Little more than

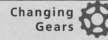

Changing Gears

Broad Run Swiss Cheese has earned countless awards for its exceptional quality. In 2001, Broad Run Swiss won the Ohio Grand Champion Cheese award.

www.broadruncheese.com

Changing Gears

Ragersville was known as "Hangtown," because it was the site of the only lynching in Tuscarawas County history.

www.bikescbc.com/ lynch.htm

a crossroad community, Ragersville has worked at retaining its history. A log cabin built to represent many nineteenth-century dwellings of the area is located in the village center. The former Evangelical Lutheran Church, erected in 1897, houses the Ragersville Historical Society. A restored one-room schoolhouse is directly across Crooked Run Road, and the adjacent house was the residence of Dr. Alta Weiss from 1946 until her death in 1964.

Alta Weiss was a dynamic individual, graduating in 1914 as the only woman in her class from the Starling Ohio Medical College, which would later become the Ohio State University Medical College. Weiss also had another career as an outstanding baseball player. In 1907, at the age of seventeen, she became the star pitcher for the Vermillion (Ohio) Independents, a men's semi-pro team. Special trains were run from Cleveland and surrounding towns for the thirteen thousand fans who saw the last seven games of the 1907 season. Alta's father, also a doctor, bought a half interest in the team at the end of the season and changed the name to the Weiss All-Stars. Weiss played ball until 1922.

Ragersville also boasts a cheese factory with a small counter where cheese can be purchased, and the Good House Restaurant and Saloon. The latter establishment has been around since 1858

Alta Weiss

Miss Alta Weiss can easily lay claim to being the only one who can handle the ball from the pitcher's box in such style that some of the best semi-pros are made to fan the atmosphere.

—The Loran Times Herald, *1907*

"I found out that you can't play in skirts . . . I tried. I wore a skirt over my bloomers and nearly broke my neck. Finally, I was forced to discard it, and now always wear bloomers, but made wide enough that the fullness gives a skirt-like effect."

—*Alta Weiss*

*A woman baseball player, circa 1918. Courtesy Library of
Congress, Prints and Photographs Division.*

and was a stagecoach stop between Akron and Columbus, offering overnight accommodations and meals for $0.25 each.

Before leaving Ragersville, I buy a soda from a machine at
a used-vehicle dealer that has eight trucks and vans on the lot.
While I am drinking, the dealer comes out. I ask about his off-
the-beaten-track location and sales. He says that he does quite
well and has many repeat customers who appreciate buying
vehicles near where they live.

I pedal out of Ragersville on Ragersville Road and pass several
farms and fields with lush crops. I continue south for a spell until
Ragersville Road turns west. I ascend two modest hills, stopping
at the top of the second one to enjoy the spectacular vista.

On the steep descent, I brake to control my speed. The last
pitch into Baltic, Ohio, is very precipitous with a crossroad at the
bottom, so I am careful not to build up a head of steam. I cross

Changing Gears

Ragersville, Ohio Cheese Factories, 1908

E. Ladrach
Espenhied
Gerber
G. Ladrach
Steiner

From Annual Report, Ohio State Board of Agriculture, *State Printers, 1908*

the road, continue on Baltic's main street and stop for lunch at Miller's Dutch Kitch'n.

Baltic is a small community (around seven hundred people) that straddles Coshocton, Holmes, and Tuscarawas counties. I had made my way from Tuscarawas to Holmes County before rolling onto Baltic's main street.

Baltic was platted in 1815 by Lewis Row and named Rowville. Early settlers migrating westward from Pennsylvania found an excellent water supply in the area. From 1847 until 1883, the post office was called Buena Vista or "beautiful view," a name that certainly described my ride into town. The village was incorporated in 1903 as Baltic because the name was short and easily pronounced. Baltic is the location of the historic Baltic Mills, one of Ohio's oldest flour mills, still in operation, and the Steiner Cheese Factory, the first cheese house established in Ohio. Baltic is a place where you go outside at night and enjoy the "peace and quiet country."

The National Fire Brick Company

This plant is located at Strasburg, Ohio, and the company owns the largest body of flint and plastic clay in Ohio, the vein averaging from four to six feet in thickness. . . . Brick made from this clay has gained an enviable reputation all over the country. . . . The large, modern kilns have a capacity from 90,000 to 125,000 brick each. The factory is located in close proximity to the clay mines, and the manufacture is under the careful supervision of trained and experienced men. . . . The factory being designed with great floor and dryer capacity, the most difficult shapes in large quantities can be made up and shipped promptly. The brands manufactured here are especially suitable for Blast Furnace Stoves, Open Hearth Checkers, or any place where brick are subjected to similar conditions. This plant makes a specialty of Blast Furnace Stove Brick, Open Hearth Checkers and has the largest capacity in the country for that class of work.

From Catalog Containing Useful Information and Tables Appertaining to the Use of Fire Brick, *The Stowe-Fuller Company, 1914*

MILLER'S DUTCH KITCH'N
108 East Main Street, Baltic, OH 43804
330-897-5481
Open year-round

HOURS
Summer
Monday–Friday: 5:30 A.M. to 8:00 P.M.
Saturday: 6:00 A.M. to 8:00 P.M.
Closed Sunday

Winter
Monday–Thursday: 5:30 A.M. to 7:00 P.M.
Friday: 5:30 A.M. to 8:00 P.M.
Saturday: 6:00 A.M. to 8:00 P.M.
Closed Sunday

SPECIALTIES
Broasted Chicken

Miller's Dutch Kitch'n, family owned since 1973, features an Amish-style cuisine. I order a hot turkey sandwich with real mashed potatoes steeped in gravy. The meal includes tasty rolls and apple butter. I savor the entire lunch.

My first challenge after eating is to ride up the steep hill I had descended on my way into town. After sitting for thirty minutes at lunch, my muscles have cooled down. I pedal up the hill with my legs complaining the whole way. (***Tip:*** I suggest you take a few warm-up laps around town before trying the hill. A lighter lunch might help, too.)

Over that hill, I turn left onto the aptly named Pleasant Valley Road, which nicks the corner of Holmes County. I pass Holmes County farms and varied rural scenery on the Tuscarawas County side. Back in Tuscarawas County, I turn right onto

Crooked Run Road (the same Crooked Run I was on earlier, only now farther west).

I climb out of the valley and continue to Ragersville, this time from the west. I pass a home festooned with a large assortment of outdoor decorations and plants. Across the road from the house is a small lake surrounded by flags with statues, a gazebo, and fountains. I assume the building and grounds must be a commercial venture, perhaps a greenhouse or florist. I ask a gentleman in town and he tells me the place is a private home and the owner likes to decorate. My surprise is the home's out-of-the-way location.

I pass through Ragersville quickly and make my way to the northern leg of Ragersville Road. I pass more farms and fields filled with crops. The area is a picturesque postcard.

After several miles, I turn right onto OR39 and pass by the Dutch Valley Restaurant, which resembles a sprawling country farmhouse. The spot is popular with both locals and the tourists who visit Ohio's Amish Country, sometimes by the busload. (Note: Miller's Dutch Kitch'n and the Dutch Valley Restaurant are closed on Sundays for religious reasons. The Good House Restaurant and Saloon in Ragersville serves a Sunday brunch and the Tavern of Ragersville, across the street from the Good House Restaurant, also serves food.)

I take OR39 across SR39 and turn left on Spooky Hollow Road. I pedal up to Prysi Road, turn right, and head north. I eventually descend and have a grand view of valley. Prysi Road brings me to Broad Run Dairy Road.

At Winfield, Ohio, I turn left on State Route 516 (SR516) for a couple of blocks, then right onto Winfield–Strasburg Road, and immediately climb toward a large farmhouse. I have a spectacular view of the broad valley ahead of me and see a section of Winfield–Strasburg Road cutting through it. I stop to take in the scenery before pedaling the final stretch to Strasburg.

Ride 19
Tents of Grace

Route: Zoar to Gnadenhutten loop
Counties: Tuscarawas
Terrain: Flat to rolling
Distance: 53 miles
Lunch: Tents of Grace, Gnadenhutten: 740-254-1082
Points of Interest: Zoar Village, Gnadenhutten memorial
How to get there: Zoar, Ohio, is a small community south of Canton, Ohio. From Interstate 77 (I-77), take the exit for State Route 212 (SR212). State Route 212 will lead directly into Zoar.

R ide 19 is distinctive because two communities on the trek, Zoar and Gnadenhutten, were originally founded as religious societies. While the villages still exist, the religious societies are gone. The ride also includes a stop at Schoenbrunn State Park and Memorial. Schoenbrunn, Ohio, was an early missionary enclave set up by the Moravian sect that later founded Gnadenhutten.

The ride passes through a wide variety of terrain, follows a good bit of the Tuscarawas River and visits communities large and small. The sister communities of Dover and New Philadelphia, Ohio, are the cities, but have only a combined population of about thirty thousand people. The path I have selected through this area is a practical one for cycling.

Zoar, Ohio, was founded in 1817 by a group of German religious dissenters called the Society of Separatists of Zoar. The town was named Zoar after the biblical city that welcomed Lot after his flight from doomed Sodom. The community held material goods in common and prospered under the leadership of Joseph Bimmler.

During the construction of the Ohio and Erie Canal, the Zoarites were paid $21,000 to dig a seven-mile stretch of the canal and later operated four canal boats providing substantial income for the community. Eventually, after the advent of railroads, younger members of the group left the colony and the remaining members eventually divided the property and abandoned the community. Some present-day residents of Zoar are descendents of the original separatists. [See inset, page 217, for further information on Zoar.]

Today, Zoar is a residential community and museum village. The Zoar Village State Memorial, operated by the Ohio Historical Society, includes many restored buildings of the Zoarite community. I walk around Zoar before starting my ride and visit the earlier era. Even the historic buildings that are not part

Changing Gears

Christmas at Zoar
The historic village recreates the Christmas customs of the German Separatists, which includes Krist Kind, who distributes candy and sweets to good boys and girls.

www.ohio.com

Early eighteenth-century log house at Zoar, Ohio. Courtesy of Rob Matheny.

of the museum village are well maintained. The two "villages" offer a pleasing combination of past and present.

After my brief tour, I wheel out onto State Route 212 (SR212), Zoar's main street and I turn south onto Dover Zoar Road. I pass over the top of a large earthen levee designed to prevent the Tuscarawas River from flooding the village. From the top of the levee, I have an excellent view of Zoar. Soon, I pass over the river and the old bed of the Ohio & Erie Canal. Even though trees and other vegetation grow within the former canal, its course is still

---

The Ohio & Erie Canal

The community of Zoar in Tuscarawas County received $21,000 for building the canal through their property, which then consisted of twelve thousand acres of land. Sections of the canal were sold to contractors who hired the laborers. Thirty cents and a jigger full of whisky a day was the wage rate at first, for work from sunrise to sunset.

From Bulletin, *The Ohio Agricultural Experiment Station, 1918*

The Zoar Tavern. Courtesy of Rob Matheny.

unmistakable. The canal's towpath has been cleared to become part of the Ohio & Erie Canal Towpath Trail, a recreational corridor from Cleveland to New Philadelphia, Ohio. (See ride 5, page 56, and ride 12, page 131, for other routes that include stretches on the Towpath Trail.) I ride under a bridge of the railway that once carried Zoarites to Akron, Canton, and Cleveland.

I pedal into the country on Dover Zoar Road, a well-paved, low-traffic route. Since there is no continuous valley through the area, I travel around hills, between them, along their cusps,

Other Houses in Dover on the National Register of Historic Places

Katherine Cooper House, 118 West Seventh Street
John Deis House, 203 West Sixth Street
Jeremiah Reeves House and Carriage House, 325 East Iron Avenue
Christian H. Rinderknecht House, 602 North Wooster Avenue
Dr. Joseph Slingluff House, 606 North Wooster Avenue

Editor's Note

around their hips, and over them. When I round each bend, I face dips, climbs, curves, and straights. This uncertainty makes my ride a source of challenge and enjoyment. Finally at the top of a hill, I enter Dover, Ohio, and roll down to Front Street.

Dover was laid out in 1806, but didn't have many residents until the Ohio & Erie Canal came through in the mid 1820s. Canal trade gave the community a boost and it kept growing, incorporating as a village in 1842 and as a city in 1901. By 1840, the community had become a flour-milling center, and later a steel production site. For many years, the town was called Canal Dover to distinguish it from other towns named Dover in Ohio.

In 1908, Dover voters passed an ordinance making the town a dry community, putting twenty-two saloons and two breweries out of business overnight. [See inset on Canal Dover and Local Prohibition, page 218.] After passage of the Volstead Act, Dover became somewhat infamous for circumventing the law.

The Separatists at Zoar, Ohio

The Separatists: A society of German origin, which settled in Zoar, Tuscarawas County, Ohio, 1817–19. The movement gathered first in Württemberg around Barbara Grubermann, a Swiss refugee to Germany, whom those who separated from the German State Church (whence the name) accepted as their leader. On her death Joseph Baumeler (Bimeler; d. 1853) became the head of the movement, and, securing the aid of some English Quakers in the persecution which followed, led the emigration of his followers to the United States. The first intention was not to adopt the communistic principles, but the diversity of station among the members and the great inequality of means seemed to make this necessary. Marriage was discouraged in the beginning, but was adopted a few years later. The society reached its largest membership about 1832 through immigration from Germany, when it numbered about 500 persons. The original enthusiasm continually declined and the society was finally dissolved. On Sept. 13, 1898, the property was allotted to the remaining members, 222 in number.

From The New Schaff-Herzog Encyclopedia of Religious Knowledge, *Funk and Wagnalls, 1909*

I enter Dover from the northeast on Front Street, with its modest, residential houses, until I arrive at 912 East Front Street, a gorgeous Victorian-style house, beautifully restored and freshly painted. Jabez Reeves, the vice-president and superintendent of the Reeves Iron Company, owned the home in the early 1900s. I pass by several other grand houses, including a Queen Anne-style structure at 211 East Front Street, listed on the National Register of Historic Places as the Frederick Bernhard House.

I follow Front Street, and it joins State Route 800 (SR800). I turn left onto Wooster Avenue and cross the Tuscarawas River.

Canal Dover and Local Prohibition

Canal Dover was the center of observation in regard to the enforcement of local prohibition. It is a busy manufacturing town, a Pittsburgh in miniature. The business section, consisting of about 15 blocks centering at the intersection of two streets, does not contain any buildings of pretension. With the exception of those upon one street, the residences are apparently those of laborers who constitute possibly 80 percent of the population. About one-fifth of the inhabitants are Germans. The city is said to be in good financial condition and boasts an excellent electric and good railway service.

In Canal Dover the State law governing saloons was supplemented by a local ordinance requiring them to close at ten o'clock p.m., Saturdays at eleven o'clock. As a matter of fact, no attention was paid to this regulation. In some of the mills a night shift changes soon after midnight, and many saloons remained open on that account. Election Day was fairly well observed. Some time ago stalls were removed from all saloons provided with them.

At the time of this investigation the illicit traffic was carried on under the guise of selling soft drinks in the same places and by the same men who previously paid tax as saloon keepers. Twenty-three such places were in operation and handled beer as well as spirits. Some of the more timid ones sold beer in bottles labelled "near-beer." The majority, however, took no such precautions and drew beer from faucets. To those who are known to the venders there was not the slightest difference from license conditions as regards the opportunity for buying liquor. Strangers must be vouched for.

From The Yearbook of the United States Brewers' Association, *United States Brewers Association, 1910*

Wooster Avenue is fairly busy, but has two lanes in each direction allowing vehicles to pass me easily. I turn off of Wooster Avenue onto the less busy Union Avenue and make my way south to New Philadelphia. If I had not seen the sign welcoming me to New Philadelphia, I wouldn't have noticed crossing into a new community, as the two communities now run together.

New Philadelphia was founded in 1804, and thrived, like Dover, in the canal era. John Knisely, a man who wanted to create a new "city of brotherly love," developed the town. He hired a surveyor to lay out the area to resemble Philadelphia, Pennsylvania. New Philadelphia became a marketing center for agricultural products and after 1854, when railroads came through, a home to coal mining and steel manufacturing. The town was incorporated as a city in 1895, and in 1898, the public square was paved.

Bicycling long stretches makes me very aware of the pavement. When the bicycle was first introduced in the United States in 1877, the new means of transportation caught on quickly. In 1880, the first national bicycle organization, the League of American Wheelmen, was formed and continues today as the League of American Bicyclists. By 1898, the League of American Wheelmen had more than 102,000 members, including the Wright Brothers,

New Philadelphia, Ohio

New Philadelphia, Ohio, city, county-seat of Tuscarawas County; on the Tuscarawas River and the Ohio Canal, and on the Pennsylvania and the Cleveland, L. & W.R.R.'s; about 100 miles northeast of Columbus and 90 miles south of Cleveland. It was settled in 1805 and incorporated in 1808. It is in an agricultural region, but its good water-power and facilities for transportation have contributed toward making it a manufacturing city. Some of the manufactures are pressed, stamped, and enameled goods, steel products, flour, woolen goods, brooms, canned goods, tile, and wagons and carriages. Shorenbraun Springs and Springer's Park are of interest. The mayor is elected biennially, and the council appoint or elect the administrative officials. Pop. (1910) 8,542.

From The Americana, *Scientific American, 1912*

Wheelmen in "a red hot finish," 1894. Courtesy Library of Congress,
Prints and Photographs division.

Diamond Jim Brady, and John D. Rockefeller. The League cam-
paigned for paved roads and other highway improvements. In
response, the Department of Agriculture established the Office
of Road Inquiry in order to study "the systems of road management throughout the United States, to make investigations in
regard to the best methods of road-making, and to enable [the
Secretary of Agriculture] to assist the agricultural college and
experiment stations in disseminating information on this subject." So when you ride on well-paved roads, thank a bicyclist.

I pedal down Union Avenue and other streets in order to
bypass New Philadelphia's downtown and travel to Schoenbrunn Village.

Schoenbrunn, Ohio [see inset, page 223, for further history],
was settled before Dover or New Philadelphia. Founded in 1772 by
the Moravian missionary, David Zeisberger, to teach Christianity

to Native Americans, the settlement of more than three hundred inhabitants included the first school and Christian church built in Ohio. Nicholas Cresswell, a twenty-five–year-old diarist from Derbyshire, England, visited Schoenbrunn in 1775 and noted:

> *Christianized under the Moravian Sect, it is a pretty town consisting of about sixty houses, and is built of logs and covered with Clapboards. It is regularly laid out in three spacious streets which meet in the centre, where there is a large meeting house built of logs sixty foot square covered with Shingles, Glass in the windows and a Bell, a good plank floor with two rows of forms. Adorned with some few pieces of Scripture painting.* (From the Journal of Nicholas Cresswell: 1774–1777, *Nicholas Cresswell, Dial Press, 1924.*)

League of American Wheelmen Description of Tuscarawas County Roads (1892)

In regard to the roads, etc., Mr. Charles Axx, of New Philadelphia, says:

To Canal Dover, elegant; thence to Dundee and Dundee Rocks, hilly, but good.

Canal Dover to Strasburg: level, part sandy, but in all, very good; from near Strasburg to Bolivar, rolling and fair.

To Falrfield, Mineral City and Sandyville, hard, hilly, and fine coasting.

To New Cumberland, hard, hilly, and good coasting.

To Rockford, tough—decidedly tough!

To Uhrichsville, Dennison and Newport, rolling and very fine.

To Trenton, Gnadenhutten, Port Washington and New Comerstown, elegant!

Gnadenhutten to Gilmore and Westchester, rough, tough, and N.G.!

To Yorktown, Phillipsburgh and New Comerstown, rolling, and generally fine.

To Ragersville or Shanesville, hilly, but solid; not an easy run.

To Zoar, via Canal Dover, hilly and sandy.

To Zoar Salt Well, hilly, but hard; good coasting.

We have few points of interest for the tourist, except fair country scenery.

From The Handbook of the Ohio Division L. A. W., *C. H. Thomson, 1892*

Log house at Schoenbrunn. Courtesy of Rob Matheny.

I had visited the site with my family on another occasion, so
I don't stop. From Delaware Drive, on which I now pedal, I get a
good view of the village. I turn south on 21st Street, and after I
pass over US Route 250 (us250), the road becomes Schoenbrunn
Road. I cross the Tuscarawas River again and maneuver left onto
State Route 416 (sr416), taking me south by the water.

On ride 13, the Hartville to Atwater loop, I passed very close
to the source of the Tuscarawas River. At that point, the river is no
wider than a drainage ditch. Where I now ride, the Tuscarawas is
wide enough to deserve the designation of "river." Its waters flow
into the Muskingum River, a tributary of the Ohio River, a source
of the Mississippi River that empties into the Gulf of Mexico.

I now travel a wide roadway with a very different topography.
I am in a broad flat valley, where I pedal easily, and see hills in
the distance. sr416 follows the river until the river begins to snake
its way eastward. sr416 continues due south to Tuscarawas, Ohio.

The community, also known as Tusky, has a population of fewer than a thousand people and was initially called Tuscarawas Town and later, Trenton. The town grew steadily during the canal years. I pump through the small town quickly and stop at a small park on the west side of the highway where I find the remains of an old canal lock. After I leave Tuscarawas, I pass another lock that is very close to the roadside.

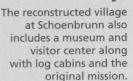

Changing Gears

The reconstructed village at Schoenbrunn also includes a museum and visitor center along with log cabins and the original mission.

www.museum.com

State Route 416 narrows and before long, I see the river again. In several places, the surrounding land is flood plain, and the roadbed had been built up to keep the area open to traffic when the river rises.

Schoenbrunn, Ohio

Schoenbrunn (Ger.: "beautiful spring"). A Moravian town, of Munsee Indians, situated about 2 m. below the site of New Philadelphia, Ohio. Zeisberger went from the station (Friedensstadt), on Beaver r., Pa., to Tuscarawas r., where the three stations of Schoenbrunn, Gnadenhuetten, and Salem were established. The Moravian Indians moved from the Beaver to these villages in 1773. The first meetinghouse and schoolhouse in the present state of Ohio were built at this station, which was also the birthplace of the first white child born within the state. The Indian village was a prosperous settlement. The Revolution brought these villages on the line between the British at Detroit and the Americans at Ft Pitt. In Aug. 1781 De Peyster, the commander at Detroit, becoming convinced that these Indians were giving information of the British movements, sent Capt. Matthew Elliott with a party of Wyandot, Delawares, and Shawnee, and a small band of French-Canadians, to remove these Indians to Sandusky, a task which they performed with great harshness, the Indians being robbed of nearly everything they had. When the Moravians were massacred at Gnadenhuetten (q.v.) in Mar. 1782, the village at Schoenbrunn was burned by the same troop of Pennsylvanians under Col. Williamson. There was also a small settlement on the opposite side of the river called New Schoenbrunn, which was established in 1779 and destroyed in 1782.

From Handbook of American Indians North of Mexico, *Government Printing Office, 1910*

The Gnadenhutten Memorial. Courtesy of Rob Matheny.

State Route 416 ends on US Route 36 (US36). I turn east, cross the river for a fourth time, and turn left onto the Gnadenhutten, Ohio, entrance ramp. Gnadenhutten, which means "Tents of Grace," was established in 1772, five month after Schoenbrunn, by Mohican Indians who had converted to Christianity under the ministry of Moravian missionary David Zeisberger.

During the American Revolution, life became difficult for the residents of Gnadenhutten because non-Christian Delawares supported England while the Christian Indians wanted to remain neutral. In 1781, British authorities ordered the Christian Delawares to abandon Gnadenhutten and relocate to northern Ohio along the Sandusky River. Facing food shortages, Zeisberger sent a group back to Gnadenhutten in March 1782 to harvest whatever crops remained in the fields. Mistakenly believing that these peaceful Indians were responsible for raids in Pennsylvania, militiamen, under the leadership of Lieutenant Colonel David Williamson attacked the village, captured the inhabitants, and then murdered them.

What became known as the "Gnadenhutten Massacre," left the village deserted for sixteen years. In 1798, John Heckewelder— one of the Moravian missionaries who had worked at Gnadenhutten—helped to restore the village. Many Pennsylvania Dutch and native Germans emigrated to the area and the town was incorporated in 1824. Today, the village is home to about 1,300 people.

After pedaling off the entrance bridge, I ride down Walnut Avenue, one of the village's two major streets. I spot my lunch

The Mallet of Gnadenhutten

Breathing the spirit of the Scalp Law, in 1782, an expedition, from Southwestern Pennsylvania, under the command of Col. David Williamson, set out, ostensibly to break up the villages of the hostile Indians on the Sandusky; but a majority of the lawless men from the frontier converted erelong the little army into a band of assassins the record of whose butcheries, summed up in the Mallet of Gnadenhutten, is the foulest blot upon the bloody page of the early history of this region—the fountainhead of the River of Blood in appalling reality. In their course lay the villages of the Moravian converts to Christianity, on the Muskingum. Where, having arrived without creating an alarm, they entrapped ninety-six men, women, and children into two houses, and deliberately butchered them as they might have killed a pack of wolves in a pen: one of the murderers taking up a cooper's mallet and knocking the heads of the old and the young, until he had killed fourteen, when, his arm failing him, he handed the weapon of death to a companion, with a word of encouragement, in God's name, to go and do likewise!

From Southwestern Pennsylvania in Song and Story, *Frank Cowan, 1878*

TENTS OF GRACE CAFÉ
120 N. Walnut Street, Gnadenhutten, OH 44629
740-254-1082
Open year-round

HOURS
Monday–Saturday: 6:30 A.M. to 9:00 P.M.
Closed Sunday

SPECIALTIES
Fried Dough, Stuffed Pepper Soup

stop, but decide to visit the Gnadenhutten Memorial site first. The site is located a few blocks from the village center and has a reconstructed church and log cabin that houses a museum. I view the monument that is made of Indian marble, and rises thirty-seven feet high. The inscription reads "Here Triumphed in Death Ninety Christian Indians. March 8, 1782."

I retrace my path to Walnut Street and enter the Tents of Grace Café. This eatery has a family-style menu. I order a Reuben sandwich and potato salad. The combination is scrumptious.

After eating, I pedal northeast on Main Street, which becomes Wolfes Crossing Road. I am still riding on a plain, surrounded by hills. I continue northeast on US36 toward Uhrichsville, a city of

Uhrichsville, Ohio

Uhrichsville is part of the area that once claimed it was the "clay center of the world" and inaugurated National Clay Week in 1951. Today, Clay Week, incorporated as the Twin City Community Projects and National Clay Week Council, Inc., is held in June. The town was established in 1804 by Michael Ulrich of Pennsylvania. The town was first called Waterford.

Editor's Note

some 5,600 people. US36 is a busy road, running along the opposite side of the Tuscarawas River from SR416, but the road is wide and creates no traffic problems. Closer to Uhrichsville, SR36 is a four-lane highway with a wide paved shoulder that allows bicycle traffic. I leave the highway at the exit for US Route 250 (US250) West, and State Route 800 (SR800) North. I maneuver on several local streets along the edge of Uhrichsville and exit the town heading northwest on Eastport Road. Beside it, I can see a tributary of the Tuscarawas River, Stillwater Creek.

A series of back roads takes me through two small hamlets: Midvale, Ohio (population 500), and Barnhill, Ohio (population 365). Midvale was platted in 1888 as a place midway between New Philadelphia and Uhrichsville. Barnhill prospered from 1880 through the early 1900s due to the rich coal deposits in the area. Barnhill, once called Pike's Run, was named for Judge Barnhill, a Tuscarawas County judge who helped the community get a post office.

I continue on Barnhill Road to Roswell, Ohio. I am now in hill county with the plains of the Tuscarawas River well behind me. Roswell is another small community (population 275) that has some prominence due to coalfields, and as a town on the railroad. I really don't see the town since my route is on SR39, which bypasses Roswell. I turn north onto Henderson School Road, a hilly, winding byway that is one of a maze of roads situated between SR39 and State Route 212 (SR212), my destination.

Somerdale, Ohio, Train Crash Report

[1898] *January 12.* Toledo and Wheeling R.P.O., train 1 was wrecked at Somerdale, Ohio, at 2.12 p.m., by running into an open switch and striking some loaded coal cars. The mail car was slightly damaged, but no injury resulted to the mail or clerk. Delayed two hours and fifteen minutes.

From Annual Reports, *United States Post Office, 1898*

When I reach SR212, I turn northwest, heading to Zoar. I pass through Somerdale, another boomtown of the coal-mining era, I jog south on SR800, pick up a back road to Zoar, and cross the Tuscarawas River again. I turn northwest on Canal Road, a quiet route that takes me to Dover Zoar Road. I cross the Tuscarawas for the sixth time and pedal on the levee to Zoar.

Zoar, Ohio

All clothing was made in the common tailor and seamstress shops, the material coming from the society's looms and mills. Cradles, baby carriages, and household furniture were made on the same patterns. To the common bakehouse and dairy some member of each family came to draw the daily portion. When cider was made, it was drawn in a cart from door to door to be distributed. Men and women alike worked in the fields when necessary. . . . Children at the age of three were taken from the parents and placed in the society's institution for children, but this plan was gradually abandoned. Attendance on the community school was compulsory, the boys going until sixteen and the girls until fifteen years of age. . . . There was no time for reading. The only amusement afforded the young people was to collect in the public garden on Sunday evenings and sing German songs.

From The Chautauquan, *Chautauqua Press, 1900.*

Ride 20
Granny's Delight

Route: Magnolia to Carrollton and back
Counties: Stark, Carroll
Terrain: Rolling to very hilly
Distance: 44 miles
Lunch: Archer's Restaurant, Carrollton (330-627-3135)
Points of Interest: Atwood Lake, Algonquin Mill Village
How to get there: Magnolia, Ohio, is located on State Route
183 (SR183). The ride starts at the Canal Park located on
Basin Street. From Interstate 77 (I-77), take the exit for State
Route 800 (SR800). Head south on SR800. Near the village
of East Sparta, turn east (left) onto Westbrook Street SE.
Turn south (right) onto Willowdale Avenue and follow it
into Magnolia. Turn west (right) onto Canal Street. Canal
Street curves and becomes Basin Street.

A friend asked me to summarize Carroll County, Ohio in a phrase. I said the county is "a tumult of hills." Since forty miles of this ride is in Carroll County and the portion in Stark County includes the incredibly steep Grovedell Hill, I have named this ride "Granny's Delight." Getting personally acquainted with the region's peaks will force you to shift down into the low, low "granny" gear repeatedly.

I start in Magnolia, Ohio (population one thousand), a community founded in 1834 by Richard Elson, who built a flour mill on the Sandy & Beaver Canal. Elson had travelled in the south and gave the name of the flowering tree to the town and his brand of flour. The mill is still standing and now operates as a feed mill. An impressive three-and-a-half story structure painted barn red, the mill was owned by members of Elston's family from 1834 until 2005. The Stark County Park District now owns the property, but the mill produces corn meal, animal feed, and various crop seeds.

My friend Wayne Ostrander is joining me on this ride. At seventy-three, Wayne is eleven years older than me, but I know I will be struggling to keep up. A retired United Methodist minister, Wayne rides forty-mile stints, three times a week, and does so every week. Youthfully trim, Wayne thankfully curtails his speed when we ride together.

We drive to Magnolia in my truck and park next to Canal Park on Basin Street, south of the old mill. The mill and most of Magnolia are located in Stark County, but about a quarter of the village is in Carroll County. Canal Park straddles both counties.

Wayne and I head east out of town on County Highway 23 (CH23). CH23 begins as Carrollton Street in Magnolia, and outside of town, first becomes Morges Road and then Batchelor Road. At the top of the first rise, we stop and take in the entire, verdant expanse.

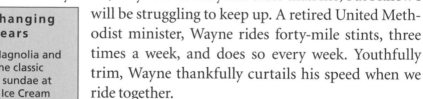

Changing Gears

Stop in Magnolia and stay for the classic "Bittner" sundae at Taggart's Ice Cream Parlor in the Historic Isaac Miller Inn located across from Canal Park.

The large, hilly slopes of the Sandy & Beaver Canal Dam near Canal Park make for excellent sled riding on a crisp winter day.

Courtesy of Kaitlin Trushel

Magnolia Mill, Stark County, Ohio. Courtesy of Aviva Bowman.

We travel over the modest rises and falls of Batchelor Road and come to Morges, Ohio, a tiny settlement on a hilltop surrounded by lush farmland. The focal point of the community is the high-steepled St. Mary's Catholic Church. We turn south at the crossroad, just before the church, and pedal down Bark Road.

Bark Road is an excellent example of the variation in terrain on the ride. During our more than five-mile stretch on the road, several upgrades are "hilly" but not "extreme" and they do not require us to downshift before reaching the top. The series of hills is like unevenly spaced ocean waves rolling toward shore. We pedal vigorously to the top of each crest, glide swiftly to the bottom of the dips and let our momentum carry us partially up the next hill. We pound the pedals, sometimes standing up out of the saddle, to carry our momentum forward to reach the top of each upgrade without shifting to low gears. Along Bark Road, we are treated to hills and dales, tidy barns, fields with crops, and tree farms with acres of evergreens, a sight we would continue to see.

On one of the rare flat stretches, Rose Road, a gravel lane, crosses Bark Road. Union Valley Cemetery sits at the northeast corner of the intersection. A flat, empty space on which a church once stood is adjacent to the graveyard. Many older cemeteries in Ohio started as churchyards where the faithful were interred. Until recently, independent and community cemeteries were rare. For many church members, being buried within the borders of sanctified ground—the center of worship life—linked the generations in their belief.

The church, a Methodist one, was closed in 1988, sold and moved to Sherrodsville, Ohio, another community in Carroll County, where it now houses a craft business.

Wayne and I soon come to the end of Bark Road near Atwood Lake, a body of water created in 1937 when the Army Corps of Engineers built an earthen dam on Indian Fork Creek for flood control, recreation, and fish and wildlife management. The lake covers some 1,540 acres and has two marinas. We turn left on State Route 542 (SR542), a route that takes us along the lake's shoreline, across a bridge at the lake's eastern end, and roll into the village of Dellroy, Ohio. Compared with Dellroy's population of fewer than three hundred people, Magnolia looks large.

State Route 542 and State Route 39 (SR39) cross in the middle of Dellroy. The community caters to visitors who come to the area to use the lake, vacation in the lakeside cabins, or stay in the lodge that is part of the Atwood Lake Resort. As an advertisement

The Atwood Dam

The Atwood Dam is a rolled-earth fill with impervious core, 65 feet high, 3,700 feet long, with a top width of 30 feet, and a base width of 360 feet.

From U.S. Army Corps of Engineers

Sailing on Atwood Lake. Courtesy of Harry Wilson.

notes, you "can lose yourself and find yourself at the exact same time in our lush setting overlooking beautiful Atwood Lake."

Wayne and I turn away from the lake and head east on SR39. This state highway is not heavily traveled and presents no problems for cyclists. We stay on the road for less than two miles and turn south onto Cactus Road—a quieter byway—so quiet in fact, I hear only my own grunting as I labor up the grade. Wayne pulls away from me as he ascends and graciously waits for me at the top.

We pedal along Cactus Road to Antigua Road, which runs along a high ridge. In this section of Ohio, the flats are from nine hundred to a thousand feet above sea level and the ridge we are riding on is around 1,200 feet. The characteristics of the elevation, however, give it an alpine feel. The foreground is populated with acres of evergreens. There are native trees in the distance, and the whole area looks windswept. Also, the first house we see has brown wood siding and a green roof, a dwelling similar to those found in a Swiss town. Antigua Road has climbs steep enough to make Wayne and me work to get to several summits.

We veer right onto Canyon Road at a "Y" intersection and begin the long run down from the ridge. We pass a farm where cattle are grazing on the steep hillside. Finished descending, we continue on a level section of Canyon Road, to Petersburg, Ohio, a spot in the valley where Canyon Road crosses State Route 332 (SR332).

Petersburg was platted in 1867, but the plat was never recorded. A mill built by George Tope around 1826 on the McGuire Fork of Conotton Creek brought business to the area. The Algonquin Mill, in operation until 1938, is the anchor of the Algonquin Mill Complex, which includes many representative build-

Wickliff Fry of Dellroy, Ohio

This claim arises by reason of the loss of a horse by Wickliff Fry, the claimant, who resided at Dellroy, Ohio, who had by written contract hired the same to the United States Geological Survey, wherein claimant was to deliver this horse to the agents of the Government, contract providing feed and stabling of outfit, shoeing, and ordinary repairs away from the stable to be paid for by the United States Geological Survey, and the horse was hired at a fixed rate per day. . . . On the 19th day of July, 1910, Mr. Charles C. Bonnell and Mr. W. S. S. Johnson, in charge of the said survey work, took the horse . . . then tied the horse to a willow tree, leaving him hitched to the buggy. This was about 7:30 in the morning, and left him there unattended while they performed their work, and returning to this place about 11:30 o'clock . . . when they returned they found the horse dead. . . . [T]he Department of the Geological Survey, acting upon the unsworn statements of the two employees of the Government, refused to make payment of this bill and recommended that the matter be taken up in Congress . . . your committee has concluded that the bill be reported favorably, but in view of the conflicting statements have recommended that the amount as asked in the bill, to wit, $185, be stricken out and that $135 be substituted . . . and that the bill do pass.

From United States Congressional Serial Set, *Government Printing Office, 1912*

Algonquin Mill. Courtesy of the Carroll County Historical Society.

ings of that earlier era, including a small railroad depot (Watheys Station), a stagecoach inn, several houses and cabins, and a one-room schoolhouse.

Wayne and I dismount, look around the grounds, and meet John Miday, the current miller. Mr. Miday tells us about the mill and identifies buildings that have been moved to the site. He is preparing for the Algonquin Mill Fall Festival, an annual three-day craft and pioneer-style event held during the second weekend of October as a fundraiser for the Carroll County Historical Society.

After our visit, we continue on Canyon Road and pedal up the steep, granny-gear climb out of Petersburg. The effort coupled with the heat causes me to warm quickly, but I do not have to stop. (Note: I pay attention to my body temperature. I have ridden my bicycle across America. When pedaling in summer over the mountains of the far West, I stopped to cool down after getting overheated. I learned if I didn't, my energy was deplet-

Changing Gears

The Algonquin Mill Fall Festival features two working steam engines that display the lumber-cutting techniques of earlier days.

Courtesy of Kaitlin Trushel

ed much sooner in the day and the rest of the day's trek became a grim struggle.) On the top of the ridge, we roll by farms and well-maintained homes, both new and old. The natural beauty and vista add to the pleasure of the ride. We pass the white-frame Mount Pleasant Church. Obviously, others have noted the pleasant view, too.

We drop into the valley on Canyon Road and see four huge metal towers strung with power lines. We turn north onto Alamo Road, glide down long descents, and pedal up steep inclines. After a few roller-coaster miles, Alamo Road becomes 3rd Street SE in Carrollton, Ohio, the county seat of Carroll County. Carrolton is a village of about 3,200 residents, but its bustling nature makes it feel larger.

We turn right onto South Lisbon Street and pedal into the southern end of the public square in Carrollton. The courthouse is on our right. The structure was built in 1885 out of Berea sandstone and replaces a smaller one built in 1835. The bell from the original courthouse, cast in 1842, is now in the square.

Carrollton was laid out in 1815 as Centreville and was located in Columbiana County. Centreville was about the same dis-

Carrollton, Ohio

The present Wheeling & Lake Erie Railroad had its origin in Carrollton, Ohio, and is the outgrowth of the primitive road organized in 1849 by John Arbuckle, Gen. Henry A. Stidger, Hon. Isaac Atkinson, John Riley, James M. Davis, John B. Moody and others, known as the Carroll County Railroad. Town and township bonds and private stock subscription to the amount of $40,000 put the Carroll County Railroad in operation. The road extended from Carrollton to Oneida, a distance of ten miles, where it connected with the Sandy & Beaver Canal and the Sandy Valley branch of the Cleveland & Wellsville Railroad, now the Cleveland & Pittsburgh Division of the Pennsylvania Lines. The first steps toward organizing the road were taken in 1849, and on May 24, 1852, the first train was run into Carrollton.

From The Railway Library, Gunthorp-Warren Printing Company, 1916

ARCHER'S RESTAURANT
100 Public Square, Carrolton, OH 44615
330-627-3135
Open year-round

HOURS
Monday–Saturday: 7:00 A.M. to 2:00 P.M.
Sunday: 8:00 A.M. to 1:00 P.M.

SPECIALTIES
Potato Pancakes, Sausage Gravy and Biscuits

tance from Lisbon, New Philadelphia, Canton, and Steubenville, Ohio, and was a convenient stopover for stagecoach passengers or travelers on horseback. Carroll County came into existence in late 1832 as a conglomeration of lands from five existing counties, with Centreville as the county seat. Less than a month later, in January 1833, the Ohio legislature passed an act changing the new county seat's name to Carrollton, in honor of Charles Carroll, the last surviving signer of the Declaration of Independence. Carroll died six months later at the age of ninety-six.

Across from the courthouse is Archer's Restaurant, our lunch stop. I order the meatloaf dinner, and Wayne orders the ham dinner and asks the waitress to substitute applesauce for the usual side of potatoes and gravy.

When our salads arrive, Wayne volunteers to offer a mealtime prayer. In it, he not only thanks God for the food, but also for the privilege of being in the outdoors, of having adventures, of seeing new places, and of being with a friend. Exactly what cycling is all about.

After eating, we visit the restored McCook house, a brick structure built in 1837 as a home and store by Daniel McCook. The home, operated by the Ohio Historical Society, is a memori-

Washington, D.C. Maj. Gen Alexander M. McCook (center) and staff on porch of quarters, 1864. Courtesy Library of Congress, Prints and Photographs Division.

al to the "Fighting McCooks," a nickname given to Major Daniel McCook and his nine sons and six nephews because of their participation in the armed services of their country prior to, and especially during, the Civil War. Fourteen of the McCooks became officers. Four of them died in service to their country.

New Harrisburg, Ohio

New Harrisburg is a small village five miles northwest of Carrollton, and which in 1883 contested with it for the county-seat. This was the birthplace of Jonathan Weaver, bishop of the United Brethren church and president of Otterbein University. The village has 1 Presbyterian, 1 Christian church, and about 200 inhabitants. In the little churchyard adjoining the town, "in a valley of dry bones, amid the silent monuments of death and desolation," is a marble slab, twelve by eighteen inches, bearing the simple inscription as annexed*: a remarkable instance of longevity.

*Jonathan Lewis. Aged 104.

From Historical Collections of Ohio, *Henry Howe & Son, 1891.*

We climb back on our bikes and pump through the square onto North Lisbon Street. As we pass through town, we notice two adjacent establishments, Sweeney's furniture store and the Sweeney Dodds funeral home. A furniture emporium and funeral home partnership was once common in many communities. In an early era, when a coffin was needed, people went to the local furniture maker, a craftsman who had the lumber and skill to make the casket. The arrangement progressed and the furniture maker eventually became the funeral director, too. (Note: Sweeney's furniture store closed in 2008.)

We take village streets and a short stretch on busy Canton Road to the edge of the village. We turn left on Bacon Road and follow its undulating path to New Harrisburg, a very small village on State Route 171 (SR171). The hamlet has two churches, several houses, and a convenience store appropriately named "The Little's Store." New Harrisburg once vied with Carrollton for the

---

The Fighting McCooks

The Ohio McCooks acquired a wide popular reputation during the civil war as the "Fighting McCooks." In the various current notices of them they are spoken of as one family, but were really two families, the sons of Major Daniel McCook and Dr. John McCook. Of the former family there were engaged in military service the father, Major Daniel McCook, Surgeon Latimer A. McCook, General George W. McCook, Major-General Robert L. McCook, Major-General A. McD. McCook, General Daniel McCook, Jr., Major-General Edwin Stanton McCook, Private Charles Morris McCook, Colonel John J. McCook—ten in all. Another son, Midshipman J. James McCook, died in the naval service before the rebellion.

Of the latter family there were engaged in the service Major-General Edward M. McCook, General Anson G. McCook, Chaplain Henry C. McCook, Commander Roderick S. McCook, U.S.N., and Lieutenant John J. McCook—five in all. This makes a total of fifteen, every son of both families, all commissioned officers except Charles, who was killed in the first battle of Bull Run, and who declined a commission in the regular army, preferring to serve as a private volunteer.

From Historical Collections of Ohio, *Henry Howe & Son, 1891*

county seat. The quiet atmosphere of New Harrisburg clearly shows the outcome.

We continue on back roads, successively Arrow, Bronze, and Avalon Roads, to Malvern, Ohio. All three roads include residential homes, a smattering of farms, and stretches of undisturbed scrubland and woods. Prior to modern transportation, Carroll County and its surroundings were not easily accessible. Thanks to the now-paved roads, Wayne and I wheel along, slowed only by the upgrades.

A long downhill run on Avalon Road brings us to Malvern (population 1,200). At the village boundary, Avalon Road changes to Carrollton Street. We turn left onto Porter Street.

Malvern started as two separate villages—Lodi (now the southeastern part of Malvern) and Troy, platted in 1834 by William Hardesty. Wayne and I come in from the south and find a traditional main street (Porter Street) with residences at both ends and on side streets. The town has a typical small Midwestern-community look. On a previous ride, I entered Malvern from the north, a part of town that is almost entirely residen-

Lewis Vail

We have digressed a little here for the honor of the family. We will return to the line of direct interest. Davis Vail's second son, Lewis Vail, was a civil engineer who early in the last century settled in Ohio, at that time a Western wilderness. Here he built canals, highways, bridges, dams—doing a pioneer's share in the reconstruction of the world.

Among the children of Lewis Vail was the second Davis Vail. Born, 1811, in Ohio, he came as a youth to Morristown, where for a time he studied medicine, then entered his uncle's manufacturing plant, the Speedwell Iron Works, to learn the trade. Here he remained until 1834; on November 27th of that year he married Phebe Quinby, daughter of Judge Isaac Quinby of Parsippany, and returned with her to Ohio where he established an ironworks on his own account

From One Man's Life: Being Chapters from the Personal & Business Career of Theodore N. Vail, *Harper & Brothers, 1921*

A portrait of David Bates Douglass, who did survey work for the Sandy & Beaver Canal and later was president of Kenyon College from 1840– 1844. Greenslade Special Collections and Archives, Kenyon College, Gambier, Ohio. Used By Permission

tial, with tree-lined streets, churches, a school, but no designated downtown. The two segments are of approximately the same size, joined only by one street that crosses at a bridge, and are not directly across from each other, but situated like two dominoes matched on a common number.

The construction of the Sandy & Beaver Canal determined Malvern's geography. In 1816, William Hardesty built a sawmill north of Sandy Creek and later platted the town of Troy. In 1836,

Portrait of General Anthony Wayne. Courtesy Library of Congress, Prints and Photographs Division.

a portion of the town, now called Malvern, was partitioned into thirty-three lots by Lewis Vail and John Reed, because the canal, including a toll station, was to be built through the area. Lodi, established in 1836 by James Reed and William E. Russell, was situated on the left bank of the Beaver Creek halfway between Minerva and Waynesburg. Initial maps showed the town as part of the canal route. In 1845, the new canal engineer, Milnor Roberts, changed the canal's path and bypassed Lodi. When the canal brought prosperity to Malvern, the town annexed Lodi.

Wayne and I stay on the south side of the village, pass through the small business district, and roll out of town on Morges Road. (Though the name of the road is the same, the road is not the related to the one in Magnolia.) Morges Road becomes Citrus Road, a path leading through a part of Carroll County that has not been extensively developed. We pedal past thick woods and make our way uphill. By this point, my climbing is labored, but Wayne does well and waits at the crest until I catch him. The ascent takes us out of Carroll County and into Stark County. We speed down a steep decline and wheel onto State Route 171 (SR171) into the east end of Waynesburg, Ohio (population one thousand).

Changing Gears

If you would like an alternate option for lunch or want to grab an early dinner, stop in Waynesburg at Cibo's Italian Restaurant, in a beautifully restored theater. If especially hungry, go for the "Mixed Plate."

Courtesy of Kaitlin Trushel

Waynesburg was platted in 1814 by Joseph Handlon and incorporated in 1833. The town prospered in the canal building days. A warehouse for shipped goods and general store were run by the town's first mayor, Robert K. Gray. He was also the proprietor of the grist mill and the town's tavern. The town was named for General Anthony Wayne, whose eighteenth-century accomplishments at the Battle of Fallen Timbers made him popular.

Battle of Fallen Timbers

The Battle of Fallen Timbers, fought on August 20, 1794, is one of the most significant events relating to post-Revolutionary War America. Major General "Mad" Anthony Wayne led the Federal Army, known as The Legion of the United States against a confederacy of Native Americans led by Miami Chief Little Turtle and Shawnee war chief Blue Jacket. Defeat in battle and lack of help from their nearby British allies disheartened the tribes and lead to the 1795 Treaty of Greenville. The Treaty secured United States control of the Northwest Territory and ultimately resulted in the formation of five new states—Ohio, Indiana, Michigan, Illinois, and Wisconsin.

From Ohio State Marker (Battle of Fallen Timbers) located in Maumee, Ohio

Pedaling to Lunch

We pedal through town to Grovedell Street, a fitting end to Granny's Delight. Grovedell Street is a monster climb with four inclines. Wayne and I climb the first two hills without much problem. The third hill is a supreme challenge for me. I shift to my lowest gear and stay completely focused to avoid rolling backward near the pinnacle. I rest at the top, where Wayne has been waiting for me, and gladly take in the stunning view. We glide down the slope picking up enough speed to get to the final peak with ease. We stay on Grovedell to Willowdale Road and pedal the final mile to Magnolia.

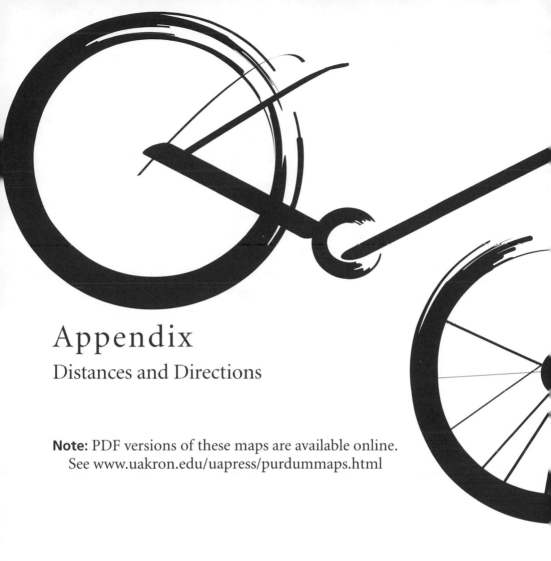

Appendix
Distances and Directions

Note: PDF versions of these maps are available online.
See www.uakron.edu/uapress/purdummaps.html

Ride 1

Miles	Directions
0.0	Leave Fairport Harbor Lakefront Park, heading south on High Street
0.1	Turn left onto Second Street
0.5	Turn right onto East Street
0.9	Turn left onto Fairport Nursery Road (SR535)
4.1	Turn left onto Blase-Nemeth Road
4.7	Cross Bacon Road; continue on Blase-Nemeth Road
5.7	Turn left onto North Ridge Road/US20
6.5	Turn left onto Lane Road
7.3	Turn right onto Niagara Avenue
7.5	Turn left onto Blackmore Road
8.2	Turn right onto Clark Road
8.9	Turn left onto Perry Park Road
9.3	Enter Perry Park; follow road to lakefront and back out of park
9.6	Turn left onto Parmly Road
11.4	Turn left onto North Ridge Road/US20
12.3	Turn left onto Antioch Road
13.9	Cross Lockwood Road, enter Lakeshore Reservation and turn right on park drive
14.1	Enter parking lot
14.1	Return to park entrance
14.3	Turn left onto Lockwood Road
15.7	Turn left onto McMackin Road
16.3	Turn right onto Chapel Road
16.6	Turn left into Bill Stanton Community Park and follow park drive to lake and back out of park
17.0	Turn left onto Chapel Road
18.3	Turn left onto Red Bird Road
19.2	Turn right onto Lake Road
20.0	Madison Township Park
20.9	Turn left onto Bennett Road

Miles Directions

Miles	Directions
21.5	Turn right onto Lake Road
22.5	Turn left onto Dock Road
22.9	Turn right into Arcola Creek Park
22.9	Exit park, turning left onto Dock Road
23.4	Turn left onto Cashen Road
23.7	Turn left onto County Line Road
24.5	Turn right onto Lake Road
25.0	Enter Geneva State Park; continue on Lake Road
27.2	Turn left onto SR534
28.1	Turn right with SR534 onto Lake Road; SR534 ends shortly thereafter; continue on Lake Road, which is now also SR531
28.9	Lunch, Sunrise Café
28.9	Head west on Lake Road/SR531; where SR531 ends, continue on Lake Road, which is now also SR534
29.9	Turn left with SR534
30.6	Turn right onto Lake Road
33.4	Turn left onto County Line Road
34.2	Turn right onto Cashen Road
34.5	Turn left onto Dock Road
37.5	Cross North Ridge Road/US20 onto Arcola Road
38.3	Turn right onto Middle Ridge Road
39.7	Cross SR528; continue on Middle Ridge Road
45.0	Turn left onto Center Road
46.1	Turn right onto Main Street, which becomes Narrows Road
48.4	Turn left onto North Ridge Road
48.6	Turn right onto Blase-Nemeth Road
49.5	Cross Bacon Road; continue on Blase-Nemeth Road
50.3	Turn right onto Fairport Nursery Road (SR535)
53.4	Turn right onto East Street
53.8	Turn left onto Second Street
54.2	Turn right onto High Street
54.3	Enter Fairport Harbor Lakefront Park

Pedaling to Lunch

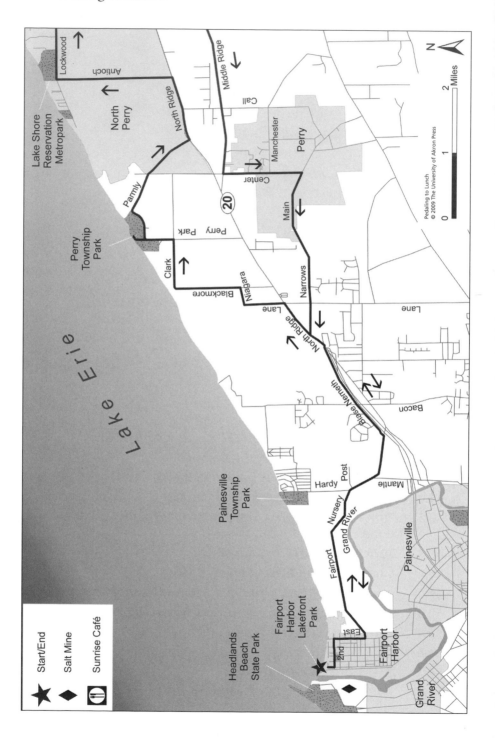

Start/End

Salt Mine

Sunrise Café

Ride 1, Map 2

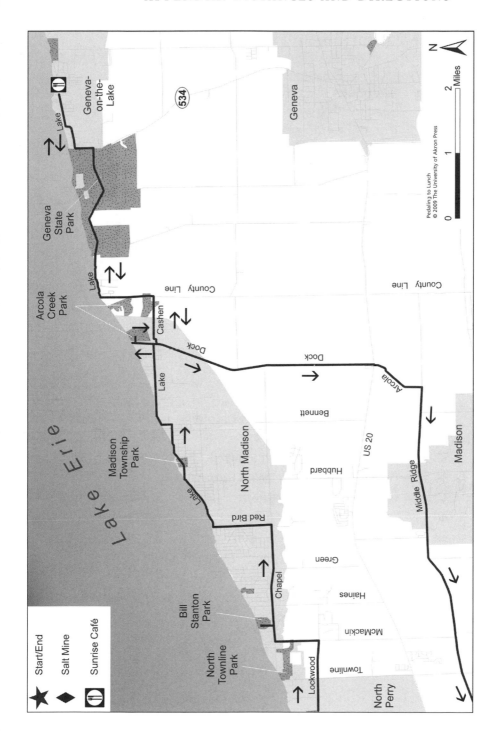

Lake Erie

Arcola Creek Park

Geneva State Park

Geneva-on-the-Lake

Geneva

534

County Line

County Line

Cashen

Dock

Dock

Arcola

Lake

Bennett

US 20

Madison

North Madison

Hubbard

Middle Ridge

Madison Township Park

Red Bird

Green

Haines

Bill Stanton Park

Chapel

McMackin

North Townline Park

Lockwood

Townline

North Perry

N

Pedaling to Lunch
© 2009 The University of Akron Press

0   1   2
Miles

Start/End
Salt Mine
Sunrise Café

Ride 2 (Starting and Ending in Kinsman)

Miles	Directions
0.00	Head north from Kinsman square on SR7
1.9	Turn right onto Kinsman-Pymatuning Road
4.8	Turn left onto Ward North Road
5.2	Turn right on Stanhope-McCormick Road; then follow curve left onto Simons South Road
7.6	Cross US322, continue on Simons South Road
8.5	Turn right on Slater Road
8.7	Follow curve left on Pymatuning Lake Road
10.4	Go straight onto park road
11.7	Turn right onto Pymatuning Lake Road
13.3	Cross SR85
20.7	Turn right onto US6
20.9	Turn left onto Creek Road
24.1	Turn right onto Marcy Road
25.5	Turn left onto Middle Road
26.4	Cross SR167 [note: At Beckwith/Rick Road (345), Middle Road makes a short jog west as it heads north.]
33.3	Turn right onto SR84
33.9	Turn left onto Furnace Road
39.2	Turn left onto US20 (Main Street)
40.2	Turn left onto State Street
40.3	Lunch, State Street Diner
40.3	Head north on Broad Street
42.0	Turn left into Port Authority beach parking lot
42.0	Head south on Broad Street
43.8	Turn right onto Main Street
44.5	Merge left onto US20
44.9	Turn left onto Center Street, which becomes Center Road

Miles	Directions
46.1	Turn left onto Gateway Avenue
46.3	Turn right onto SR7
47.0	Turn right onto Underridge Road
47.2	Turn left onto Center Road
48.6	Merge right onto SR7
49.2	Turn right onto Hatches Corners Road
51.6	Turn right onto State Road to north end of covered bridge
51.8	Turn around on State Road and head south
53.5	Cross SR84 (at some point after this, State Road becomes Stanhope-Kelloggsville Road, but I could not ascertain the exactly where. But by either name, it is all one road.)
55.7	Covered bridge at Root Road
59.4	Covered bridge at Graham Road (to the right of the road, in dip)
60.6	Covered bridge at Caine Road
61.4	Cross SR167
71.8	Cross US6
76.9	Cross US322
82.5	Cross SR87
83.2	Arrive Kinsman square

Ride 2 (Starting and Ending in Conneaut)

Miles	Directions
0.0	Exit Port Authority beach parking lot and head south on Broad Street
1.7	State Street Diner
1.8	Turn right onto Main Street
2.5	Merge left onto US20
2.9	Turn left onto Center Street, which becomes Center Road
4.1	Turn left onto Gateway Avenue
4.3	Turn right onto SR7
5.0	Turn right onto Underridge Road
5.2	Turn left onto Center Road
6.6	Merge right onto SR7
7.2	Turn right onto Hatches Corners Road
9.6	Turn right onto State Road to north end of covered bridge
9.8	Turn around on State Road and head south
11.5	Cross SR84 (at some point after this, State Road becomes Stanhope-Kelloggsville Road, but I could not ascertain the exactly where. But by either name, it is all one road.)
13.7	Covered bridge at Root Road
17.4	Covered bridge at Graham Road (to the right of the road, in dip)
18.6	Covered bridge at Caine Road
19.4	Cross SR167
29.8	Cross US6
34.9	Cross US322
40.5	Cross SR87
41.2	Arrive Kinsman square; proceed south on SR7
41.3	Lunch, Times Square Restaurant

Miles Directions

Miles	Directions
41.3	Head north on SR7
41.4	Proceed around Kinsman square and head north on SR7
43.3	Turn right onto Kinsman-Pymatuning Road
46.2	Turn left onto Ward North Road
46.6	Turn right on Stanhope-McCormick Road; then follow curve left onto Simons South Road
49.0	Cross US322, continue on Simons South Road
49.9	Turn right on Slater Road
50.1	Follow curve left on Pymatuning Lake Road
51.8	Go straight onto park road
53.1	Turn right onto Pymatuning Lake Road
54.7	Cross SR85
62.1	Turn right onto US6
62.3	Turn left onto Creek Road
65.5	Turn right onto Marcy Road
66.9	Turn left onto Middle Road [note: Middle Road makes a short jog east on Beckwith/Rick Road (345), as it heads south.]
67.8	Cross SR167
74.7	Turn right onto SR84
75.3	Turn left onto Furnace Road
80.6	Turn left onto US20 (Main Street)
81.5	Turn left onto State Street
81.7	Turn right on Broad Street
83.4	Turn left into Port Authority beach parking lot

Ride 2, Map 1

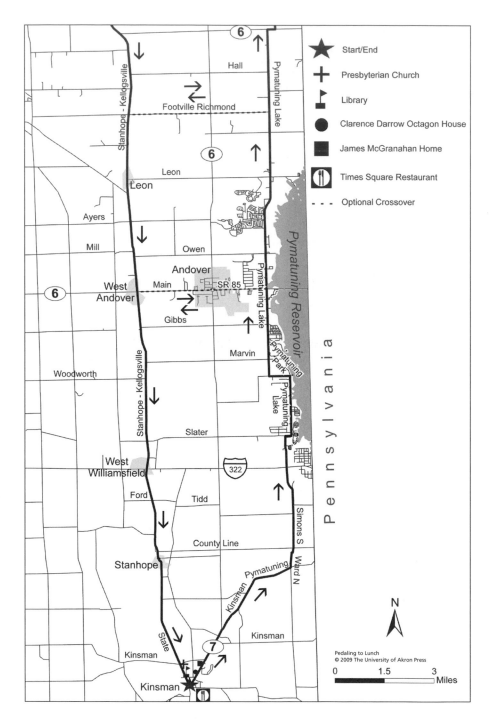

Start/End

Presbyterian Church

Library

Clarence Darrow Octagon House

James McGranahan Home

Times Square Restaurant

Optional Crossover

Pedaling to Lunch
© 2009 The University of Akron Press

0   1.5   3
Miles

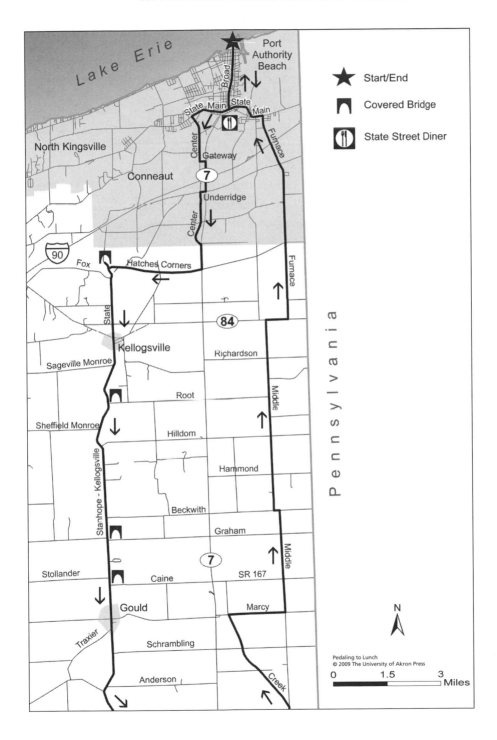

Lake Erie

Port Authority Beach

Broad

State Main State

State Main

North Kingsville

Center

Gateway

7

Conneaut

Center

Underridge

90

Fox

Furnace

Hatches Corners

84

State

Pennsylvania

Kellogsville

Richardson

Sageville Monroe

Sheffield Monroe

Root

Middle

Hilldom

Stanhope - Kellogsville

Hammond

Beckwith

Graham

Stollander

Caine

7

SR 167

Middle

Gould

Marcy

Traxier

Creek

Schrambling

Anderson

★ Start/End

▢ Covered Bridge

🍴 State Street Diner

N

Pedaling to Lunch
© 2009 The University of Akron Press

0   1.5   3
▭ Miles

255

Ride 3

Miles	Directions
0.0	Head north on SR534 (mileage started at south end of Mesopotamia Commons at SR87)
4.0	Octagon house
5.5	Cross US322; go straight onto Noble Road
6.5	Turn right onto New Hudson Road
7.5	Turn left onto Winsor-Mechanicsville Road
11.3	Cross US6, continue on Winsor-Mechanicsville Road
15.2	Turn right onto Footville-Richmond Road
17.8	Enter Rock Creek; Footville-Richmond Road becomes Water Street
18.2	Turn right on Main Street/SR45
18.2	Lunch. Pasta Oven is on the west side of Main Street
18.2	Head south on Main Street/SR45
18.6	Turn left onto Rome-Rock Creek Road
19.6	Follow Rome-Rock Creek Road as it turns south
21.1	Turn left onto Callender Road
21.4	Turn right onto continuation of Rome-Rock Creek Road
23.1	Turn left onto Lunar Lane and continue around the park, where Lunar Lane resumes
23.4	Turn right onto Evening Star Drive
23.9	Cross US6, continue straight onto Dodge Road
27.3	Turn right onto Windsor Road
27.8	Turn left onto Bogue Road
28.3	Turn right onto Hague Road
29.1	Turn right onto Staley Road
29.6	Enter Orwell
30.0	Turn right onto US322
30.3	Turn left onto Penniman Road

Miles	Directions
32.2	Turn right onto Winters Road (where road beside trail turns right)
33.2	Turn left onto SR45
33.7	Turn right onto Rice Road
34.2	Turn left onto Creaser Road
35.0	Turn right onto Flagg Road
36.0	Turn left onto Bloomfield-Geneva Road
37.1	Turn right onto Donley Road
40.5	Turn left onto SR534
41.2	Enter Mesopotamia
41.7	Arrive Mesopotamia Commons, south end

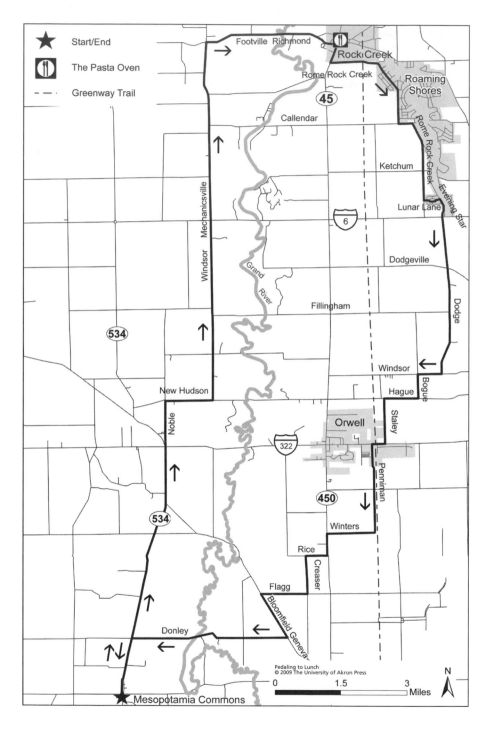

Ride 4

Miles	Directions
0.0	Leave Scenic Park Picnic Area, heading south on the All-Purpose Trail, paralleling Valley Parkway (mileage count started at entrance of the picnic area)
9.8	Cross Cedar Point Road
12.9	Berea Falls Scenic Overlook
13.4	Cross Bagley Road
14.3	Turn left onto North Quarry Lane
14.5	Turn left onto S. Rocky River Drive
14.5	Turn right onto E. Bridge Street
14.6	Lunch, Sandwich Delights
14.6	Retrace route back to Scenic Park Picnic Area
29.2	Arrive Scenic Park Picnic Area

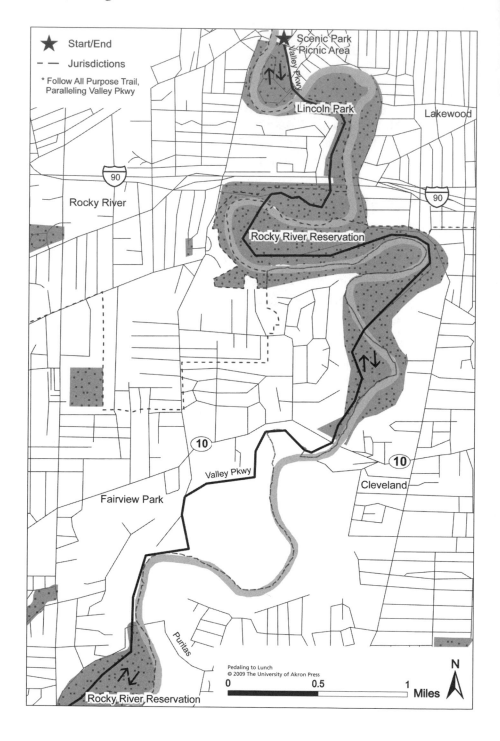

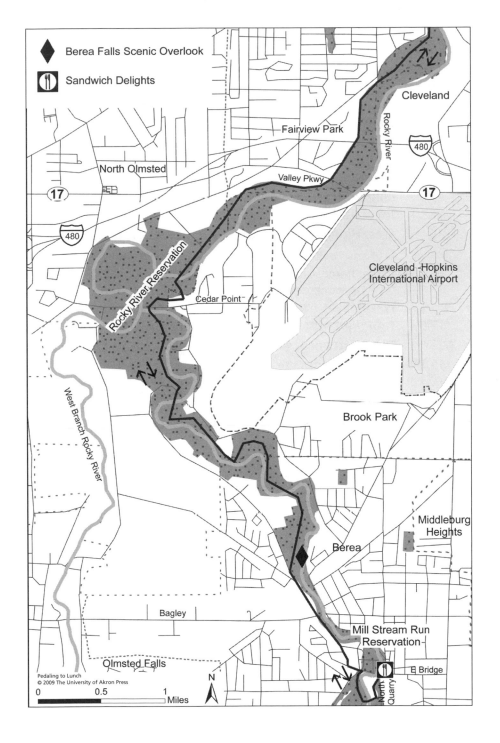

Berea Falls Scenic Overlook

Sandwich Delights

Cleveland

Fairview Park

Rocky River

480

North Olmsted

17

480

Valley Pkwy

17

Rocky River Reservation

Cleveland -Hopkins
International Airport

Cedar Point

West Branch Rocky River

Brook Park

Middleburg
Heights

Berea

Bagley

Mill Stream Run
Reservation

Olmsted Falls

Pedaling to Lunch
© 2009 The University of Akron Press

0   0.5   1
                              Miles

N

E Bridge

North Quarry

Ride 5

Miles	**Directions**
0.0	Leave Canal Visitor Center, heading south on Towpath Trail
4.5	Pass under Chippewa Road Bridge; continue on Towpath Trail
4.7	Station Road Bridge
6.4	Connector trail to Bike & Hike Trail, continue on Towpath Trail
7.2	Cross Highland Road; continue on Towpath Trail
9.1	Cross Boston Mills Road; continue on Towpath Trail
11.4	Arrive Peninsula Towpath Trail parking lot; exit parking lot, cross railroad tracks and turn left onto West Mill Street
11.6	Turn right onto North Locust Street
11.7	Turn right onto Main Street/SR303
11.7	Lunch, Fisher's Café and Pub
11.7	Head west on Main Street/SR303
12.0	Turn right onto Riverview Road
13.6	Cross Boston Mills Road; continue on Riverview Road
14.6	Turn left onto Columbia Road
16.9	Turn right onto Dewey Road
17.7	Turn left onto Snowville Road
18.8	Turn right onto Brecksville Road
19.3	Turn left onto Miller Road
20.7	Turn right onto Barr Road (road is named Townsend to the left)
21.6	Turn right onto Valley Parkway
23.1	Cross Brecksville Road; enter multi-use trail

Miles	Directions
25.0	Turn right onto Chippewa Creek Road, enter multi-use trail
25.5	Turn left onto Riverview Road
25.7	Cross Chippewa Road/SR82
28.8	Turn right onto Brookside Road
28.9	Turn right onto Pleasant Valley Road
29.5	Turn right onto Canal Road entrance
29.6	Cross Canal Road; take Fitzwater Bridge to Towpath Trail
29.7	Turn right onto Towpath Trail
31.2	Arrive at Canal Visitor Center

Pedaling to Lunch

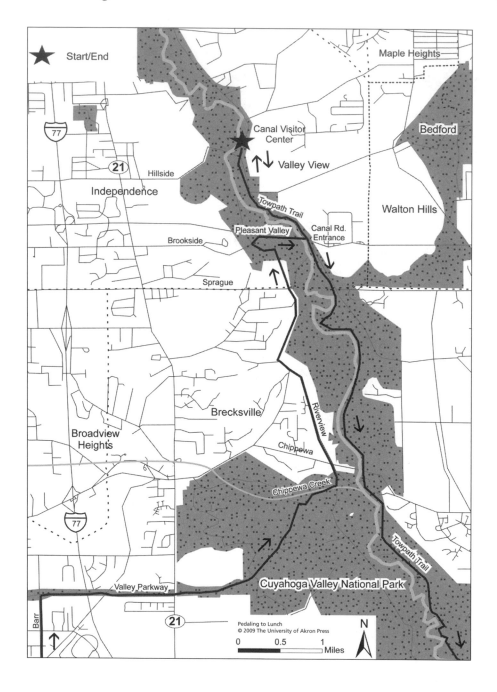

★ Start/End

Maple Heights

77

21   Hillside

Canal Visitor
Center

Bedford

Valley View

Independence

Towpath Trail

Walton Hills

Pleasant Valley

Canal Rd.
Entrance

Brookside

Sprague

Brecksville

Riverview

Broadview
Heights

Chippewa

77

Chippewa Creek

Towpath Trail

Valley Parkway

Cuyahoga Valley National Park

Barr

21

Pedaling to Lunch
© 2009 The University of Akron Press

0   0.5   1
Miles

N

264

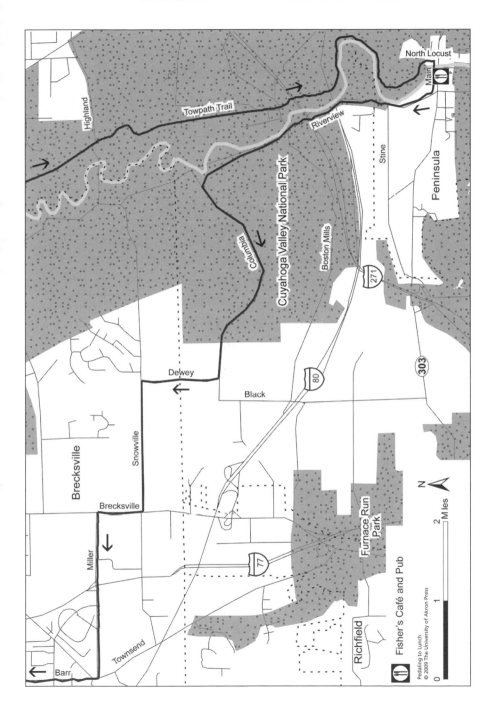

Ride 5, Map 2

North Locust

Main

Highland

Towpath Trail

Riverview

Stine

Peninsula

Cuyahoga Valley National Park

Columbia

Boston Mills

271

Dewey

Black

303

80

Brecksville

Snowville

Brecksville

Miller

Furnace Run Park

N

Miles

77

Townsend

Richfield

Fisher's Café and Pub

Barr

Pedaling to Lunch
© 2009 The University of Akron Press

0   1   2

Ride 6

Miles Directions

0.0   Leave the corner of Main Street and Prospect heading east on Prospect

0.3   Turn right onto High Street

0.9   Turn left onto Peck Road

2.1   Turn left onto Pioneer Trail

3.2   Turn sharp right onto Sheldon Road

3.2   Historic site of Mantua Glass Company

4.1   Cross SR82, continue on Sheldon Road, which eventually becomes Fox Road

8.9   Turn left onto Rapids Road

9.9   Cross US422, continue on Rapids Road

12.6   Turn right into Eldon Russell Park

13.1   Retrace route to Eldon Russell Park entrance

13.6   Turn right onto Rapids Road

16.4   Enter Burton

16.6   Turn right onto Carlton Street

17.1   Turn left onto Cheshire Street

17.4   Enter Burton Square

17.5   Lunch

17.5   Continue around Burton Square

17.8   Turn right onto Cheshire Street (SR700, SR168); when SR700 splits off, continue straight onto SR168

20.3   Bear right onto Jug Street

22.9   Jog right onto Patch Road then left onto Jug Street

24.7   Cross US422, continue on Jug Street

27.0   Turn right onto Grove Street, which becomes Allyn Road

27.9   Cross SR700, continue on Allyn Road

Miles	Directions
29.0	Enter Hiram Rapids
29.1	At west side of park bear right onto Winchell to the bridge over the river
29.2	At bridge reverse direction
29.2	Turn right on Abbot Road
29.4	When Abbot Road swings right, continue straight onto Alpha Road
31.3	Turn left onto SR82
31.5	Turn right onto Ryder Road
32.5	Turn right onto Pioneer Trail
33.4	Historic Johnson Home
34.6	Turn left onto Vaughn Road
35.7	Turn right onto Mennonite Road
36.7	Enter Mantua; Mennonite Road becomes High Street
37.2	Turn left onto Prospect Street
37.5	Arrive at Main Street

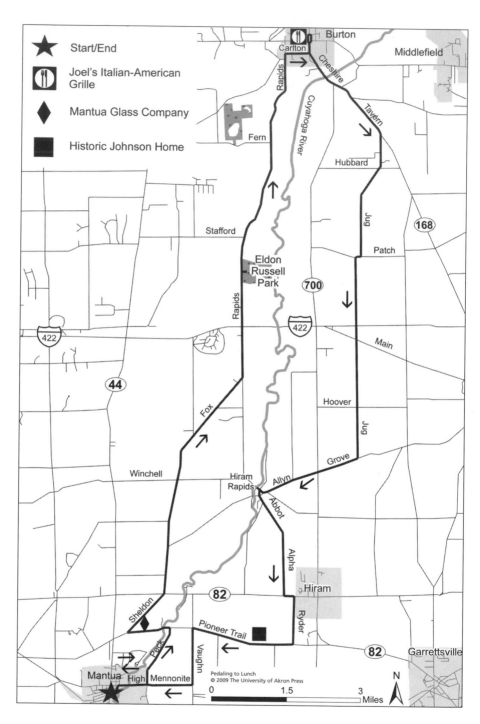

Legend:
- ★ Start/End
- 🍴 Joel's Italian-American Grille
- ◆ Mantua Glass Company
- ■ Historic Johnson Home

Ride 6

Pedaling to Lunch
© 2009 The University of Akron Press

0   1.5   3
Miles

Ride 7

Miles Directions

0.0   In Lodi, leave the village square, heading southwest on Bank Street/SR421

1.1   Turn right onto West Drive, which becomes Richman Road

2.4   Cross US224

2.5   Turn left onto Sanford Road

3.5   Turn right onto Congress Road

7.8   Cross SR162, Congress Road becomes Spencer Mills Road

10.2 Cross SR301, continue on Spencer Mills Road

11.2 Turn left onto Hunter Road

11.3 Turn right onto Bursley Road

12.4 Turn right onto Firestone Road

13.8 Turn left onto Smith Road

14.8 Turn right with Smith Road

15.6 Turn left onto Jones Road

16.2 Turn right onto Hawley Road

17.6 Turn left onto SR18

18.0 Enter Wellington; SR18 is also Herrick Avenue in Wellington

18.8 Lunch, Bread-N-Brew

18.8 Head south on Main Street/SR58

19.6 Turn left onto Cemetery Road

20.8 Turn right onto Hawley Road

22.7 Jog right onto Pratt Road, then follow curve left onto Hawley Road

25.0 Cross SR162, continue on Hawley Road

27.3 Turn left onto New London-Eastern Road

30.9 Cross SR301, continue on New London-Eastern Road

Pedaling to Lunch

Miles   Directions

Miles	Directions
33.5	Turn right onto Pawnee Road
35.1	Turn left onto Sanford Road
37.4	Turn right onto Richman Road
37.5	Cross US224; Richman Road becomes West Drive
38.7	Turn left onto Bank Street
39.8	End at Lodi village square

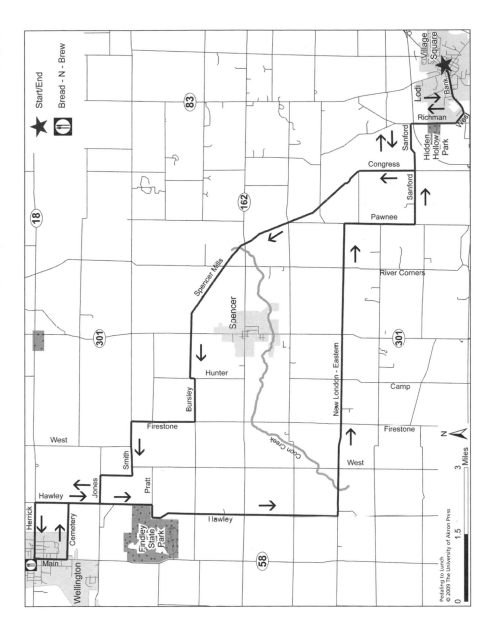

Ride 7

★ Start/End

🥖 Bread - N - Brew

N

Miles
0   1.5   3

Pedaling to Lunch
© 2009 The University of Akron Press

Ride 8

Miles	Directions
0.0	From the southeast corner of Medina Public Square, head south on Broadway Street
0.1	Turn left onto Smith Road
2.9	Turn right onto River Styx Road
3.6	Turn left onto Ridgewood Road
5.0	At junction with Windfall Road, turn right with Ridgewood Road
6.8	Turn right onto Beach Road
8.0	Turn left onto Sharon-Copley Road/SR162
9.2	Proceed halfway around Sharon Center traffic circle; continue on Sharon-Copley Road
10.2	Turn left onto State Road
13.1	Cross SR18; continue on State Road
15.1	Bear left with State Road
19.0	At Hinckley Reservation, turn left onto multi-use trail beside West Drive
20.6	Turn left onto Bellus Road
21.9	Turn right on Ridge Road/SR94
22.6	Cross SR303; turn left into Foster's Tavern parking lot
22.6	Head south on Ridge Road/SR94, retracing path to Bellus Road
23.2	Turn right onto Bellus Road
24.2	Turn left onto Stony Hill Road
24.7	Turn right onto Laurel Road
25.9	Turn left onto 130th Street
26.6	Turn right onto Sleepy Hollow Road
29.6	Cross Pearl Road; continue on Sleepy Hollow Road

Miles	Directions
31.6	At Marks Road, jog left and then right; continue on Sleepy Hollow Road
32.4	Turn left onto Muntz Road
32.8	Turn left onto Abbeyville Road
37.6	Turn left on to W. Liberty Street/SR18
39.1	Turn right with SR18 onto Elwood Street
39.2	Turn left with SR18 onto Washington Street
39.3	End at Medina Public Square

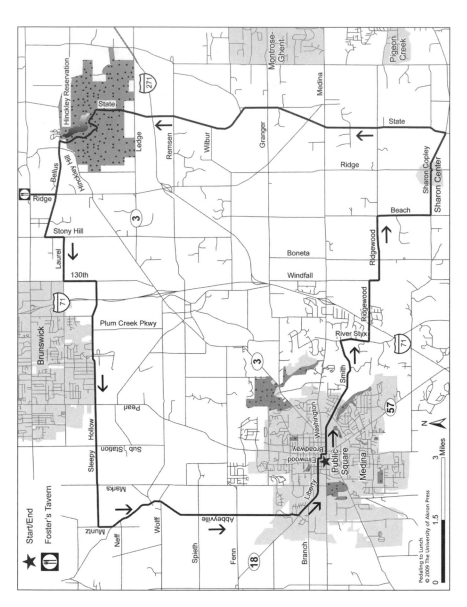

Ride 8

★ Start/End

⊖ Foster's Tavern

Pedaling to Lunch
© 2009 The University of Akron Press

N

0   1.5   3 Miles

Ride 9

Miles   Directions

0.0   Exit Havre's Woods Park, turning left onto New Milford Road

0.4   Turn right onto Main Street

0.6   Bear left onto Newton Falls Road

4.4   Cross center of Charlestown, continue on Newton Falls Road

7.3   Merge left onto SR5

8.5   Turn right onto Wayland Road

9.0   Turn left onto Newton Falls Road

11.9   Turn left with Newton Falls Road (which is McClintocksburg Road to the right), which becomes Ravenna Road

14.2   In Newton Falls; Ravenna Road becomes Church Street

14.4   Turn left on Canal Street

14.5   Turn right on Broad Street

14.8   Turn left onto River Street; view covered bridge

14.9   Reverse direction and return on River Street

15.0   Cross Broad Street, continue on River Street, which becomes River Road

19.0   Turn right onto County Line Road

19.3   Turn left onto Grandview Road

19.5   Lunch, Olde Dutch Mill Restaurant

19.5   Continue on Grandview Road, entering Craig Beach

20.2   At village park, reverse direction and return to County Line Road

21.2   Turn left onto County Line Road, which becomes Cable Line Road

25.1   Cross SR225; continue on Cable Line Road

Miles   Directions

27.5   Entrance to West Branch State Park. At curve just beyond park entrance, Cable Line Road becomes Alliance Road

28.5   Turn right onto Calvin Road

29.8   Turn left onto Porter Road

29.9   Turn right onto Hughes Road

31.1   Turn right onto Rock Spring Road

32.0   Turn left onto Cable Line Road

34.3   Turn right onto SR14

34.8   Bear left onto Hayes Road

36.1   Turn right onto New Milford Road

36.9   Cross SRs 5/44

37.1   Turn left into Havre's Woods Park

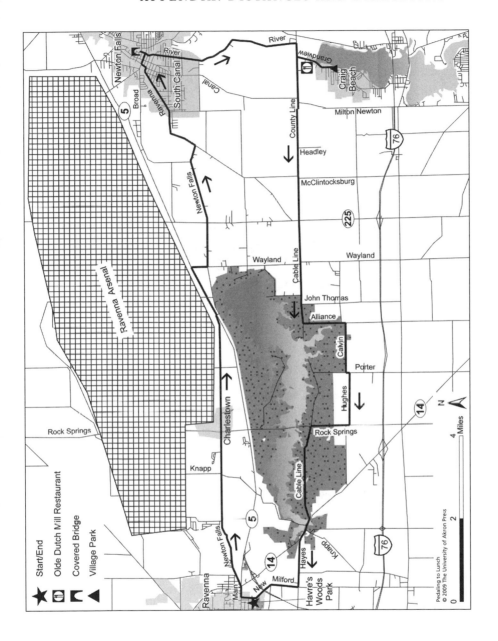

Ride 9

★ Start/End
⊞ Olde Dutch Mill Restaurant
◄ Covered Bridge
◄ Village Park

Pedaling to Lunch
© 2009 The University of Akron Press

Ride 10

Miles **Directions**

0.0 In Orrville, turn left out of Heritage Museum parking lot onto Market Street

0.9 Turn right onto Crown Hill Road

1.1 Turn left onto High Street

2.2 Turn right onto Chippewa Road

3.2 Turn left onto Smucker Road

5.5 Enter Smithville; Smucker Road becomes Center Street

5.9 Bear right onto Milton Street

6.3 Turn left onto Main Street/SR585

6.8 Turn right onto Smithville Western Road

9.9 Cross Cleveland Road/SR3; continue on Smithville–Western Road

11.2 Cross Burbank Road/SR83; continue on Smithville–Western Road

14.3 Turn right onto Overton Road

14.8 Turn left onto Cedar Valley Road

16.1 At fork, bear right with Cedar Valley Road

19.2 Turn left onto Pleasant Home Road

19.8 Turn right onto Congress Road, SR539

20.5 In Congress, turn left with SR539 onto Oak Street/SR604

20.9 Bear right with SR539 onto Congress Road/West Salem Road

22.2 Leave SR539 and continue straight onto Kline Road

24.1 Turn left onto Ruff Road

24.2 Turn right onto SR301

24.7 Enter West Salem; SR301 is also Main Street

25.6 Turn right onto East Buckeye Street/US42

26.0 Lunch, The Village Cornerstone

Miles	Directions
26.0	Exit left from restaurant and turn left immediately onto Hazel Street
26.1	Turn left onto Britton Street, which becomes Britton Road
31.7	Cross SR83; continue on Britton Road
34.8	Turn right onto Canaan Center Road
36.9	Cross SR604 at Canaan; continue on Canaan Center Road
38.9	Turn left onto Pleasant Home Road
40.3	Cross SR3; continue on Pleasant Home Road
41.0	Turn right onto Geyers Chapel Road
41.9	Jog right onto Fulton Road and then left onto the continuation of Geyers Chapel Road
43.5	Turn left onto Hutton Road
44.5	Jog left onto Honeytown Road and then right onto Hutton Road
46.4	Turn right onto Apple Creek Road
46.9	Cross SR585 and then immediately turn left onto Five Points Road
47.2	Turn right onto Crown Hill Road
52.3	Turn left onto Market Street
53.3	Turn right into Heritage Museum parking lot

Ride 10

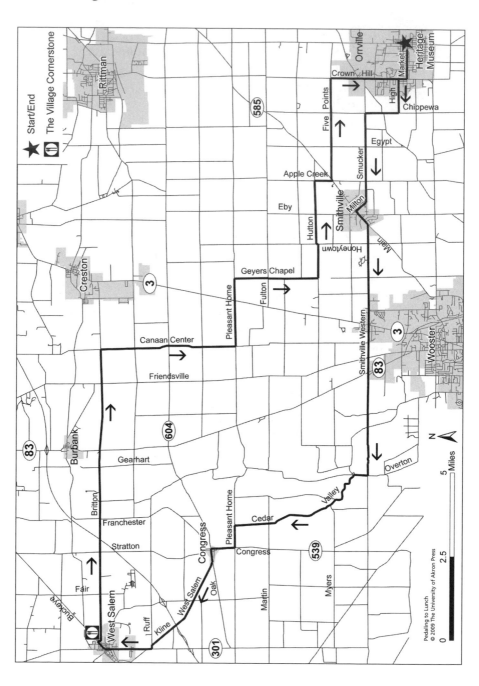

Start/End

The Village Cornerstone

Orrville

Heritage Museum

Crown Hill

Market

High

Chippewa

Five Points

585

Egypt

Smucker

Apple Creek

Eby

Smithville

Milton

Hutton

Honeytown

Main

Geyers Chapel

Fulton

3

Creston

Pleasant Home

Canaan Center

Smithville Western

Friendsville

3

Wooster

604

83

Burbank

Gearhart

83

Britton

Overton

Franchester

Congress

Pleasant Home

Valley

Stratton

Cedar

Fair

West Salem

Congress

539

Buckeye

West Salem

Oak

Myers

West Salem

Martin

Kline

Ruff

N

301

Miles

Pedaling to Lunch
© 2009 The University of Akron Press

0   2.5   5

Ride 11

Miles   Directions

Miles	Directions
0.0	Turn right out of Towpath lot onto North Street
0.1	Turn right onto Main Street
0.2	Turn right onto Cleveland-Massillon Road
0.3	Turn left onto Clinton Road
1.8	Cross Route 21
2.6	Turn right onto Hametown Road
2.8	Turn left onto Clinton Road
4.1	Enter Doylestown,
4.8	Cross Portage Street
5.0	Turn left onto Cleveland Street
5.1	Turn right onto Collier Drive
5.6	Collier Drive becomes Doylestown Road
7.1	Cross Mt. Eton Road (Route 94)
8.5	Cross Route 57
8.8	Cross Ohio Avenue, Doylestown Road becomes Sunset Drive
9.7	Cross Main Street; Sunset Drive eventually becomes Doylestown Road
13.8	Turn left onto Seville Road
14.3	Enter Sterling
14.7	Bradley's Restaurant
14.7	Continue south on Seville Road
15.5	Cross Sterling Road
16.6	Turn left onto Easton Road (Route 604)
17.0	Turn right onto Apple Creek Road
18.0	Turn left onto Steiner Road
21.0	Turn right onto Benner Road
22.0	Cross Route 585
23.0	Turn left onto Fulton Road
24.1	Cross Route 57
25.1	Enter Marshallville

Miles	Directions
25.6	Turn right onto Main Street
25.7	Turn left onto Market Street, which becomes Fulton Road
30.3	Turn left onto Deerfield Avenue
31.7	Enter Clinton; Deerfield Avenue becomes 2nd Street
32.7	Veer right onto Hickory Street
33.2	Turn right onto Main Street
33.2	Turn left onto North Street
33.4	Turn left into Towpath parking lot

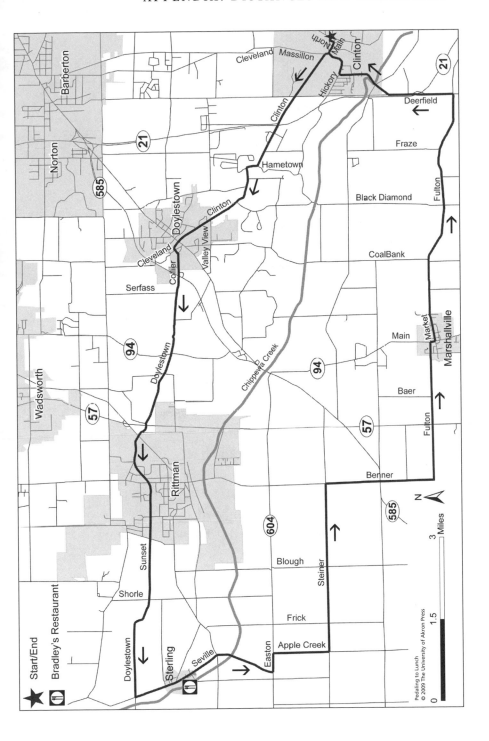

Ride 12

Miles	Directions
0.0	Leave Nimisila Campground parking lot heading east on the park drive
0.4	Turn right onto Christman Road
2.5	Turn right onto Stoner Road
3.5	Turn left onto Comet Road
5.6	Turn right onto Manchester Road/SR93
5.9	Turn left onto Comet Road
8.6	Enter Clinton
9.4	Cross Van Buren Road, Comet Road becomes North Street
9.5	Turn right into Towpath Trailhead, proceed north onto Towpath Trail
11.1	Cross Center Road; continue on Towpath Trail
13.3	Turn right onto Vanderhoof Road
14.3	Turn right onto Grove Road
14.8	Turn left onto Johns Road
16.2	Turn right onto Manchester Road/SR93
16.3	Turn left onto Renninger Road
17.0	Turn right with Renninger Road
17.4	Turn left onto Caston Road
18.4	Turn left onto South Main Street
18.7	Turn right onto East Caston Road
19.1	Turn right onto Christman Road; lunch at Falcon Restaurant
19.1	Head south on Christman Road
20.3	Turn left onto E. Nimisila Road
21.3	Cross Arlington Road
22.1	Turn left onto Greensburg Road
22.3	Turn right onto King Drive
22.8	Turn left onto Shriver Road

Miles	Directions
23.3	Turn right onto Steese Road
23.6	Turn right onto Massillon Road/SR241
23.9	Turn left onto Wise Road
25.5	Turn left onto Mayfair Road
26.0	Turn right onto Heckman Road
26.8	Turn left onto Kreighbaum Road
27.8	Turn left onto Raber Road
27.9	Turn right onto Myersville Road
31.7	Turn right onto Flickinger Road
32.0	Turn right onto Sanitarium Road
32.2	Turn left onto Lake Road
32.5	Turn left onto Church Street
32.8	Turn right onto Sunnyside Ave, which becomes Lakeside Drive, which becomes Lake Road
33.8	Turn left onto Hillbish Avenue
34.3	Turn right onto Krumroy Road
34.8	Cross Massillon Road/SR241
35.2	Turn left onto Pickle Road
36.6	Turn right onto Killian Road
37.6	Cross Arlington Road
38.2	Turn left onto Conlin Drive
38.8	Turn right onto Jarvis Road
39.3	Turn left onto Cottage Grove Road
41.8	Turn right onto East Caston Road
42.3	Turn left onto Christman Road
43.5	Turn right onto Nimisila Campground road
43.9	Arrive at Nimisila Campground parking lot

Ride 12, Map 1

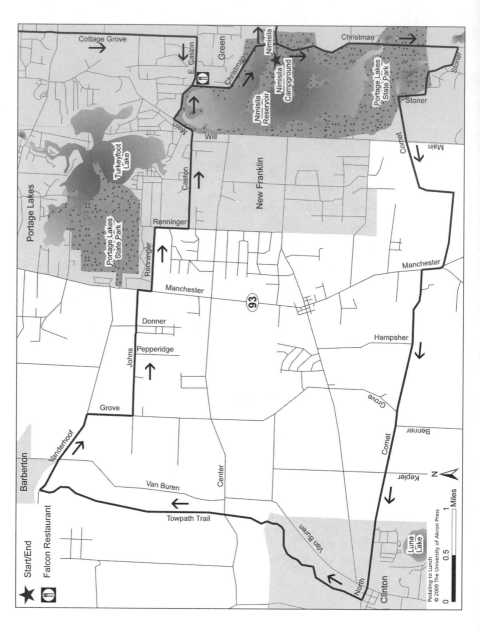

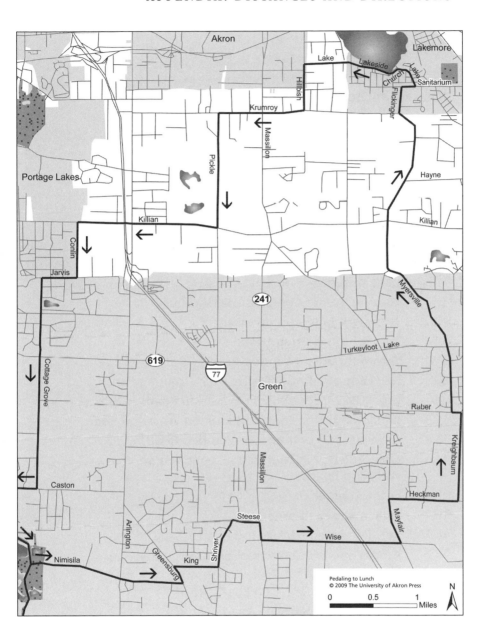

Ride 12, Map 2

Pedaling to Lunch
© 2009 The University of Akron Press

0   0.5   1
Miles

N

Ride 13

Miles	Directions
0.0	Exit parking lot, turning right onto Grand Trunk Avenue
0.1	Turn left onto Sunnyside Street
0.8	Turn left onto Prospect Street; proceed through traffic light
1.6	Prospect Street becomes Congress Lake Avenue
2.0	Turn right into Quail Hollow State Park
2.7	Bear right at road fork
2.9	At mansion, turn around and retrace route to park entrance
3.9	Turn right onto Congress Lake Avenue
4.8	Turn right onto Pontius Street
5.5	Turn left onto Griggy Road
8.1	Turn right onto Waterloo Road
8.7	Our Lady of Lourdes Grotto at St. Joseph's Parish
9.9	Cross US224, continue on Waterloo Road
11.3	Randolph traffic light; continue on Waterloo Road
13.2	Cross US224, continue on Waterloo Road
14.3	Cross five-points intersection; continue on Waterloo Road
15.5	Enter Atwater
16.7	Lunch, Kinsey's Korner
16.7	Retrace route on Waterloo Road
19.2	At five-points intersection, proceed straight onto Eberly Road
22.1	Cross SR44, continue on Eberly Road
23.4	Turn left onto Hartville Road
25.8	Cross Pontius Street; Hartville Road becomes Duquette Avenue
28.3	Turn right onto Edison Street (SR619)

Miles	Directions
28.5	Turn left onto William Penn Avenue
30.0	Turn right onto Smith Kramer Street
31.3	Cross SR43, continue on Smith Kramer Street
31.5	Turn right onto Geib Avenue
32.7	Cross Woodlawn Street; Geib Avenue becomes Crestmont Avenue
33.2	Turn left on Menlo Park Street
33.3	Follow turn to right onto Grand Trunk Avenue
33.5	Turn left into parking lot

Pedaling to Lunch

Ride 13

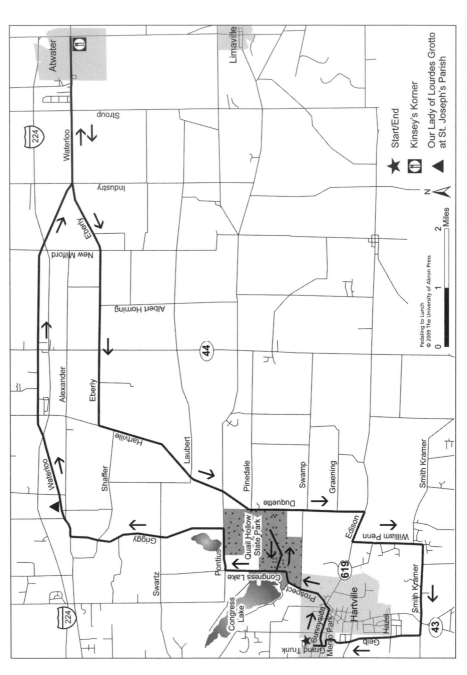

Legend:
★ Start/End
⊖ Kinsey's Korner
◄ Our Lady of Lourdes Grotto at St. Joseph's Parish

Pedaling to Lunch
© 2009 The University of Akron Press

0   1   2 Miles

290

Ride 14

Miles	Directions
0.0	Exit the Walborn Marina lot and turn right onto Price Street
1.5	Enter Limaville
2.0	Cross SR183, continue on Price Street
4.5	Turn left onto SR225
4.7	Turn right onto Lowe Road
5.7	Angle right onto North Benton West Road
8.0	Miller Airport (at driveway to café and office)
9.5	Turn left onto 12th Street
9.6	Turn right onto Center Street
9.7	Turn left onto Heisel Road
9.8	Cross SR14
9.9	Turn right onto Western Reserve Road
11.1	Turn left onto Bedell Road
11.7	Noah's Lost Ark Animal Sanctuary
12.9	Mill Creek Campground (at entrance)
13.6	Cross US224, continue on Bedell Road
16.0	Turn left onto Shilling's Mill Bridge
16.1	Turn right onto Mill Road
16.8	Turn right onto Ellsworth Road (Country Road 116)
17.6	Turn left onto SE River Road
19.7	Turn left onto Mahoning Avenue
20.4	The Sand Trap Restaurant
20.4	Continue west on Mahoning Avenue
21.2	Turn left onto Mahoning Road
23.7	Turn right onto Yale Road
28.8	Yale six-point corners; cross SR14
30.1	Turn left onto Porter Road
32.8	Cross US224

Pedaling to Lunch

Miles	Directions
35.2	Turn right onto German Church Road
36.3	Cross SR183
37.7	Turn left onto McCallum Avenue
38.5	Turn right onto Price Street
38.9	Turn left into the Walborn Reservoir Marina lot

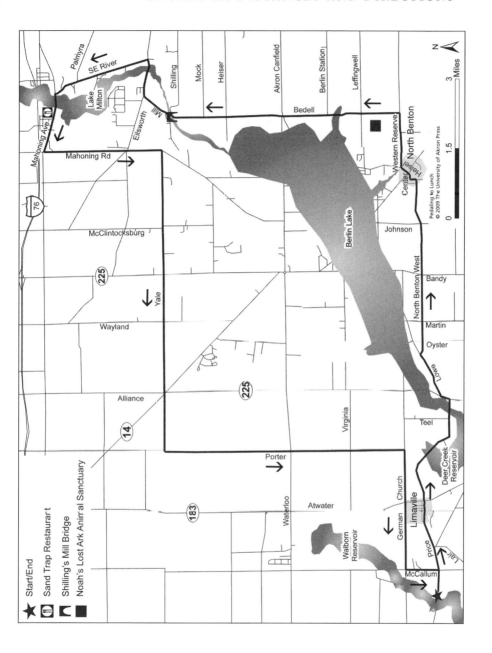

Ride 14

Start/End
Sand Trap Restaurant
Shilling's Mill Bridge
Noah's Lost Ark Animal Sanctuary

Ride 15

Miles   Directions

Miles	Directions
0.0	Brewster, head south from the intersection of Wabash Avenue/SR93 and Main Street
0.2	Turn right onto Seventh Street, which becomes Mt. Eaton Street, which becomes Harrison Road
5.7	Merge left onto Massillon Road/SR241, which becomes E. Chestnut Street
5.9	Turn left onto Canton Street
5.9	Turn right onto Main Street/ US250 and proceed through Mt. Eaton
6.3	Turn left onto Harrison Road
10.9	Center of Maysville; continue on Harrison Road
15.5	Center of Fredericksburg; continue straight on W. Clay Street, which becomes Harrison Road
19.8	Cross SR83; continue on Harrison Road, which becomes Centerville Road
21.7	Turn right onto Shreve Eastern Road
24.6	Enter Shreve; Shreve Eastern Road becomes E. Wood Street
24.8	Turn left onto Market Street/SR226
25.0	Lunch, Des Dutch Essenhaus
25.0	Head south on Market Street
25.1	Turn right onto South Street
25.2	Turn left onto South Main Street, which becomes South Jefferson Road
26.1	Turn left onto Centerville Road
26.3	Turn right onto CR318
28.5	Turn left onto CR329
33.3	Turn left onto CR320
33.6	Enter Holmesville; CR320 becomes Main Street
34.1	Turn left onto SR83
34.1	Turn right onto E. Jackson Street

Miles	Directions
34.5	Turn left onto Holmes County Trail
38.6	Turn right onto Clay Street in Fredericksburg
38.8	Turn left onto N. Main Street
38.8	Turn right onto Jackson Street
39.1	Turn left onto Henry Street
40.3	Turn right onto Carr Road
41.0	Turn left with Carr Road
44.9	Cross 250; continue on Carr Road
45.2	Turn right onto Emerson Road
48.9	Center of Kidron; continue on Emerson Road
49.0	Bear left onto Jericho Road
51.6	Cross SR94, continue on Jericho Road
53.8	Turn right onto SR241
53.9	Turn left onto Elton Road, which becomes Elton Street
56.0	Hamlet of Elton; continue on Elton Street
57.2	Turn right onto Manchester Road/SR93, which becomes Wabash Avenue
58.3	Arrive at intersection of Wabash Avenue/SR93 and Main Street

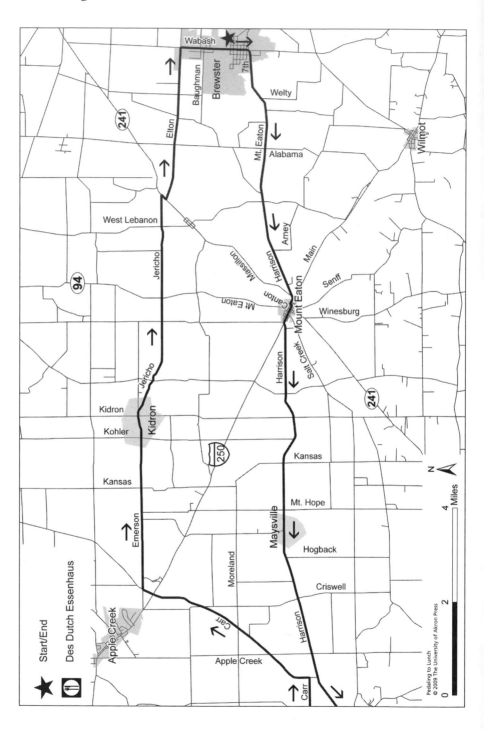

Ride 15, Map 1

Wabash
Brewster
7th
Baughman
Elton
241
Welty
Mt. Eaton
Alabama
Wilmot
West Lebanon
Jericho
94
Arney
Main
Massillon
Harrison
Canton
Mt Eaton
Senff
Mount Eaton
Winesburg
Jericho
Harrison
Salt Creek
Kidron
Kidron
Kohler
Kidron
250
Kansas
241
Kansas
Mt. Hope
Emerson
Maysville
Hogback
Moreland
Criswell
Start/End
Des Dutch Essenhaus
Apple Creek
Apple Creek
Carr
Harrison
Carr
N

Pedaling to Lunch
© 2009 The University of Akron Press

0   2   4 Miles

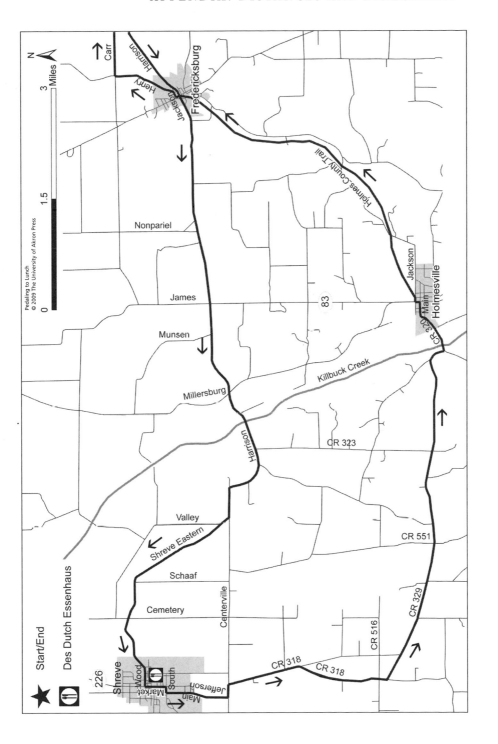

Ride 15, Map 2

★ Start/End

🍴 Des Dutch Essenhaus

N

0   1.5   3
Miles

Pedaling to Lunch
© 2009 The University of Akron Press

Carr

Harrison

Fredericksburg

Henry

Jackson

Holmes County Trail

Nonpariel

Jackson

James

83

Main

Holmesville

CR 329

Munsen

Killbuck Creek

Millersburg

Harrison

CR 323

Valley

Shreve Eastern

CR 551

Schaaf

CR 329

Cemetery

Centerville

226

Shreve

Wood

South

CR 516

Market

Jefferson

Main

CR 318

CR 318

Ride 16

Miles	Directions
0.0	Leave East Canton Village Park, turning left onto Werley Road
0.2	Turn left onto Noble Street
0.4	Right onto Berger Street
0.5	Cross Nassau Street/US30; continue on Berger Street
0.7	At Church Street jog slightly left and continue on Berger Street
1.6	Turn right onto Orchard View Drive
1.7	Turn left onto Argyle Road
3.0	Cross Mapleton Street onto Crestlawn Drive
3.1	Bear right onto Argyle Road
3.7	Turn left onto Waynesburg Drive
4.9	Turn right on Baum Street
5.0	Cross Zwallen Way/SR43; continue on Baum Street
7.9	(approximate, no sign) Enter North Industry
8.2	Turn left onto Ridge Avenue
8.3	Turn right onto 53rd Street
8.5	Cross Cleveland Avenue/SR800, continue on 53rd Street
8.8	Bear left onto Fohl Street
10.9	Turn right onto Dueber Avenue
10.3	Turn left onto Fohl Street
11.3	Cross I-77, continue on Fohl Street
16.0	(approximate, no sign) Enter Navarre; Fohl Street becomes Wooster Street
17.0	Turn left onto Main Street/US62/SR21
17.4	Turn left onto Canal Street
17.4	Lunch, Kiki's Café
17.4	Head east on Canal Street, which becomes Hudson Drive
18.1	Craig Pittman Memorial Park

Miles	Directions
18.2	Bear left onto Brinker Street
23.8	Turn right onto Dueber Avenue
25.0	Turn left onto Battlesburg Street
28.4	Jog left with Battlesburg Street onto East Sparta Avenue and then right to continue on Battlesburg Street
28.5	Cross Cleveland Avenue/SR800, continue on Battlesburg Street
30.8	Turn left onto Willowdale Avenue
31.8	Cross Zwallen Way/SR43
31.9	Turn left onto Waynesburg Drive
32.7	Turn right onto Westfall Street
34.2	Turn left onto Indian Run Avenue
36.6	Turn left onto Orchard View Drive
36.8	Turn right onto Wood Avenue
37.6	Enter East Canton
37.8	Turn left onto Church Street
38.1	Turn right onto Berger Street
38.3	Cross Nassau Street/US30, continue on Berger Street
38.4	Turn left onto Noble Street
38.5	Turn right onto Werley Road
38.7	Turn right into Village Park

Pedaling to Lunch

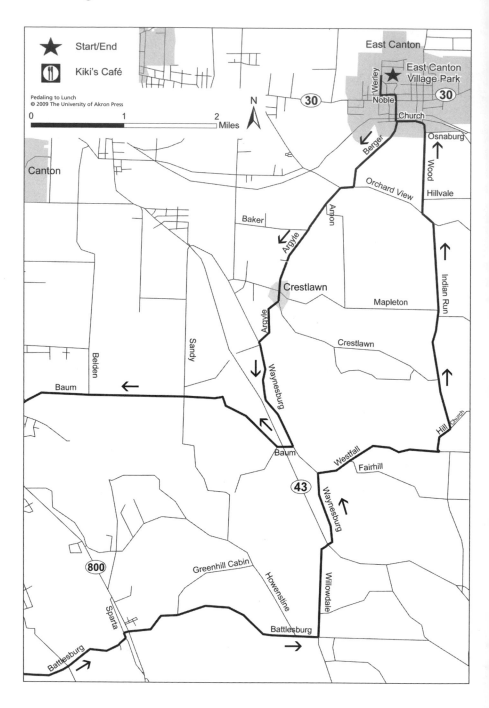

Ride 16, Map 1

300

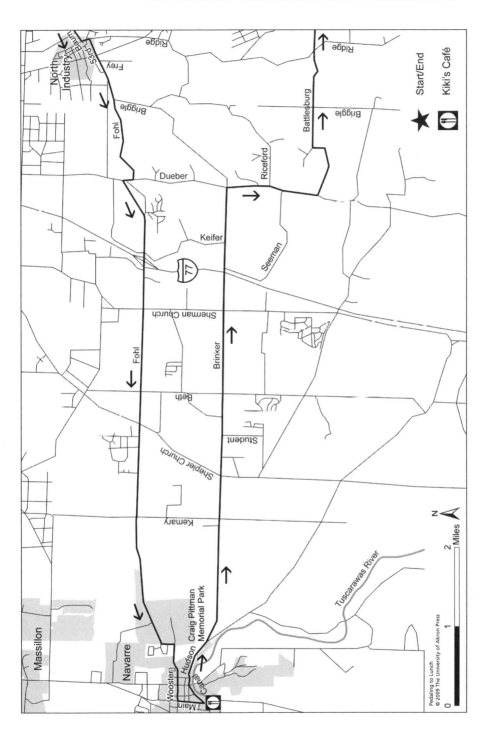

Ride 16, Map 2

Pedaling to Lunch
© 2009 The University of Akron Press

★ Start/End

🍴 Kiki's Café

Ride 17

Miles	Directions
0.0	From the Old Stagecoach Inn, head south on Rochester Road
1.0	Turn left onto Winona Road
2.9	Turn right onto McCann Road
3.9	Jog right on Mountz and then left on McCann
5.4	Cross SR172; continue on McCann, which eventually joins Ellyson Road
7.6	Merge left onto Buffalo Road/Clinton Street (no sign I could see)
8.8	Cross SR9; continue on Clinton Street
8.9	Turn right onto Plymouth Street
9.0	Spread Eagle Tavern on left (optional lunch stop)
9.0	Continue past Spread Eagle Tavern
9.1	Turn left onto Howard Street
9.3	Cross US30 and go straight onto Haessley Road
11.3	Turn right onto Gavers Road
12.2	Enter Dungannon; continue on Gavers Road
12.8	Turn left onto Lisbon Dungannon Road
14.7	Turn right onto Trinity Church Road
14.9	Turn left onto Lisbon Dungannon Road
16.7	At junction with Freeman Road, bear right, continuing on Lisbon Dungannon Road
17.7	Turn left onto Wayne Bridge Road
18.7	Turn right onto US30
19.3	Enter Lisbon; continue on US30, which is also Lincoln Way
20.0	Lunch, Steel Trolley Diner
20.0	Head south on Jefferson Street
20.1	Turn right onto Washington Street
20.4	Turn left onto Lincoln Avenue/SR164

Miles   Directions

20.6   Turn right into Greenway Trail lot and enter Greenway
        Trail (sometime after mile 2 of the trail, its path joins
        St. Jacob-Logtown Road for about a half mile; the trail
        then resumes.)

25.8   Leave Greenway Trail and turn left onto Eagleton Road

25.9   Teegarden Centennial Covered Bridge

26.0   Turn left onto Teegarden Road (no sign)

26.1   Turn right onto Yates Road

27.1   Bear left onto Winona Road

27.8   Jog left onto Depot Road, then right onto
        Winona Road

29.7   Enter Winona

30.9   Cross SR9

31.9   Turn right onto Butler Grange Road

32.9   Turn left onto King Road

35.0   Turn left onto Georgetown Road

36.0   End at North Georgetown

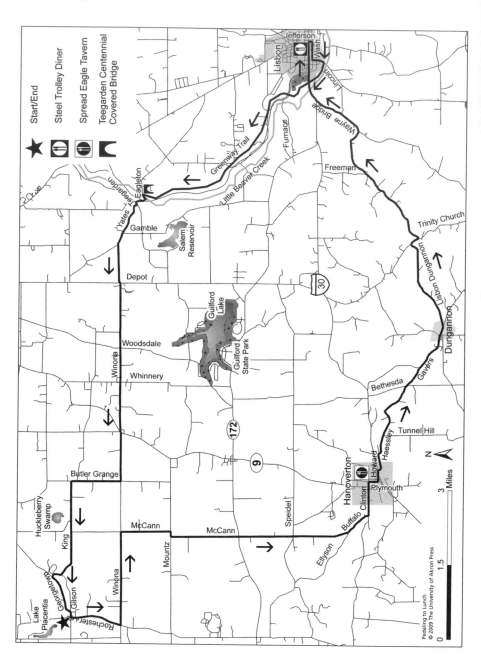

Ride 18

Miles Directions

Miles	Directions
0.0	In Strasburg, turn right out of Hardee's onto US250 and then right onto 9th Street
0.1	Turn left onto Race Road
3.2	Turn right onto Schneiders Crossing Road
3.7	Cross SR516 at Winfield; proceed straight ahead on Broad Run Dairy Road
5.7	Bear turn left with Broad Run Dairy Road
6.6	Turn left onto Old Ohio 39
6.7	Turn right onto Schilling Hill Road
6.9	Cross SR39; continue on Schilling Hill Road
9.3	Turn sharp right onto Crooked Run Road
15.2	Enter Ragersville
15.3	Turn left at Ragersville center onto Ragersville Road
18.1	Turn right with Ragersville Road
20.7	Enter Baltic
21.0	Lunch, Miller's Dutch Kitch'n
21.0	From restaurant, turn left onto Main Street
21.1	Cross SR93; proceed straight ahead on Ragersville Road
22.1	Turn left onto Pleasant Valley Road
24.2	Proceed straight off of Pleasant Valley Road onto Crooked Run Road
25.6	Enter Ragersville
26.1	Turn left onto Ragersville Road
30.2	Turn right onto Old Ohio 39
31.2	Cross SR39; proceed straight ahead on Old Ohio 39
31.4	Turn left onto Spooky Hollow Road
31.6	Turn right onto Prysi Road
33.1	Proceed straight onto Broad Run Dairy Road
34.9	Turn left onto SR516

Miles Directions

35.1 Turn right onto Winfield–Strasburg Road

37.8 Turn right with Winfield–Strasburg Road
(road is Cherry Run to the left)

38.6 Turn right onto 9th Street

38.9 Turn left onto US250

39.0 Turn left into Hardee's lot

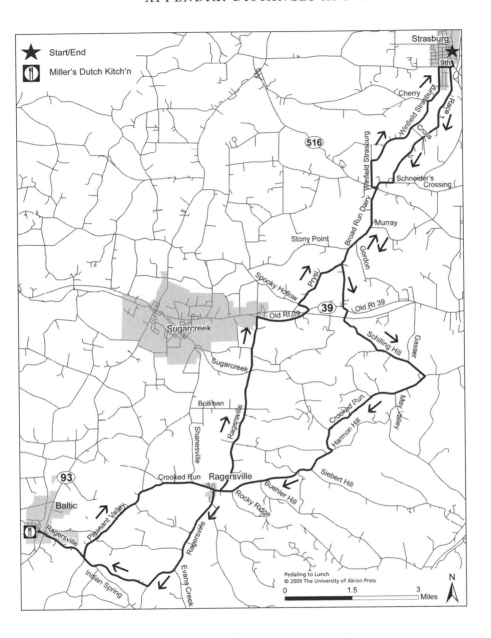

Start/End

Miller's Dutch Kitch'n

Strasburg

9th

Cherry

Winfield Strasburg

Cross

Race

516

Schneider's Crossing

Broad Run Dairy

Winfield Strasburg

Murray

Stony Point

Gordon

Pvts

Spooky Hollow

Old Rt 39

39

Old Rt 39

Sugarcreek

Schilling Hill

Gasser

Sugarcreek

May Valley

Bollman

Ragersville

Crooked Run

Harmon Hill

Shanesville

93

Crooked Run   Ragersville

Siebert Hill

Baltic

Buehler Hill

Rocky Ridge

Ragersville

Pleasant Valley

Ragersville

Evans Creek

Indian Spring

Pedaling to Lunch
© 2009 The University of Akron Press

0   1.5   3
                         Miles

N

Ride 18

Ride 19

Miles   Directions

0.0   Turn right onto SR212

0.1   Turn right onto Dover Zoar Road

6.4   Enter Dover, continue straight onto Front Street

7.1   SR800 joins Front Street

7.7   Turn left with Route 800 onto Wooster Avenue

8.1   Bear right onto Union Avenue

8.8   Enter New Philadelphia

9.8   Union Avenue becomes 7th Street

9.9   Turn left onto Fair Avenue. Continue on Fair Avenue, crossing successively, 4th Street/SR800 (10.2), Broadway/SR416 (10.5) and Beaver Avenue/SR39 (11.0)

11.4   Jog left onto 8th Street NE and then right onto Fair Avenue

11.6   Turn right onto 8th Drive NE

11.7   Turn left onto E. High Avenue/US250

12.3   Turn right onto Delaware Drive

13.1   Schoenbrunn State Park and Memorial on left

13.1   Continue on Delaware Drive

13.4   Turn right onto 21st Street

13.6   Cross SR250; 21st Street becomes Schoenbrunn Road

14.1   Turn left onto SR416

17.6   Enter Tuscarawas; continue on Route 416

22.2   Turn left onto SR36

22.8   Turn left onto Gnadenhutten entrance ramp, which becomes Walnut Avenue; enter Gnadenhutten

23.4   Turn right onto Main Street

23.5   Turn left onto Cherry Street

23.7   Museum and memorial

23.7   Return on Cherry Street

24.1   Turn right onto Main Street

Miles	Directions
24.2	Turn left onto Walnut Street
24.2	Lunch at Tents of Grace Café
24.2	Turn right onto Walnut Street
24.3	Turn left onto Main Street, which becomes Wolfes Crossing Road
26.2	Turn right onto SR36
29.7	Take exit right for Routes 250 West, 800 North
30.0	Turn right onto Water Street
30.2	Turn left onto 11th Street
30.5	Turn left onto Eastport Avenue
30.8	Turn left onto Eastport Road
32.4	Turn left onto Wolf Run Road
33.6	Enter Midvale
34.0	Turn right onto Main Street, which becomes Nagley Road
34.8	Turn right onto Barnhill Road
34.9	Bear right with Barnhill Road
37.2	Turn left onto SR39
38.0	Turn right onto Henderson School Road
43.5	Turn right onto Tabor Ridge Road and then left onto SR212
46.2	Enter Somerdale; continue on SR212
48.6	Turn left onto SR800
49.3	Turn right onto Canal Road
52.2	Turn right onto Dover Zoar Road
52.7	Turn left onto SR212
52.8	Enter Zoar

Pedaling to Lunch

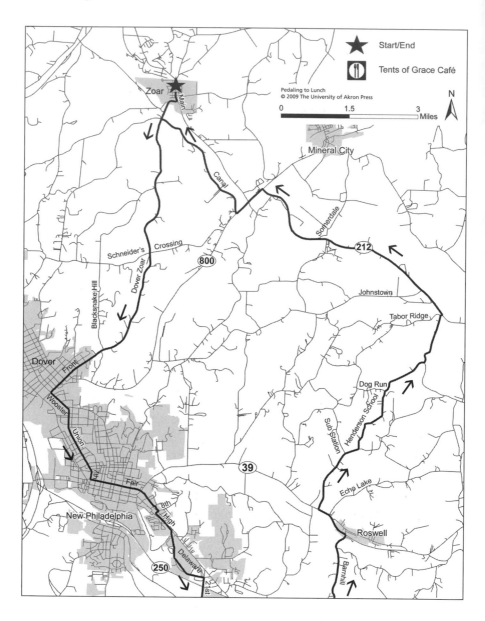

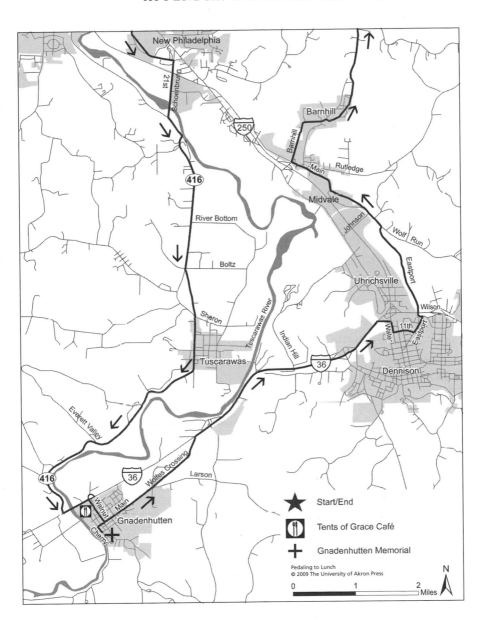

Start/End

Tents of Grace Café

Gnadenhutten Memorial

Pedaling to Lunch
© 2009 The University of Akron Press

0   1   2
Miles

N

Ride 20

Miles	Directions
0.0	In Magnolia, leave Canal Park heading south on Basin Street
0.1	Turn left onto Carrollton Street
0.3	Bear right onto Morges Road (also called Bachelor Road)
3.1	Turn right onto Bark Road
7.4	Union Valley Cemetery
8.7	Turn left onto SR542
10.0	Enter Dellroy
10.2	Turn left onto SR39 East
12.0	Turn right onto Cactus Road, C51
13.4	Turn left onto Antigua Road, C11
15.0	Bear right onto Canyon Road
17.4	Turn left with Canyon Road
17.7	Cross SR332 at Petersburg; continue on Canyon Road
20.3	Turn left onto Alamo Road
22.4	Enter Carrollton; Alamo Road becomes 3rd Street SE
22.9	Turn right onto S. Lisbon Street
22.9	Enter Public Square
23.0	Lunch, Archer's Restaurant.
23.0	Follow traffic flow around square to its north end
23.0	Cross SR39; continue straight ahead on N. Lisbon Street
23.1	Turn left 2nd Street NW
23.5	Turn right onto Lincoln Avenue NW
23.9	Turn left onto 8th Street NW
24.2	Turn right onto Canton Road (SR43)
24.6	Turn left onto Trump Road
25.2	Turn left onto Bacon Road
28.6	Cross SR171 at New Harrisburg; continue straight onto Arrow Road

Miles   Directions

29.4   Bear left onto Bronze Road

31.4   Turn right onto Avalon Road

33.6   Enter Malvern; Avalon Road becomes Carrollton Street

33.9   Turn left onto Porter Street

34.5   Porter Street ends; turn left onto Morges Road

34.8   Morges Road becomes Citrus Road

35.4   Turn right with Citrus Road

38.7   Turn right SR171

38.9   Enter Waynesburg

39.1   Turn left with Route 171 onto Lisbon Street

39.4   Turn right onto SR183 (initially called Main Street); follow through a left and right turn

39.9   Turn left onto Grovedell Street (turn is immediately after bridge)

41.6   Continue straight onto Willowdale Avenue

42.9   Enter Magnolia

43.3   Turn right onto Canal Street

43.3   Turn left onto Basin Street

43.4   Arrive at Canal Park in Magnolia

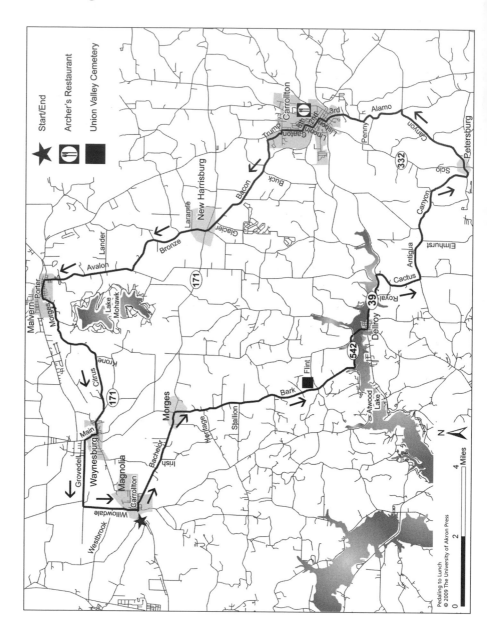

Start/End

Archer's Restaurant

Union Valley Cemetery

About the Author

Stan Purdum is a writer, editor, and pastor who has written for both general and religious journals. A long-distance cyclist, Stan is the author of *Roll Around Heaven All Day*, an account of his cross-nation ride, and *Playing in Traffic*, which recounts his bicycle journey from Niagara Falls, New York, to El Paso, Texas, on US62. He has also written a book of short stories, *New Mercies I See*, and a study of the ministry of Jesus, *He Walked in Galilee*. He lives in North Canton, Ohio.

About the Book

Pedaling to Lunch was designed and typeset by Amy Freels. The typeface, Minion, was designed by Robert Slimbach in 1990 for Adobe Systems. The display type, Frutiger, was designed by Adrian Frutiger and released in 1976 by Stempel/Linotype.

Pedaling to Lunch was printed on 60-pound Glatfelter Offset Natural and bound by Cushing-Malloy of Ann Arbor, Michigan.